DESIGI

QUESTION OF

HISTORY

DESIGN, HISTORIES, FUTURES:
SERIES INTRODUCTION

This series aims to advance knowledge on the wider historical significance of design, and, in doing so, go beyond the current scope of 'design history'. It will also strive to demonstrate that a historical engagement with design necessitates engagement with the wider crisis of the discipline of history itself.

The contributing authors to the series will no doubt bring very different perspectives to the realization of the series aim and the intellectual challenges it presents. However, they will all share an understanding of the significance of design thought and design action for sustaining the future well-being of humanity and the environments of our dependence. They will also recognize that for this potentiality to be realized, the scope of historical inquiry has to be significantly widened, become more critical, and surpass the limitations of existing concerns with disciplinary boundaries.

The actual directional consequences of designing and of the designed worlds of human occupation, historically and futurally, are still not adequately understood either in or beyond design education, practice, history and theory. Without understanding design as both historically situated and futurally directional, the ethical character of design – as a negotiation between creation and destruction, care and uncaring – cannot be adequately grasped. This series aims to expand the scope of discourse and comprehension of the directional agency of design, extending understanding and prompting speculation toward this end.

Tony Fry, Lisa Norton and Anne-Marie Willis
Series Editors

TITLES IN THE SERIES

DESIGN AND THE QUESTION OF HISTORY

Tony Fry, Clive Dilnot and Susan C. Stewart

Bloomsbury Academic
An imprint of Bloomsbury Publishing Plc

B L O O M S B U R Y
LONDON • NEW DELHI • NEW YORK • SYDNEY

Bloomsbury Academic

An imprint of Bloomsbury Publishing Plc

50 Bedford Square	1385 Broadway
London	New York
WC1B 3DP	NY 10018
UK	USA

www.bloomsbury.com

BLOOMSBURY and the Diana logo are trademarks of Bloomsbury Publishing Plc

First published 2015

British Library Cataloguing-in-Publication Data
A catalogue record for this book is available from the British Library.

ISBN: HB: 978-0-8578-5476-6
PB: 978-0-8578-5477-3
ePDF: 978-1-4725-8934-7
ePub: 978-1-4725-2160-6

Library of Congress Cataloging-in-Publication Data
Design and the question of history / Tony Fry, Clive Dilnot, Susan C. Stewart.
pages cm. — (Design, history, futures)
Includes bibliographical references and index.
ISBN 978-0-85785-476-6 (hardback) — ISBN 978-0-85785-477-3 (paperback)
1. Design and history. I. Fry, Tony. II. Dilnot, Clive. III. Stewart, Susan C.
(Susan Catherine Huston)
NK1520.D456 2014
745.409—dc23
2014012207

Typeset by RefineCatch Limited, Bungay, Suffolk

CONTENTS

PREFACE, PRE-FACE ESSENTIAL READING

What is this book?

Let's start with what it is not. It is not a work of design history, although it has a great deal to say about design and history.

It is not a resolved continuous dialogue of three authors speaking with one voice. Rather the three of us cut across each other and present the reader with the task of disclosing to themselves the commonalities, repetitions and differences within the deployed explicatory approaches, linguistic styles, arguments and issues addressed from which the text is constituted.

It is not an object of closure, an attempted last word.

So now what is it?

It is an opening—the opening of a series of books that all in some way are to look at the relation between design and history otherwise and without the constraint of just writing for the "design community" (however perceived), for design is more important than any form of disciplinary constraint. So said, it is a facing, *a facing of design now*, this in a world that is still being partly created and still being partly destroyed by design.

It is a mixture of meditation, advocation, and polemic. It is also a work of friendship, of solidarity in difference, an act of design cultural politics —which means its ambition is to make "a something happen" at the very least for some of those people who have occasion to think about design, history and futures. This is to say, contra to a certain strain of intellectual fashion of recent decades, it invites a reader to "take a position." It thus seeks engagement over agreement.

Now why is this book?

Above all it exists because of the necessity of "care." We can all say we "care," but in ontological reality care is not what we say but the consequence of what we do, not least by forms of design(ing), making, educating that negate the wasteland, the arrival of which Friedrich Nietzsche warned, and of which design, in its ambiguity, has been deeply implicated in creating, extending, aesthetizing and concealing.

The point of this project can be simply stated: to establish that design history dominantly fails to recognize the historical significance of design, and thus by implication its futuring agency, while equally ignoring the contemporary "crisis in the discipline of history."

This situation places an enormous intellectual challenge before design thinkers that instantly arrives—a challenge that demands to be urgently met. Stated in its most overt and simplified form: the fate of humanity to a very significant degree rests upon what is now designed, and how. So contextualized, the project before us is to move design out of what in the critical scheme of things is a trivial modality of history, into a position wherein its actual historical importance, and thus its futural significance, is understood and engaged.

The approach to be taken by all three contributors will substantiate these opening claims while questioning those narratives in which design and history travel in wedlock, as with design history. Rather what will follow will be more of a weaving together of the problems and possibilities of design and history as they circle around each other. However, the overall objective is straightforward: to expand how design is understood, to expose history as a problem begging far more serious consideration, and to pose ways to establish a far more dynamic and critical relation between the two.

ESSAY ONE

WHITHER DESIGN/ WHETHER HISTORY

Tony Fry

INTRODUCTION

History, as a serious practice and rigorous discipline, is having a hard time.

Certainly in contemporary Western culture, history has been diminished by its reduction to image in popular media. This means that increasingly it carries imaginaries. As such, rather than telling us who we are, it authors who we imagine ourselves to be. This is especially seen in film and television, where an enormous amount of effort is expended on the construction of authentic and detailed historical description and visual appearance. With some notable exceptions, "narrative history" has, at best, only a thin critical historical grounding. In the company of "the political," and elemental to it, history is being reduced to entertainment. What results when the political is so negated, as Carl Schmitt prophetically pointed out in the 1930s, is "the world" rendered merely "a world of entertainment," a world without "seriousness."[1] Thus for Schmitt it is "the political"—that domain of decision that goes well beyond just institutionalized politics—that stands between humanity and a reduction of "all and everything" to entertainment.

Academic history has suffered, in the company of other disciplines, from the diminished status of the Humanities within higher education. Along with these general trends has been a growing epistemological and increasingly Eurocentric critique of the foundations of the discipline itself. In sum, as will be shown; the authority of history is in decline, with the discipline itself becoming ever more fragmented. Notwithstanding this situation, there is a strong argument for the standing of "the historical" to be revived and for associated practices to be remade. At the core of this argument is the recognition that in the deepening complexities of the late modern world there is an increasing need for an understanding of the presence of the past. To recognize this then requires asking: what form should this understanding take, and how can it accommodate actual and substantial differences of power and perspective? Equally one asks: does not the imperative of revitalizing "history" beyond existing regimes of disciplinary ownership and practice actually mean the creation of something else, something new? Exploring these two questions will be central to our inquiry and its relation to design.

On design and history

Design history is dominantly disarticulated from those "questions of history" that have preoccupied historical studies.

It can be characterized as a subdiscipline of history that arrived in the space, and adopted the methods and values, of art and architectural history. But by the late 1970s design history had attempted to break away from these links and establish itself as a project in its own right. While some "in the field" might claim that it has done this, frankly it still carries many traces of the perspectives of its origins. Most significantly, what did not arrive during this period of transition, or subsequently, was what historical studies was fully aware of; that history itself, as discipline, practice and method, was in deep trouble.

Against this backdrop, rather than moving design and its agency into a wider and more critically engaged relation to debate of the "question of history," design history took it mostly in the opposite direction. Thereafter, design's history became historically dislocated. At best, it was supplemented by social context (again an art-historical trope). So while design history dominantly "established itself" as a "history" of canonized objects, images, organizations, movements, people, and events (often gathered under the rubrics of graphic design, industrial design, interior design, fashion design, jewelry design and so on) the practice frequently veered into antiquarianism and connoisseurship.[2] It was in this modality that a dominantly Western canon was constructed. When the non-Western was inducted (often as the exotic) it was done so within values, norms and topologies of the then "established field."

What has not been engaged by design history is the huge complexity of the "world-within-the-world" of human fabrication, wherein everything within this world has been created by design: as such, it is often invisible, mostly anonymous (as Siegfried Giedon told us well over half a century ago[3]), of little stylistic interest, a manifestation of the force of will (and now capital) and is always, to a greater or lesser extent, an elemental force of futuring or defuturing consequence. Design, so grasped, is historically directive of both "worlding" and "deworlding." By implication, under-standing design historically is far harder and enormously more important than design history recognizes and communicates. But as remarks already made imply, a naive appeal to history as self-evident is no more viable than is such an appeal to design. Like it or not, neither design, history or design history are resolved objects of inquiry.

As should be now clear, what follows is a continuation of engagement with design as problematic, linked to an acknowledgement of the inadequacy of design history (already argued in prior publications by Dilnot and by Fry), meeting what gets characterized as "the crisis of history." Fundamentally, this "crisis" has had two moments: the first at the end of the nineteenth century when there was a recoil against the claim of history as a science; and the second in recent decades coming from critiques arising in postmodern theory, centered on the epistemological claims of historical narrative. What debate around the crisis of history has exposed is:

- That the notion of there being an evolutionary *telos* of "human society" is totally flawed, and that the historical narratives associated with this *telos* are now dysfunctional areas of knowledge. Such a view was given profile through the discrediting of those master narratives that underpinned modernity, this in significant part triggered by the critique proffered by Jean-François Lyotard in 1979.[4]

- The loss of authority of the discipline of history that has increased with its fragmentation, coming not just as a result of critiques of its practice but also from its diminishment of status within the academy, as the position of the Humanities has been made weaker in the course of the instrumentalization of higher education around the world post-1968.

- The contestation of the authority of Eurocentric paradigm of history coming from decolonial theory that showed how, and from where, the dominant practices of the historian were formed, and how these practices were generalized and thus constituted the history other cultures.[5]

The result of this crisis is not that history no longer has a presence in the world, but rather that the nature, value and ability of history to critically inform (which was always less than adequate) is fading fast. At the same time, the need for historical understanding (which is not the same thing as history) constantly increases—not least in relation to design. History so qualified not only acts to conceal, but retains a certain appropriative ability in that we are historical beings. Historical understanding arrives with the potential to disclose this condition and the anthropocentric essence of history (we are history and it does not exist without us). More than this, the overwhelming force of human centeredness is indivisible from the lack of focus on, or concern with, the issue of being itself.[6]

Responding to this situation is the substantial task at hand. It is undertaken not because of some deep-seated desire to rescue history for design, but as a necessary task, if we are to comprehend and deal with so many of the problems elemental to the contemporary world. These are problems that need to be better understood historically and, in many cases, as a consequence of design's limitations, flaws and errors. In other words, what is needed is a general recognition of design, within orders of power, as an historical actor in and upon the world. Such an understanding requires the creation of radically transformed notions of both design and history. Placed in this context, design history—the practice and its product—has unwittingly acted to conceal the historical significance and agency of the designed world of human habitation.

At its simplest what design historians (among others in "the world of design") have failed to recognize is *that everyone, or at the very least all thinking people, need to grasp that it is not possible to comprehend the worlds of human existence without design, its agency, function and presence, being adequately understood in both historical and contemporary terms.* At its most basic, what this requires is gaining ascent for an understanding of the historical assent and prefigurative agency of design as generative of, and exercised by, things, processes, systems, social structures, built forms, and environments as they converge to constitute the ontologically designing forces of (and within) the uneven and inequitable distribution of power of the "world-within-the-world" of human creation.[7]

While in our animality "we" are of the biophysical world, as the human we are the producers and the product of another world, by design and artifice, named here as "the world-within-the-world." In this world all that is brought into being by design takes on a life of its own and, in some form, returns to us to actively influence and, in part, materially direct, what we are, what and how we see, and how we act (and upon what). Thus, while the formative act of design employs the inscriptive intention of an act of will, the designed object itself is directively independent in its designing—as such it constitutes ontologies—but in, and from, conditions of global(izing) inequity.

Currently, so many of the people who lead and direct the affairs of "the world" only have a very partial (if any) understanding of the significance and agency of design. It follows that as a result of their limited (or nonexistent) understanding they only have a limited comprehension of the world of human existence itself. This remark in fact equally applies in large part to almost all designers and design academics. Bluntly: design practice, history, theory and journalism have failed to grasp and communicate, especially to leaders and decision-makers, just how powerful is design's distributive and compound directive agency.

With these comments in mind, the intent is to turn design (obviously reconsidered beyond its characterization by design history) toward history, but with a corresponding intent of turning history (reconsidered) toward design.

Of course the ambition is not to resolve all the challenges the discipline of history faces, but rather to problematize them within a remit that recognizes the historico-worldly importance of design and then strives to communicate it to, and beyond, the design community.

Design history and history

As indicated, the formation of design history partly, but only partly, displaced the methods, values and agenda of art history. This meant it constituted a history outside the epistemological issues, arguments, politics and debates over, in and about history. Of course it would be misleading to suggest that the rise of design history was a coherent, consensual and consciously managed project. It was not—the practice was contested when it first arrived and ever remains so.[8]

Bringing the perspectives so far adopted leads us to ask the question: *how* does one start to think about and engage design in history as a contested domain of knowledge?

To do this, four key meta-design observations need to be made.

1   Observation one is that as a species the ability to prefigure what we intend to make before doing so is elemental to our being; this is designing at its most fundamental. Not only have *Homo sapiens* always been able to do this (as were some of the hominoid predecessors) but also this ability at a deep level contributed to our becoming what we now are.[9] Prefiguration is thus one of the defining characteristics of our becoming human.

2   Observation two is that from the ability to prefigure (as it directed both the creation and use of tools and, subsequently, the development of practices of making), human beings incrementally

created *by design* what has been named here as a world-within-the-world—a world that in its complexity is now beyond our ability to comprehend.

3   Observation three is that the situation in which human beings now find themselves—demographically, geopolitically, biophysically, psychosocially and environmentally—is one wherein the future with a future for "us" can only be reached by design.

4   Observation four is that design is currently implicated in the world of uneven human development, dominantly in the service of inequality.

As just a few moments of reflection reveals: to comprehend and explore these four observations demands historical inquiry, and for this inquiry to be possible a new kind of dialogue between design and history has to be created. Design has to be ripped away from that clean, sanitized and risk-free engagement with "the world" as delivered by design history. The directional imposition integral to the essence of design (what "it," as a situated willing, designs) folds into the dialectic of sustainment. What this means is that design, as an act, draws the line between creation and destruction, and determines what falls on which side, but at present mostly unknowingly.

Critical issues, centering on the world that design(ing) has brought into being and has negated, are extraordinarily complex. Consider that almost everything in the environment around us is designed—stand at a window in a city, any city: is there anything to be seen, beyond a given relation to the biophysical substrate, which is not designed (including the very way we see what we are looking at)? Such designing arrives by both intent and ontologically (the designing of things/things designing, which is why one can say that we are in part a product of design).

Clearly the significance of the corpus of design history scholarship and its textual output is trivial if measured against the overwhelming active and relational complexity of the designed. There is simply no correlation between the totality of the transformative agency of the designed and the assembled discourse of design. Design discourse in fact strives to secure its "coherence" by exclusion. But in harmony with Jacques Derrida's famous line "the world is a text" (by which he meant "world" as an object of interpretation) it can be pointed out that "the text is designed" (which is to acknowledge that what we see, and/or how we see, are a product of design as disclosed via a play of object, image, idea and interpretation).

As is becoming more evident to a growing number of people: the negative dimension and consequences of design have had a profound worldly impact. A great deal of what has been brought into being by design, from coal-fired power stations to asbestos, from herbicides to jet-skis, from cigarettes to cluster bombs, all combine to take the future away. They "defuture." In particular, industrial society has brought these, and a myriad other defuturing things and forces, into being. As members of such a society, we find ourselves at the currently comfortable epicenter of the condition of unsustainability that defuturing animates. To know this is to realize that design has had much more significant historical agency than has been realized. To know this can, and should, be seen to have huge implications in how its history is constructed, understood and viewed. Even more important—to gain such an historical understanding is to acquire a crucial source of knowledge directive of how "designing the future" is thought and undertaken, and by whom. What is implied here is far more than just "learning from history" (because this history does not yet exist).

History, the past, is always a construction of the present by those powers that control it. This means *how and why* the past is made present (as a transformation of "what was") is as critical to understand as *what* is actually (re)presented, and who and how it can be contested. What is at stake in the creation of history—as George Orwell famously pointed out in his book *Nineteen Eighty-Four*—is the future.

History, the historical and historicity cannot be gathered into a single discourse. Its fragments can never again be reassembled. The very notion of a possible unified discourse has gone. It follows that nobody any longer has the authority to speak for history (those who did so in the past now look to be delusional, and those who do so in the present are critically unaware). Yet even so one can find and create historical assemblages for particular ends, including gaining an understanding of relations between design and narratives of change over time (which may or may not be claimed as "history").

But for the moment our aim is merely to start orientating the reader to the nature and the scale of what has to be resolved in order to think and talk about "design" as it is present *in* historical process. Much more on this will be said in the essays, so what follows is a first pass.

History totalized

We are, and will be, writing against history totalized, naturalized and narrativized. That is, learning from Nietzsche, we are writing against the history of historians (especially those who claim "historical truth" from (their) account of the historical). But likewise we are writing against the "genetic theory of the modern world," expressed in Hegel's philosophy of history, whereby European nations surpassed the Asiatic world in an evolutionary schema emanating from the Greeks, and characterized by linear and unstinting drive called "progress." Essentially, Western metaphysics underscored the Hegelian view, negated the history of other civilizations and was oblivious to the "darker side of modernity."[10] Likewise, the beginning of the West so characterized marked, as Heidegger recognized, the start of a history of forgetting—not only was this moment of first thinking forgotten for centuries but its significance still dominantly remains unremembered, silent, unthought (thus the casting of "our" destiny is overlooked).[11] Here history becomes positioned in the project started by Nietzsche, and continued by Heidegger, as an object through which to think the meaning of Western thought, how the West thinks and its fate.[12]

By implication, history is refused as an ordered gathering of typologies of events configured in a universalized chronology. There is no "world history." There is no mode of representation that can "speak for the world"; there are no direct or supportable links between the author, referent and the represented. One might ask, for example, when were "The Crusades" and who speaks for them? In the West they are cast into the past and long forgotten but for cinematic fictive traces. But in the Middle East they still cast a shadow and occupy a significant place as a historical marker of a European ideology of war underwritten by the Christian church.[13] As such they remain of the present and retain future determinant agency, and as such still have a continuing effect upon everyday life. "The historical" thus is never simply "the past." To cast it as this, as many historians do, is to negate an ability to comprehend the nature of the present and future, as well as of time itself.

That narrative ordering from "the zero" point that discounts all Other(s), is so familiar within, but so ignored in practice by, the *habitus* of the historian. The past is not "there," and the viewpoint is not simply "here." Moreover, future events rewrite the past. For instance, at one time the Soviet Union looked like an eternally present force, yet it evaporated. The fall of the Berlin Wall acted symbolically to mark its demise while also opening up a moment of major historical revision. Likewise, postcolonial studies started rewriting the narrative of modernity; now the discourse of decoloniality has divested all remaining claims of modernity's global authority. The apocryphal arguments for the progressive dimension of modernity, delivered by, for example, Anthony Giddens and Jürgen Habermas, stand condemned by many thinkers from the underside of modernity inspired by the enduring significance of Frantz Fanon and the Latin American philosopher Enrique Dussel.[14] There is an emergent recognition that structural unsustainability, as inscribed in the very essence of human being, will have an even larger impact as population numbers increase, and "consumerist" demands for planetary resources grow.

As indicated, the ethnocentric notion of "world history" is anathema (including a world history of design) because there is no valid locus of observation (or defence against the perceptual coercion that arrives when it is adopted). This is not only because this mode of history is exclusive, and written from the "zero point," but also because it assumed there is an essential being ("man") available to be employed as the common denominator, the common figure, linking all events over time and space. "Man" is not a singularity as humanism would have it, and therefore cannot provide the basis and figure for a unified history. As Michel Harr put it: "There is no autonomous history of humanity." "Man," as the subject of "world history," is the product of a particular and imposed historical construct (from Enlightenment metaphysics) that dismisses all other ways, ancient and modern, by which our *dasein* has been enacted.[15] We can emotionally align ourselves with Emmanuel Levinas when he says "Humanism has to be denounced only because it is not sufficiently human," yet we equally need to intellectually contest this view because it excludes our plurality, animality and technicity.[16]

On forgetting history

History is forgotten (individually and culturally) but this does not mean that the forgetting of the historical can be sanctioned.

The notion that history had a *telos* with an end point is now a discredited idea carrying the mark of Hegel. There has never been a totality, history has never had a totality (only a particular discourse with varied narratives): there was never a destination to reach, an end point, an end state. Events continue. Some will end, some will not, others will commence. That which continues implies memory and "the not completely forgotten." However, memory is at risk. It is being industrialized, externalized and ruptured from mind.[17] Memory is never just a servant of the past, a given. Remembering is directly linked to becoming futural. It is a key to liberation from forms of oppression lodged in, and continued from, the past. Likewise, forgetting is not overcoming what has passed: the future, directional choice, demands remembrance.

History, as Michel Foucault made clear in his seminal essay "Nietzsche, genealogy, history," does not function as truth but as "counter-memory."[18] History from the underside of modernity is this writ large. "We" can survive without history, but not without memory.

Keith Jenkins claims that a whole raft of contemporary thinkers, including Roland Barthes, Gilles Deleuze, Jacques Derrida, Jean-Francois Lyotard, Ernesto Laclau, Stanley Fish, Richard Rorty, Julia Kristeva and Gayatri Chakravorty Spivak, functioned, and managed perfectly well, without making reference to history—they (at least those who are still alive) "can forget history."[19] This sweeping claim is not true. It rests on the reduction of history to the "output" of historians. Just to take one of the Jenkins examples: Derrida. Not only did his oeuvre trade on historical reference, but equally it is evident that his own history (especially in relation to his Algerian background and the Jewish tradition) underscored many of his concerns (one clear example was his writing on racism[20]). Then there were texts like his *Spectres of Marx* that registered a certain kind of presence of history that exposed a past existing in the present as futural. So while "history" is undoubtedly extremely problematic, and begs to be treated with a great deal of critical caution—it is not (able) to be wished away or simply erased by critique. Certainly there is much that must not be forgotten. Here witnesses are at large in the world, and their memories of modernization and colonization, continually question the positions and perspectives of the historians.

History and humanism

The Enlightenment welded history to its fabricator/fabrication ("man")— the individuated rational humanist subject. Metaphysics, in this context, validated the history/man nexus. In recoil, Theodore Adorno and Walter Benjamin grounded the being of both in another of the Enlightenment's project's "discoveries": "nature." Seemingly they were going somewhere, but as we shall see, in the end they went nowhere. "Man" is ripped from "nature" by humanism negating "our" animality. Moreover, there is no binary: man/nature (the animal that "we" are, no matter who we tell ourselves we are, rips the nature/nurture debate to pieces). "We" remain the "wonderful and terrible" (understood as *deinon*: that overpowering power of our being unsurpassed in its strangeness[21]).

The challenge before us goes beyond Eurocentric errors of constructed history (as it marginalized and erased the historical significance of Others). It exceeds all such errors in its global and continuing consequences. This challenge cannot be met by searching for authentic history (notwithstanding that for some it will be felt and claimed as authentic). Science does not provide a way forward—it certainly does not provide truth or fact supported by observation. Rather science creates a worldview that clarifies "idealizations" endemic to itself.[22] Historically it thus created a position of observation that arrived, and appeared to observe nature from a position outside it ("man").

The combination of the Enlightenment's fabrication of "man," globalized by Eurocentric colonialism, imposed a universal construct of "the human"—a "civilized and civilizing being" that was deployed in ways that dehumanized all being deemed Other.[23] This protracted action not only repressed our own understanding, and our dealing with "the animal that we are," it was equally a refusal to recognize those Others whose sense of being was not predicated on the binary division human/animal but on a continuum of the being that we are. The human was, is and remains an epistemological imposition.

Ontology and history

The challenge before us thinkers of, or about, design is to hold the ground of the advancement of "history" counter to consciousness. What this means is holding the space of possibility opened by Heidegger's recognition of the interpretation of history centering on the historical being an ontologically foundational structure. The nature of this structure is not recoverable in itself, rather it arrives in the form of interpretations emanating from a new ontology, which itself is an effect of a practice of transformation. "History" (the historical) here is placed before design as agency—as historical events that in significant part ontologically design subjects that interpret them (the past). Historical agency is therefore lodged in foundational events that, in part, bring them, as subjects, into being. It follows that there is simply not "us" and historical events *for we are historical*—even though "we" (in all our differences) have little or no awareness of our being as such. As historical beings we are a trace of more than the past experiences of our "self."

There can be no appeal to our coming out of nature. Humanity has no natural history (as Adorno and Benjamin would have it[24]). We *Homo sapiens* are not historically or ontologically "natural" beings, albeit that we humans created the world-within-the-world out of, and in, that which is deemed "nature." Our very coming into being was a rupture from the "general economy" of exchange ("life") that insured the formation of a history that fused the "natural" and the artificial. As argued at length elsewhere, "we" arrived as an animal onto-technologically predestined to become a biological/technological (world-designing) hybrid.[25] The animal that we were was ontologically designed by the use of basic (stone) tools to become the human-animal that we now are. In this sense, "we" did not invent technology; rather, technology invented us (and continues to do so). The persistent idea that technology is merely a tool we use de facto feeds a dangerous illusion.

The decentering of historical consciousness brings the notion of historical experience into question. The assumption has been that it is possible to gain a genuine experience of one's own historicity (this as we are bound to objects of experience).[26] However, ontological design (across the full range of the conditions of being that "we" as a species occupy) reveals the gap between the agency of the object of experience and knowledge of experience and, as such, exposes a structural lack of awareness of design, not least by designers. Thus, a hermeneutical engagement with experience does not necessarily get to the ontological production of what is being examined here. A simple example makes the point: the passage from instruction to intuition is not retained as a remembered experience (one does not remember learning to talk, what it was like to learn how to walk nor, perhaps, the first time a pencil was held and used; other memories blur, like learning to ride a bike, to tie one's shoe laces etc.). Formative experience is not available for interpretation, or free from re-presentation (the constructed memory in childhood by "an other" is a part of what "I" take to be "my" memory). Moreover, one must not assume that experience implies and equates with authenticity. As Edmund Husserl, in his examination of scientific thought made very clear, idealization travels ahead of us as "we" experience "the world" and as such prefigures a great deal of what is experienced.[27]

Yet there can be no argument that experience begs interrogation, is of great complexity, and folds into the condition of the mode of presence of the "Being-of-beings."[28] Certainly it can deliver knowledge (but once it becomes this it ceases to be experience). Thereafter experience provides subjects with objectified insights of/into their positive and the negative worldly encounters: their pain and their pleasures.[29] However, it is the case that all claims to experiential truth, and their sufficiency as causal agents, remain problematic.

Now

All things meet in the transience of "now." The past and the future are only ever viewed, understood and represented from a "now," a constant moment of time—or as Benjamin engaged it, *jetztzeit* (an everlasting now). The form of this particular figure of the displacement of history will receive much more attention later. But for the moment all we wish to do is: (i) to note that a primary characteristic of our present moment is the negation of time (a negation we have called defuturing—those actions that reduce the time of our finitude as finite beings), and (ii) acknowledge that all "nows" are not the same.

Defuturing qualifies the process whereby we are all living in a continuous structural condition of unsustainability. To better understand this moment requires gaining a clear understanding of how defuturing is reconfiguring both the past and the future, and thereafter how this knowledge is key to act counter-wise (the practice and process of futural action toward Sustainment).

Futuring education: Design and history

Design education is in flux. The technological inroad into the craft practices of design continues apace. The distinction between its subdisciplines— product/interior/visual communication design etc., continue to blur. Newer areas, like service design, are becoming more established. The demand for designers to be ever-better informed beyond the bounds of design practice and design theory (including design thinking) constantly increases. And the viability and appropriateness of simply educating designers to be "service providers" is now becoming questioned. But above all, the key issue that design and design education has to face is whether it is going to remain within its currently limited sphere of aesthetic-economic function, or enlarge its scope to more significantly engage the geoenvironmental and sociopsycho challenges arriving in this emergent age of unsettlement.

For design education to rise to the challenges posed it would have to rupture its relation to the instrumentalism that brought it into the academy and act against the more pervasive degeneration of education, not least university education, into instrumentalism (the servicing of the needs of "the economy" and the associated demands of scientific pragmatism). Such a move, of course, requires education constituting a new vision and project informed by a critique of its current modality, and clear understanding of the existing and coming imperatives of unsettlement.

Against this backdrop one is required to acknowledge that the ambitions of the Enlightenment, and the kindred project of modernity, died and were not replaced with a new and better vision. The result is that learning itself has become diminished and devalued. So much education has lost sight of what really needs to be learnt, with a great deal of what is actually delivered directed by concerns of the status quo and government (there are numerous publications and many international conferences supporting this view[30]). So positioned, the critique of education turns on two fundamental observations.

First, institutionalized education mostly educates for "the world that was" rather than "the world that is." What this means is that, from kindergarten to the postgraduate level, people are *now* "educated in error." Thus, as earlier implied, children and adults are being inducted into values, practices and knowledge that in the end serve to extend the unsustainable everyday *everywhere*. This educational debacle, and its accompanying void, did not happen by accident; rather, it was created, and can be characterized, as such, in various ways, for example, as:

- An induction into capital logic as "the appropriate" foundation of exchange (whereas, such "logic" rests upon unsustainable modes of production and consumption bonded to the notion of continual economic growth, within a finite system—our planetary system, and thus is illogical);

- An induction into the unrestrained acquisition of a world of manufactured things deployed as (conspicuous consumption) to mark worldly "success";

- An induction into consumption as an expression of freedom. At best one can say that that while institutional education may provide knowledge, plus many skills and competencies able to assist career advancement, at best it only partially educates. Certainly institutions, as they stand, fail to educate for the future—they fail to be futural, they are unable to present and deal with the complexity of the worlds of "human" habitation. What this might mean is what we are about to explore.

To become futural in this context is not an option, if humanity is to be able to learn how to sustain itself and all that it depends upon. What this means is: first, thinking and creating in the medium of time, and in the understanding that the future is already populated by many problems (including the related problems of climate change) that have been thrown into it. Then second, learning how to better track the consequences of our material actions on all the environments of our existence over far longer expanses of time.

Besides a failure of education content, there is also a failure of method. As Iain Thomson explores at length, universities have lost the essence of *paideia*. But what does this mean, and what exactly has been lost? As Thomson points out, Heidegger describes *paideia* very clearly in saying it is a means that enables us to "become what we are." As such, it teaches us "to dwell." It lays hold "of our very soul," transforms it and then returns us to the essential place of our being.[31]

What we are as a human being is not what we can be reduced to (our animality, bare life, a Eurocentrically totalized subject and so on) but rather our potentiality in difference. Heidegger's declaration that to "become what you are" is to be situated in a context of becoming, which is a condition of emergence informed by what this being desires to be, or realize (ambitions, dreams and goals).[32] But becoming is always a becoming situated somewhere in cultural space. To realize this is to transform one's potentiality. For instance, to discover one is Eurocentrically placed in the world to "become what you are" means undergoing a process of epistemological decolonialization enabling reflection upon "what you were made." The ambitions, abysmal dreams and forged goals in the wake of this reflection can but disrupt, disturb and crack the colonized identity, and in so doing open a space into which something other than that self can insinuate itself.

Education is inherently futural: it is a form of ontological designing. As such it can deliver positive or negative futures. What is lost in the negative (currently seen in the economic functionalism of instrumentalized education) is the potentiality of individuals to realize what they could become in their difference. It follows, and universally, that in the early twenty-first century universities have to be "led" away from their subordination to the instrumental and specifically:

- The continued damage they do to the already damaged Humanities (both in terms of their status, level of presence and critical content—this not on the basis that the Humanities need to be saved but rather that they be available to be transformed), and

- Vocational programs servicing the structurally unsustainable status quo (in pragmatic areas like business, tourism, marketing, public relations, nursing, project management, accountancy and of course computing) have to be eliminated or redirected. Such programs in almost all disciplines are now presented and marketed in terms of their claim to having a "use value" and delivering career prospect/jobs.[33]

Institutional managerialism accompanied the rise of such instrumentalism. Both trends have contributed to the modern university becoming a diminished institution, lacking vision and meaning within public culture. This situation is, of course, not a sudden occurrence but one that gained momentum over the last century.[34]

Against this backdrop, if we define *paideia* as "real" and "essential" education, then the view of existing instrumentalized and conformist education can be seen as not just an abandonment of our self-realization but also a fundamental failure to really identify what knowledge should be and direct—this within global contemporary sociocultural, geopolitical, economic and environmental circumstances as they harbour the defuturing forces of structural unsustainability. To acknowledge and expose the specific characteristics of this situation makes possible much of what actuality needs to be newly learnt to advance the condition upon which life, not just human life, as we know it depends—Sustainment.

Here we acknowledge that metaphysics, from its inception, directed the very form of knowledge within which all Western education became situated. Following Heidegger's critique of metaphysics, Thomson elaborated how it delivered what he called "ontological holism"—a mode of being with knowledge of which there was no exterior.[35] He suggested that "by giving shape to our most historical understanding of 'what is' metaphysics determines the most basic presuppositions of what *anything is*, including *education*."[36] Of this understanding Thomson also observes that it makes "education" possible, both as knowing what entities are and how our knowledge of them is transformed.[37] However, in a post-Enlightenment defuturing world, such education, as indicated, is now insufficient. The absence of design education (understood here not as it is, but with its true potential of disclosing world making and unmaking) is just one example of such insufficiency.

Foundationally what is established by metaphysics is the extension of a particular condition of being: a globalizing Western condition of being within an ontotheological understanding of what knowledge is and does. Effectively what this being-in-a-condition-of-belief means is that there is "what is" and a history of being with an absolute belief *that arrives with the ability bring the "what is" within the realm of knowledge.* Thus the caesura between "what is" and "how it is known" goes unseen. This condition of limitation (a condition intrinsic to the metaphysics of presence) has been universalized under the direction of a process of epistemological colonialization (as it equally colonizes the colonizer and thereafter the colonized). Such a "mode of being with knowledge has no exterior"—all other modes of knowledge are either unseen or deemed operationally inferior (esoteric). It follows that the belief in such knowledge is taken to be the total sphere of authentic knowing and, as such, completely colonizes—but it does so not as under the mantle of imposition but in the name and guise of a gift (education).

A critique of the Eurocentrically grounded metaphysics from the viewpoint of epistemological colonialism, as it layers onto the structural traces of colonialism in global inequity and conflicts, arrives as just another face of defuturing."[38] This is to say it is elemental to the ontologically designing essence of unsustainability (as it forms the basis of so much of the "knowledge" upon which defuturing actions are based). Knowledge of "what is" and "the world" cannot be divided from "knowing" how to act in and upon "the world." In a deeply structurally unsustainable world, by implication, this means people are educated into defuturing actions. Thus, countering such education and knowledge changes our knowing of every*thing*. Effectively, the arrival of such counter knowledge demands engagment in a process of unlearning, and it is this unlearning that enable "true" learning to become a possibility. All this means that in confronting the unsustainable, the very ground of education shifts.

What this shift reveals acts to confirm Heidegger's realization that education is grounded in the history of being (but with the caveat that this history is neither totalized nor of the singular). To comprehend this is again to realize that the ontotheological foundation of "our" education, as the ground of all we know, is a reaffirmation of ontological designing at its most fundamental. Education, so grasped, is absolutely directional: underlying all that is learnt is the mode of being into which the learner is placed.

Our concern with design remains central to this exposition as, by implication, we are all designed into the way we know by informal and formal education, and thereafter act in the belief in the validity of the foundational knowledge of our knowing (the taken-for-granted knowledge "we" inhabit – or *habitus*). What is to be done in this situation? For it appears to contain a double bind—namely: we only know there is a problem via the way we know, which we gain as a result of the way we have been educated into a way of knowing.

These comments take us back to the now dominant instrumental paradigm of education, and again to the recognition that the colonizing forces of education are always a displacement and imposition. At its most basic, this is characterized by the notion that "we are born an animal and are made a human by education." What education displaces is not the fact of our animality; rather, it represses its social appearance. The way we know is one thing, what we know is another. For knowing to become otherwise, as we have acknowledged, existing ways of knowing have to be disrupted by a process of unlearning.

Thomson suggests: "we need an alternative to our contemporary understanding of education, one capable of favorably resolving our education crisis by averting the technological dissolution of the historical essence of education."[39] But as indicated, "our education crisis" needs more than this.

In Thomson's terms, this means departing from instrumental "information based knowledge accumulation," and "how-to learning," to a privileging of the question of "why" and practices of "situated learning." Calling up Plato and Heidegger, he hopes to restore "meaning to the increasingly formal and empty ideas guiding contemporary education."[40] Both these proposals invite a critical response, which must include an acknowledgement of the long and dark shadow cast over education by

Eurocentrism, as well as the clearing of a space into which difference can arrive.

Let's start by looking at the issue of "averting the technological dissolution of the historical essence of education." Two problems arise immediately when considering this.

The first problem is that Thomson's statement assumes technology to be an external agent, yet he is familiar with Heidegger's notion of "the essence of modern technology" being identical with "the essence of modern metaphysics"—whereby technology is metaphysics "completed."[41] But as already established, metaphysics determines what *anything is* and as such establishes our condition of being, *ergo*: we are technological Beings-in-being. Yet what an ontological design informed critique of Heidegger's view of "man" as "world forming" reveals is that ontologically "we" have always been technological and that now, with metaphysics becoming technology, we are completed as technological beings. This of course is not to say "we" are machines," but it is to recognize that the ontological designing of technology has gone way beyond changing the way we make a world-within-the-world.

Huge numbers of us think and act within a technospheric existence. The interface has dissolved, now there is no boundary between the inside and the outside, interiority and the exterior.[42] "We" are now fully technologically "naturalized" (it is as much of our nature as "nature"). What becomes at issue, what is at stake, is contesting the *nature* of technology as: environment, as ontological form-giving, and as directionality (wherein the distinction between user and used is rendered meaningless). The key to doing this, it is suggested, is a form of "creative alienation" whereby technological being becomes an object of projective and reflective "observed observation" that is focused upon how what is observed is actually observed. Methodologically this method is indivisible from one brought to the observation of ecological systems by Niklas Luhmann.[43] This means that rather than being seen/seeing our self as singular, as monad, as an objectification (as the Enlightenment would have it, as the primary object of enquiry), we recognize that we are relational—thus co-joined by our animality to the biophysical sphere and overdetermined as a self by our social ecology. Effectively, our "modern" sense of self ruptures us from what there is to know about what we relationally actually are. This is not to suggest we are not a self but rather that we are more than it names—and that this "more" is a "cleared space" into which a difference to be learnt can arrive.

The second problem Thompson gives us is that *paideia* (as "the historical essence of education") has not actually survived "the dissolution of" metaphysics and the marginalization of ontological inquiry. However, in reframing "what is" beyond a Western metaphysical characterization, as well as "what there is to learn," a possibility arrives for a remaking. *Paideia* is learning and law embedded in the forms of designation of education. It is (ontological) design. As *habitus*, it is a historical presence that is futural (it takes us to our future).[44]

Certainly there are currently no organizational models, politically coherent projects or agreed agenda for such a fundamental reframing of education. Yet there are counter-institutional projects arriving that do strive to build a way of knowing and acting that can seriously challenge the now dominant instrumental paradigm.[45] In all cases what is shared is a substantial critique of the status quo, recoil against the structurally unsustainable, a recognition of the imperative of intercultural understanding, and of making futures that have the sustaining-ability all we depend upon, that go to what we humans should be rather than just what we are.

Notwithstanding dealing with questions of metaphysics/technology, it follows that the resolution of the "education crisis" that Thomson speaks of is as much a political challenge (geopolitically and personally) as it is an intellectual one. His hope to reinstate "meaning to the increasingly formal and empty ideas guiding contemporary education" is clearly not enough. The task is far larger than this. What is actually needed is not just "meaning" but rather a reconfiguration of what is to be learnt (this to recover, understand and redirect old critical content, and to invent new content that is apposite to the times). When moving to discuss Heidegger's belief in and commitment to "ontological education" Thomson understands this as education disclosing the "essential in all things." What he overlooks are those divisions of knowledge that disable science from delivering relational thought and action in a world where the colonizer gives due recognition to the colonized.[46]

Thomson asks: how can Heidegger's ontological education combat the metaphysical education "we" have always received? The answer given by Heidegger, which resonates with what was said on creative alienation earlier, is totally counter to the contemporary instrumental and technocentric mode. What Heidegger advocated, as indicated by Thomson, looks like a counter action.[47] This can be summarized as:

- Students breaking their "bondage to the technological mode of revealing, freeing themselves to understand the being of 'what-is' in a different way"[48]—this being linked to his understanding of *paideia* as an exposure of the essence of things (that is their "thinging").

- Students liberating themselves from the grip of metaphysics in relation to the knowledge they have acquired (here is the move from a claim to know to a motivation to understand).

- Students learning the relation to dwelling, as an attunement to the essence of things beyond their ontologically directive technological enframing (impositional form) thereby seeing the "world" of beings, and things as beings, as animated with no-thing as passive and reified.

The convergence between *paideia*, as understood so far, decolonization, and education (centering on ontological design) begs noting. While Heidegger posed education against metaphysically overdetermined education as mere "teaching," ontological design education (as education against instrumentalized design) names its pedagogic practice as "futuring." Decoloniality, while having a totally different agent and agenda, shares the same goal.[49]

Appropriation and the new university

The idea of a new form of the university does not assume a "green field project" that claims pedagogic and market difference from the "modern university." Rather, and informed by the emergent projects, it needs to be far more strategic to succeed and really have the kind of transformative impact needed.

There are strong clues on how to do this to be found in non-Western progressive institutions[50] and in the transition of the first European Universities (the first of which, the University of Bologna, was founded around 1155) to the modern university. The primary objective of these early universities was theological and legal, with their power centered on the Church. This disposition continued with the rise of the medieval university. Then at the start of the fifteenth century, prefigured by the rise of the Renaissance and an interest in the classical world (via Greek learning arriving by mediation from the Middle East), the power of reason started to ascend as a conceptually refined and directive mode of thought in the face of resistance from the Christian church.

As the Western university started to explore the agency of reason, the institution started to transform, knowledge started to divide and the influence and agency of science grew. The path to its secularization was set and over the next few hundred years the modern university developed. Increasingly as modernity became a global project the expansion of knowledge was marked by a deepening ignorance of other kinds of knowing from elsewhere.

In the present moment, prompted by the necessity of creating the kind of knowledge that Sustainment demands (which for reasons stated cannot be met by the educational status quo), what is now being called the "Urmadic University" is one example of redirective change. Its form is as a university without a place, and without cultural ownership by one culture (while rejecting pluralism), but with a dispersed community and a clear program of learning for change—as such, it is more than just another network organization. The strategic intent, learning from the formation of the modern university as it resulted from acts of appropriation enacted by the medieval university, is to mirror this process so that eventually the new knowledge displaces the old. Within such a model, the *historical understanding of design* occupies a position of major importance, in contrast to the inability of "design history" to add to a relational understanding of the consequences of the historical agency of the designed.

Obviously there are a large number of issues and questions thrown up by comments made here, and these will engaged at length in the essays to follow. The hope is that the engagement with history, design and education to be presented will generate debate, gather interest, inform action and produce change.

1 REMEMBERINGS AND DISMEMBERINGS

Whatever has a beginning deserves to have an undoing
JOHANN WOLFGANG VON GOETHE

As Friedrich Nietzsche knew, perhaps more than any thinker before or even since: the critical shatters "and dissolves something to enable" life. This is how history placed in such a frame of understanding stands before us in fragments. Insightful readers of the historical recognize this, others do not—not least because there is a covering-over, a fabricated illusion, which gets called "history." The language of history hides what has befallen it. The hidden is not only what is broken into a myriad pieces but also what is a nascent assembly. Our aim here then is to trawl through the shattering of history in order to find and expose what a process of remaking could future.

History: Points of difference in a world of fragments

World is so often mobilized as if it were a unified and unifying idea. But it is not. The physical object, the planet, is not "the world." Rather, the planet is, for us, a mere container of that difference created by the world's "we" construct, via the plurality of our ideas, worldviews, related projections, and practices. Thus the reality of what is frequently deemed to be singular is nothing more than a collection of culturally prefigured fragments, which we attempt, ongoingly, to politically force into a union (named, for example, as "world"). History has been made to conspire with this falsity, and still does so, yet history's shattering equally shatters a world of meaning and, as will be seen in a later essay, every possibility of "world history."

The noise of history

Even though it has amassed a mountain of literature, and has generated a vast amount of historical debate across millennia, history itself has no voice.

While so many have lain claim to actually speak for history nobody has or can. There is only a cacophony of voices asserting arguments, statements and making judgments about the idea or the status and qualities of the textual products that travel in its name. Likewise, and in every case, the management of historical appearances, narratives and claims to historical facts fall into an abyss from which they never reappear. Here they become entangled in, and indivisible from, perspectival problems of observation and interpretation, with the (historical) even(t) out of reach. Thereafter, all that is rendered visible arrives in the company of concealment, omissions and bias. So understood it can be said that there is no essential, resolved and closed history of the Crusades, World War II, the black death, the birth of capitalism, the Enlightenment, Rome, the colonization of Africa or any other moment registered in the vast plethora of other historical events, large or small. What are actually available are just histories framed by the exercise of power vested in acts of narrativization situated in, and by, specific powers that claim an authority to speak. Notwithstanding many valiant projects, the powerless, the less than marginal, do not produce history (they are just (dis)placed within it as "accommodated" historical actors en masse).

As we shall see, the realization that history is illusionary, and infused with fictions, has produced a number of recoils which have opened new ways to think and engage "the event" (pro)claimed as history. These recoils are basically against history constituted as encased, complete, closed and, above all as that held in the grip of the past. Equally, these recoils are also about the historian as the gatekeeper of the past who, as characterized by Mark Poster, is "an intellectual who presides over the past, nurtures it, develops it, and controls it."[1] To make this clearer, we will evoke just one "event" already named—the Crusades.

The West's history tells of nine Crusades—the first starting in 1096 and the last ending in 1291. If this history arrives in the West in the present day it dominantly does so as image: be it of knights in armor configured as the trace of an ill-understood campaign to extend the command of Christianity in the "holy land" as caricatured in film, as a movie set itself, a backdrop to a novel, an image on the wall of an art gallery or in a history textbook. Notwithstanding these images, for all but a few specialist historians, the Crusades are events of a mostly forgotten past. But for the world of Islam, the Crusades are an enduring and violent presence. They remain inscribed in space, landscape, memory, and in the sociotheological divisions of everyday life. Thus their consequences live on in mind and contemporary life, and as such continue to configure events that mark a regional geography and geopolitics. Their afterlife retains agency within conflicts in the Middle East of the present, and as a remembrance that will continue to arrive from the future.

History and historians

There are a legion of historians whom one could call upon from the past to speak for the discipline of history: Marc Bloch, Isaiah Berlin, E.P. Thomson, E.H. Carr, Arthur Marwick, R.G. Collingwood, A.J. Toynbee, Heinrich Rickert, Leopold von Ranke, and many more. All these historians recognized that the representation of history was replete with problems, but assumed that the past nonetheless was to hand as an available, meaningful object of enquiry. However, from the late-nineteenth century this assumption was challenged. The opening salvos came from Friedrich Nietzsche. Later they came from thinkers as diverse as Oswald Spengler and Karl Barth who both made their rejection of history as a domain of meaning clear. However, as we shall see, it was Martin Heidegger who went beyond the available debates on history, meaning and its locus, to provide the most radical resolution—he simply posited history in "us." As historical beings, we are history. What this move did was to reject any notion of history depending upon a logical method of inquiry or a science, and instead adopt a position based on history as historicity. Hereafter, it became "an ontological exploration of the roots of human being in the world" in order to understand what it meant "to be historical."[2] As a consequence of this major shift of focus, the way meaning and history were conceptualized dramatically changed. Charles Bambach well expressed this: "The genuine experience of history for Heidegger was not about reconstructing facts but about retrieving the meaning of the past within the situation of the present as a possibility for one's own future."[3]

What can be recognized from this reconfiguration of how history is viewed is that while historical narratives recognize the diverse forms of agency of human actors—collective and individual—in historical events what gets underplayed is that "we" are historically formed beings. As such, "we" bear the weight of our own history. History thus, as Heidegger pointed out in a letter to Karl Jaspers, "is what we are."[4] This means that the essence of history is nothing "historical" (nothing delivered by historical research or writing) but rather resides in us and our actions.[5]

Heidegger's thinking on history was not formed in isolation but under the influence of one of the most progressive historians of the day, Wilhelm Dilthey (1833–1911).[6] It is therefore most appropriate that Dilthey is given critical consideration.

For all his insights Dilthey still stands for the flawed ontology of the historian. Central to this ontology was a belief that in writing history the historian has the imaginative reach to access and recapture the past, draw out experience from it, and then represent it. In support of this, Dilthey claimed that events could be "emplotted" in ways that position meaning without the disruption of "historical facts." This argument reproduced a long established opposition between "truth" and "facts" while actually claiming the creation of new meaning. Clearly, as a consequence of retrospective reconstruction, "facts" always remain open to being contested. The second and more significant reason why Dilthey is of interest is that he acted as a vector projecting a Kantian idealist understanding of knowledge into the future. As a result his thinking acquired a foundational status for future historians, but at the same time it acted to link Kant and Heidegger's understanding of history and in doing this he essentially he drew a fundamental distinction between scientific and cultural knowledge which posited two distinct forms of experience.

In viewing "the flawed ontology of the historian" one can add that a great deal of the critique of the history of historians (including design historians) goes to their failure to confront, expose and interrogate their *habitus*. This means that their taken-for-granted knowledge—the knowledge of the practices they are inducted into—goes unexamined. These practices, like all others, arrive via an ontological designing.

Dilthey's influence on Heidegger was substantial; specifically, in his proposition that the acquisition of historical experience produces existential change. However, and problematically, Dilthey's reading and weaving together of time, culture and circumstance always resulted in a relativistic history that folded into idealism carrying truth claims.[7] Most problematically, Dilthey never resolved the epistemological problem of "history itself having the ability to reveal knowledge of the past." A key reason for this was that he deployed a faith in science to explain the nature of life, while at the same time privileging the agency of experience.[8] In spite of these limitations, Dilthey did provide Heidegger with a critical insight through his notion of "*Lebensanalyse*" (analysis of human life), which gave Heidegger his opening position in *Being and Time*. It was from this position that Heidegger engaged and developed a critical transcendence able to underscore his claim to an existential hermeneutics. As we read in *Being and Time*, this insight was informed especially by the correspondence on the topics of science, logic and history that took place between Dilthey and his friend Count Yorck von Wartenburg.[9] To this debate Heidegger brought Edmund Husserl's recognition that historical beings and natural beings are not divisible, for they both have those temporal differences that constitute their historicity.[10]

We have to see Dilthey very much as a product of his moment. During the nineteenth century history became elevated to a science (not least in Germany); many historians asserted a calculative objectivity that ran alongside, and sought to draw upon, the assent of the power of science. This was a key moment in which the truth claims of science became elevated above subjectivism. What resulted from this move was history becoming dislocated from all other modes of knowledge and projected as an independent "object for itself."[11] "The Western mind" still exists in the shadow of this moment. Here, then, is a disjuncture that, as will become apparent, Nietzsche reacted against.

The momentum given to the authority of history by its becoming claimed as science paradoxically marked a diminution of history's social status—"social history" was never able to redeem the consequences of its de-socialization. Its claim to being a science meant that history was understood to be purely accountable to itself, detached and thus without need for any kind of "check or balance." The past was removed from time by arresting it. Likewise history was placed outside and beyond the subject standing before it. As a result the history/life nexus, wherein history could be thought to appear as refracted experience (via the familiar or unfamiliar, the same or difference), became disfigured and stripped of life as lived, it thus became "an eternal non-subjectivity."[12]

Objectively "true" history is impossible. Yet the claim of objectivity, and its refutation, has been continuously debated for almost two hundred years. But as examples evident in current debate show, the argument asserting "true history" constantly gets weaker.[13] It has been virtually universally accepted in secular societies that there is no history without interpretation, and that as soon as interpretation arrives so does perspectival difference. At the same time it is equally important to understand that history is not just a "product" of interpretation but rather an act that itself "has a history of its own."[14] Even more destabilizing has been the breakdown of any notion of correspondence between objectivity and reality—this has been made clear by postmodern theory and in the more general undercutting of the authority of the discourse of history by deconstruction. It is not that "objective conditions" (the ontic) are said not to exist but rather, after postmodern theory, there is now no consensual view of the nature of reality (not that, in truth, there ever was) or of a position from which to observe it. What therefore now pertains is the absence of any form of authority able to speak from a position outside of pluralism. There is no longer a voice able to rise above the noise of the clamor of voices.

Notwithstanding that history is increasingly conceptually and practically becoming viewed as problematic (and as we proceed it will become ever more so) a question arises. It can be posed as follows: is there a widespread, intercultural and existential need for history, and does history, even as flawed, nonetheless still provide an actual sense of meaning, direction and identity? This question is neither mine nor new. It preoccupied, for instance, Eric Weil in his *Logique de la philosophie*, first published in Paris in 1950.[15] Certainly, as will be made clear, history now exists against a theoretical backdrop that totally rejects it having any value. Moreover, and more stridently, are those political movements (like Italian Futurism) and regimes (like those in China in the mid-nineteenth and twentieth centuries) that saw the past/history as an obstruction blocking a path to the future and thus requiring to be removed. While historians do not knowingly act against the future, they mostly do not grasp the history they author as a designing force—this is to say they do not sufficiently engage the "having been" as futurally determinate. As Bambach points out: "Classical historians denied this futural dimension of historical experience, preferring to explore the epistemological questions of verification and access."[16]

Now is the moment

Time is not what it is so often taken to be (the measure of duration), but is, in its essence, process, change and a "medium in which events occur."[17] It follows that there has never been one time in a historical sense. Yet there has been a violent moment of its enforcement—the forced time of "modernity" (which can be understood as time/event without unity within the context of the fragmentation of history) wherein a Eurocentric-directed ordering attempted to bring all global others into one moment of control.[18] In this respect modernity/Western colonialism was a displacement of multiple orders of difference within which specific (geographic) cultures and their modality of time arrived. Thereafter, it imposed and made dominant an ordering regime of everyday life, knowledge and thought.[19]

So although, as Heidegger recognized and explained, everything has its own time, "we" all are "now" configured within a moment, "a history"— presented as the appearance of time past—that is, continually present as that which is absent. Here the past is concealed by its simulacra (historical movies, TV series, novels, museum displays, exhibitions, heritage architecture and so on). At the same time traces remain. Contrary to appearances (textual), historians are not the keepers of these traces. Their discovery and following has shifted to cultural theorists (of which the work of Michel Foucault still remains the most influential). There are a number of reasons why this has happened, including history's internal implosion as a discipline; the more general decline of support for, and the presence of, the Humanities in universities; and uncertainty about how to deal with history in the often confused curricula of primary and secondary school education. Against this backdrop one asks, as others have before, "so what is history now"? This question is yet another question we will travel with, displace and (re)visit.

At this juncture we note that history is a discipline and practice in crisis that mostly refuses to recognize this situation, but in so doing exacerbates it. Notwithstanding this, a new practice beckons.

So what is critical?

We human beings live with both the living and the dead. We walk with the ghosts of many who have gone before us—we are haunted by their writing, thoughts, images, objects, institutions, and actions. They are present, if physically absent, as beings that in their wake leave deposits that we that mostly ignore; or occasionally uncover and sometimes try to examine. Besides memories, it is to these ghosts and deposits and traces that we turn to find out whom once we were, and it is by their perpetual presence that we are eternally haunted.

The state of history, as has been registered, is terminally fractured. While this can be deemed to be critical for history it is not a historical crisis. Such a crisis is the gathering of what is actually conjuncturally critical at the level of: life or death, the form of the future, the fate of a nation and so on. As a naming, a historical crisis is always a masking of what is actually critical, present and futural. Likewise, the critical condition of what actually threatens comes from the past as it has been lodged in the future. Crisis, it should be said, is never without ambiguity. It can, and often is, breakdown, decline, destruction, end, but equally it can be opening, transition, or opportunity. More than this, crisis is so often a crisis of omission, neglect and blindness.[20] Positioned "in crisis," our fate may be decided circumstantially and/or perceptually. History so framed, as Heidegger understood, was a crisis of the futural. As many commenters have noted, he saw history as crisis embedded in Western thought that required a return to its Greek beginning.[21] But of course even if this were possible, a journey through ruins scattered across a wasteland, and any remaking cannot simply be another Eurocentric fabrication, "time and the world" have turned. At the same time this beginning does not just remain in the past, for the ruins mark its passage towards and with "us"; but "us" are we of the West. So when Heidegger, for example, called for the West's return to its Greek beginning, or equally when he asserted "we" all think like the Greeks, he was manifesting the extent of his Eurocentric *habitus* and placing himself in what now looks like a politico-epistemological crisis.

In 1982 philosopher Reiner Schürmann posed the question: "Are we the precursors of a dawn of an entirely different world age, which has left our contemporary representations of history behind?" We are now in a position to answer his question without equivocation—yes. Such representations are now behind us and we have moved to futures that seriously reconfigure how the past is referenced. Directional figures of the future from the past, as embedded in represented material forms and events, like the West's model of "development" and "progress" fall. Although "we" en masse are not static, we have no destination and are deeply implicated, by globalism, in forces of defuturing (actions that in our finitude take time away)—thus "our time" as a species is being negated.[22] To recognize this situation is to grasp that "our age" is one of growing unsettlement grounded in the structural unsustainability of the world-within-the-world of human fabrication. In the shadow of this knowledge, it appears, at least for those who care to look, that a great deal of what has been written as "the history of human attainment" is in fact a produced liability carrying danger into the future.

There is a need in fact to place the fracturing of history within what is increasingly unfolding as critical of our age as unsettlement. While unsettlement is arriving as an age wherein serious biophysical, climatic, psychological, economic and geopolitical dangers combine in ways that can easily trigger environmental crises, conflicts and social and economic breakdowns, it is even more than this. The fracturing of history, placed in this context, makes this clear. The experience of the loss of ecologies, being forced to move because of climate change impacts, economic regression, living in a condition of deep uncertainty, are just some examples of how unsettlement disrupts and fractures history; where and what one has been attached to, the expected future that history has constructed, historically established identities, the break-up of nation, the termination of long-standing traditions—these possibilities and actualities all illustrate the point.

So contextualized, the past does not arrive "now" in ways that historians have ordered, classified and interpreted as generalities (like centuries, periods, geographies) or as neatly ordered events (such as wars, revolutions, civilizations). Time and events are becoming disordered, as the disjuncture between systems of classification and that to which they are applied increases. Moreover, the notion of "the human" as placed within a regime of continual evolution has no remaining credence: "we" and "history" are going nowhere.[23] In our difference we affirm the Nietzschean notion of "the return of the same."

Starting at the end

The notion of the end of history has been around for a long time. It was elemental to Enlightenment thought (Kant, for example, posed it as a possibility if war was brought to a total end). But more than anyone else, Hegel framed the understanding that what "the end" and "completion of history" meant was the arrival at an "Endstate" (the *telos* of reason realized as the fully rational state) wherein the developmental trajectory of history—social, political, economic—had arrived at its destined destination. This thinking had a certain revivalist moment in 1992 with the publication of Francis Fukuyama's *The End of History and the Last Man*.[24] Fukuyama argued (and subsequently distanced himself from) that the end of the Cold War marked a victory of capitalism over communism with liberal democracy arriving as the final form of political evolution. Now several decades on, capitalism is staggering and the last remaining quasi-communist force on the planet—China—is headed (be it more tentatively) toward economically overpowering the USA. Moreover, liberal democracy has shown itself to be ailing and incapable of recognizing, and so dealing with, the historical crisis of defuturing and the demands of an "age of unsettlement."[25] In a real sense it is visionless, and so "future blind."

Between Hegel and Fukuyama's failed projects can be found Alexandre Kojève's Hegelian inspired declaration on the end of history resting upon the view that Hegel had actually "drawn a line" under the very possibility of history.[26] From this point onward all that was possible was for history to repeat itself in another form and moment (which is simply meant another version of "the return of the same").

Accompanying the politico-philosophical claim of the end of history is the perception held within the practice of history itself that history has ended. Perhaps more than anyone else this view is clearly expressed by Keith Jenkins. For him historical scholarship has become just "an act of imagination (*illusio*) ever bereft of certainty . . . history has no definitive object of enquiry nor any definitive mode of enquiry."[27] The desire to know the past cannot be realized. Jenkins thus concludes that history is merely a form of rhetoric that is never for itself but always for a "someone," which is to say that "historians cannot provide any objective/universal idea of direction, aim, purpose, meaning, truth, etc."[28] Unambiguously Jenkins states: "we can now live without histories of either a modernist or postmodernist kind."[29] While these snippets caricature what is a substantial argument, they do directly communicate the extent to which the practice of history is seen by a body of more radical historical thinkers as terminal.[30]

Out of historicity: Casting back

Our concern here will be with the nature of historicity, but before discussing this there are still more qualifications of history, following Jenkins, that need to be assembled into what remains an emergent point of view to consider.

Restating: history is neither unified nor singular. Notwithstanding the construction of appearances of history in numerous forms of its representation it is never seamless or resolved by narrative. Rather history is always grounded in a specific perspective. By implication this means that it cannot be but a fabrication, an approximation of things past. "Facts" (quantified truth claims) do not overpower their deployment in a fiction called history. Whatever the telling, there will always be absent referents, gaps, repressed or ignored voices and falsehoods, but the partiality of what arrives is framed as complete and claimed as historical "truth." The image of history as ordered, clear and continuous does not correspond to "the past as event." The past cannot arrive as a document/documentation. In its dis-order it lacks all that orders.

Events are never discrete. They cannot be captured by time, for time itself is not discrete.

The relationality of historical events is always lodged in time as lived. Memory, so contextualized, thus futures and in so doing breaks the past from the past. In bringing memory to history it becomes strange, alien, and an inauthentic configuration of what has been and is. The past, of course, can only ever be viewed by "a someone" from a somewhere. The past can never have a single appearance, yet history is a negation of this truism.

Again one acknowledges that ghosts of history haunt the present. Here once more is "the return of the same" as the repetition of events in difference. But equally, history is also a domain of forgetting. As we have seen, the presence and availability of history (as text, practice and discipline) does not mean that the past is actively engaged or understood. In fact "history" (so often) obscures or erases the past and becomes its surrogate. Its representations displace and replace memory and then they become the remembered. The event and experience lodged in the past so often does not make sense, hence when represented, order replaces the memory of disorder. In "our" inability to frequently make sense of the passage of disorder of the world in which we live, and reflect upon it, history arrives with the claim to do this for us. But there is a price: the arrival of the past turned to a fiction—one at which we were not present.

Is it not so that the search and desire for knowledge of the past begs to be abandoned in favor of the acquisition of understanding of it?

"The end of history" still leaves the past in question. If there is an end of history it is not as the arrival of an Hegelian Endstate but dissolution of any possible trajectory, any pathway, that could possibly reach it (again we see there never was a *telos*). Thus what has ended is history as directional and in any way resting upon reason.

In terms of the implosion of history as a practice, arguments that the nature and agency of history no longer have validity are overwhelming. Reiterating: the foundation of the authority of the discipline of history has fallen. Yet the corpse walks with a great swathe of historians unaware of its death. Among this community of the unaware are many design historians, who in their difference, assume history as available and viable. As for readers of history, the vast bulk inside and outside the academy take history on face value. Yet it is, as it were, just another representation projected onto the wall of Plato's cave.

With these qualifications in place we now come to the issue of historicity. Gadamer tells us that "neither the knower nor the known is 'present at hand' in an 'ontic' way, but in an 'historical' one—i.e., they both have the *mode of being of historicity*."[31] To understand historicity, the difference between the *ontic* and the historical is vital to grasp.

Historicity is grounded in the constitution of the ontological condition of historical beings, whereas the *ontic* enfolds what is, in general, and as such embraces the being of all beings. Fundamentally this adds up to the difference between being situated in a specific time and space *and* being situated in the totality of "what is," in the recognition that all that is futural is absent.[32] Everything has historicity—everything thus manifests itself through the structural form of its temporality—nothing is unhistorical, but not everything can be claimed to have a historiography.[33] So although everything is situated historically, and comes into being "in itself" via the historicity of the event that brought it into being, there is much that is without a history.[34] As we have indicated, history does not necessarily expose the historical being of the thing in question.

Certainly, as Heidegger knew full well, historicity was that determinate condition that was prior to and constitutive of "historical possibility."[35] Thus, without the disclosure of historicity there is no prospect of historical inquiry.[36] Thus in itself the temporal character of historicity has no past, present, future or *telos*.

Gadamer asserts that we study history because "we are ourselves historical," and that our historicity is what enables us to do this. It appears we are thus the object and the means of inquiry. But as we have been making clear, history is a flawed tool for examining the past. Moreover, the degree to which "we study history" itself comes into question, not least because of what appears to be a major disjuncture between historical representations in circulation in popular and academic culture (of which design history is but one example) and critical historical scholarship that is aware of history as problematic.

Heidegger deals with temporality and historicity at length in chapter five of Division Two of *Being and Time*. He questions the extent to which the historical subject owns its historicity. Heidegger not only clearly understood historicity prior to "history" but also realized that for the historical subject to make its own existence transparent to its self (and so to inquire existentiality into its self) there had to be an inquiry of and into historicity, which in turn becomes an inquiry of Being itself.[37] Here what is historical can only be gathered from historicity and its rootedness in temporality.[38]

Put simply, our being is historical in so far as it exists temporally and, as such, we share the condition of historicity of all things. While all things have their own time and thus their historicity, no other beings are the (made) subjects of history (be it that history/historians induct many subjects as their historical objects).

Theodor Adorno, in a Hobbesean turn, took issue with Heidegger, claiming historicity an idealist category in defiance of history's real "natural growth."[39] He viewed historicity not as a quality of being but its condition in time, viewed as a constant moment of change. Under the influence of Walter Benjamin, Adorno also regarded change as decay, as natural, and thus he posited the relation between nature and history as a continuum.[40] But problematically his criticism of Heidegger fell into his own subjectivizing of the natural as the "totality of beings," whereas for Heidegger historicity is of the world and the world is no longer reducible to the natural.[41] Nature cannot any longer be seen as the total ground of our being or becoming. Moreover, our historicity as a species was always unnatural in so far as our rupture from pure animality was always an ontological product of artifice.[42]

In the crisis of history, what historicity essentially provides is a means to engage the past as it exists in the present, without the mediation or claims of historical practice (in their most advanced or debased forms).

We will now consider a number of thinkers who, by degree, claim to have attempted to do just this.

History without historians: Fundamental thinking

None of the thinkers we are about to briefly review will provide us with all the answers we need, but all have something to say that will assist in advancing our understanding. Our intent is simply to look at how these thinkers disrupt received ideas of history, past and present, in order to expose more adequate ways of bringing historicity to presence. Our aim is not to review the work of these thinkers more generally; these thinkers are not viewed as independent from each other for they illustrate how thought becomes interwoven—thus what we see at work is both an individual and collective (ecology of) mind.

Friedrich Nietzsche

In 1873 Nietzsche wrote an extended essay on history. It was published in draft the following year in a collection called *Thoughts out of Season*. The text first appeared in translation in English as *The Use and Abuse of History* in 1949. It was then reprinted as *On the Advantages and Disadvantages of History for Life* (translated by Peter Preuss) in 1980. This text was revised and translated in 2010.[43] The book created critical recoil on its arrival and continues to do so. For example, here is a vitriolic line from the eminent historian Hayden White: "Nietzsche hated history even more than he hated religion."[44] White is wrong. As Julius Kraft wrote in his editorial introduction to the 1949 edition of *The Use and Abuse of History*—Nietzsche has "no hatred of history but was antagonistic to 'historicist intellectualism' which 'indulges in baseless constructions of history' in contrast to aiming at 'contemplation and action.'"

Reading Nietzsche on history one is struck by his insight and ambiguity. As we shall see, for him history was bankrupt and essential; contested and surprising; an obstacle and liberating. He understood it as confounding that directionality that metaphysics posits with reason as the resolved, accounted for and considered. Likewise he saw history *deployed contingently by those who, at the very same time retained unaware positions of unknowing* (does this not remind us of the position of design history?). It existed for him as that which exposed and concealed the truth. History, in its revelation and undecidability, is distanced from the historian. According to Mark Sinclair, Nietzsche always speaks "as an oracle" and only "those with a creative concern for our lives in the present and the future are fit to interpret it."[45]

Echoing his confounding of direction, Sande Cohen points out that for Nietzsche "every discourse of goal is always partly incredible."[46] What this actually means is that whatever appearance of direction he gave, it was actually always multiple; and whatever he seemed to make certain was always actually uncertain. Uncertainty marked the very way Nietzsche viewed the use of history and in so doing the decision to act was left completely in the hands of the actor. Again as Sinclair pointed out from his reading of *On the Advantages and Disadvantages of History for Life*, Nietzsche believed that the well-being of a culture demands a limitation be placed on the exposure to historical knowledge.[47] This is because the future, and life in the present, requires that we both remember and forget. What must be recognized here is that Nietzsche was writing at a time when there was a national obsession with history in Germany. Times have changed. We now live in an age wherein neither the past nor the future are given due consideration, and are effectively rendered invisible by a plethora of imagery centered on style (historicist or futuristic). Now finding a dividing line between remembering and forgetting might not be an easy task. Nietzsche demanded more than this and required a path be steered between the historical and the unhistorical—necessary, he thought, for "the health of the individual, a people and a culture."[48]

A clue to such a "finding and taking" from Nietzsche comes from his thoughts on knowledge as being indivisible from our awareness of life and death—this as it informs living and dying either well or badly, as well as his evocation of the "study of history as a means to life."[49] He believed such study to be "only fruitful for the future if it follows a powerful life-giving influence" that is if it is " dominated by a higher force and does not itself guide and dominate."[50] Affirmatively, via the agency of "the living man," Nietzsche said "life requires the service of history" as it is active and striving, as it preserves and as it exposes suffering and the need of liberation"[51] (in contradiction to his statement on history and the "need of liberation" a counter view is posed by Nietzsche: "History belongs above all to the active and powerful ... who fights a great fight, who requires models, teachers and comforters and cannot find them among associates (sic) and contemporaries").[52]

Nietzsche's remarks on life and history go to his "vitalism" wherein "the history of man is only the continuation of the history of animals and plants." This is a line of thought that extends back to Goethe and forward to Benjamin and his notion of "natural history" (which in our age translates into a biodegradable history of decay and renewal).[53] Notwithstanding Heidegger's attempt to render Nietzsche's biologism more ambiguous than it actually was, one must again place it in the context of its moment—in Germany at the time that history was in vogue biology was rising as an influential radical science.[54] What Nietzsche could not know was how his problematic biological selectivism would travel towards a jackbooted fate that would leave an indelible stain on his name.

While warning against "shallow history" ("the history of tourism's travail of monuments, museums and galleries and the work of 'painstaking micrologists'"[55]) Nietzsche's most direct address to history in *On the Advantages and Disadvantages of History for Life* is his characterization of it as having three modes: the monumental, antiquarian and critical.

The monumental is heroic history. It is the stuff of great deeds of the past acknowledged and celebrated in the present. Monumental history thereby becomes history reified and employed as point of reference, as measure, in and for the future. Historically "the monumental ought not to arise—that is the counter watch-word. Dull habit, the small and the lowly which fills the corners of the world and wafts like dense earthly vapor around everything great, deceiving, smothering and suffocating, obstructs the path which the great must still travel to immortality."[56] However, "whenever the monumental vision of the past rules: . . . very great portions of the past are forgotten and despised, and flow away like grey uninterrupted flood, and only single embellished facts stand out as islands."[57] Such history is not to be regarded as a true "historical nexus of causes and effect."[58] In its generalities it is equated with "world history" and in its stasis it is seen as lacking the movement and chance of events.[59]

Monumental history in its use is deemed by Nietzsche to embrace both ambition and illusion, and as a "romantic celebration," he sees it turning the historical into myopic antiquarianism wherein history is made inert. Yet for all the critical barbs cast in the path of monumental and antiquarian history he does not totally discount their value to "life." As for "critical history," it is not seen to be critical at all, but rather abstracted, dismembered and dislocated from the present.

Nietzsche's position toward history, while reacting to its moment, also has a critical resonance that touches the contemporary. The tone is futural and chilling: "the past always speaks as an oracle: only as a master builder of the future who knows the present will you understand it." His view of the historian has an edge to it that is perhaps a little more appropriate to our age: "The genuine historian must have the strength to recast the well known into something never heard before."[60] Both views are seen in what Nietzsche did in writing a "History of European nihilism" wherein he speaks as an oracle recasting the partly known into the totally unfamiliar.[61]

Overall one can conclude that what Nietzsche did was to undercut the authority of history and in so doing open the way for another kind of historical engagement. This view is of course a back-reading of his agency, and thus goes more to his influence than his intent. Supporting this view is, of course, the work of Michel Foucault, as it delivered a particular kind of historical inquiry displaced from the historical practice of historians. Effectively Foucault created another kind of practice that, while historical, was not cast in the mould of history.

Martin Heidegger

In moving from Nietzsche to Heidegger, remembering his relation to Dilthey mentioned earlier, we are really not moving anywhere at all. As David Farrell Krell says in his introduction to the four-volume paperback edition of Heidegger on Nietzsche, after noting a clutch of eminent thinkers who have written on Nietzsche, "Yet none of these writers can readily separate the names Nietzsche/Heidegger. None can pry apart this lament. As though one of the crucial confrontations for thinkers today were what one might call heidegger's nietzsche, nietzsche's heidegger."[62] One could perhaps add, that what also cannot be divided is the brilliance and the tragedy of both thinkers.

In his consideration of Nietzsche on "Nihilism and history," Heidegger makes sense of the project as a recasting of history, saying it is not that nihilism has a history but that "it can be traced historically in its temporal course"; as such it "determines the historicity of this history."[63] To make sense of this we have to be clear about what nihilism named, which was essentially not just a loss of the highest values but a loss of the belief of value itself. This thinking in turn produces a psychology of life lived with lost meaning and agency in the midst of substitutes for what was absent.

If we bring such thinking to the present it can be seen that a culture of commodities (wherein culture, diminished to "happiness" is itself "things" bought and sold) can be understood as a marker of nihilism, a substitute, signifying loss. Continuous acquisition, while ever holding the promise of realized desire and value, is based on endless disappointment. More than this, with Western metaphysics constantly delivering us over into being fully technological beings (which we importantly in part have always been) instrumentalism becomes a hegemonic ontology. What this means is a vast diminishment of value and an increase of nihilism as structural.

For Heidegger historical knowledge was not a projection in the sense of direction, "the will to power"—an ordering of things according to desires, prejudices or command—rather it was a description of the temporal relations between subject and object within the dynamics of being and becoming. Moreover, as he made clear, Nietzsche's characterization of a triadic historiography (the monumental, antiquarian and the critical) was not just prefigured by *Dasien* but is unified by it: *Dasein is historical in its Being*, it is what brings historicity to presence as "history."[64] What is actually historically present with things that remain present is not the thing in itself but the trace of the world in which it existed, and to which the thing directs us.[65] Thus, all history centers on "our being here" (*Dasein*)—and, as such, always in the past, present and future[66]—which, to reaffirm, means all objects and events of "history" depend on the "subject of being."[67] We need to remember that the nature of our being here is the historical occurrence of our "being-in-the-world" and, "with the existence of historical being-in-the-world things at hand and objectively present have already been included in the history of the world (in their proximity to our being with them in engagement)."[68] World is not to be seen so situated as an all-encompassing whole but as the coming together of "a world" and a being in that world as inner worldliness that discovers itself in the extant external world.

That history has generally failed to be seen to act futurally, and so cast as past, negates recognition of its directional designing. At a fundamental level this limitation folds into a "crisis of the negation of time" (now able to be understood as the crisis of defuturing). What is evident in the way that Heidegger understands the *historizing of history*, through subjects and objects being linked together, is what can now be understood as an ontologically designing agency.[69] He recognized that authentic being (an insecure condition) understands history as temporality and as a moment of vision.

The historicality of design begs to be recognized as a specific instance of the dynamic of subjects and objects being and becoming in that "we" (*Dasein*) come into the historicity of a designed world, acquire a historically endowed design agency and, by degree, produce historical effects by design practices that create "things" that transform the conditions of being into which others will be born. So situated "we" exist as authentically futural in disclosed and determined conditions of possibility.[70] "We" essentially have our roots in the future and our being is always ahead of our past (the past then is never lived but experienced as the history of the historicity of our being).[71]

These observations are key links to our very coming into being by the ontological designing of our actual being. Here is the historicity of the very first stone tools—the basis of our historical origin as the animal becoming a human animal, and our being technological.[72]

Heidegger's history lacks a heartbeat—in common with his oeuvre in general, the biological condition of being is virtually absent. Whereas Nietzsche fell into a trap of his own making, Heidegger exercises his art of silence (much is silent in his discussion of history, not least the ghost of history given to the future by Hegel and his own history). Of the limitation of Heidegger, in his greatness, Charles Bambach points to his failure to see the political consequences of his own thinking, especially in relation to the crisis that swept over him, and his "faith" in the "saving power" of the poetic.[73]

Notwithstanding absences and the criticism of centering the subject historically the placement of the horizon of Being was and is in time— and is so presented as the event of being. Thus when Heidegger observes "that everything has its own time" he is asserting a historical difference of identity and being: identity inhabits and expresses its own time, while being is time.

Walter Benjamin

Benjamin's view of history rested upon two very different directional movements: one against Kant's (and neo-Kantian) notions of history;[74] the other toward an organic history—a "natural history."

On movement one, Kant's philosophy of history was rejected on two counts.[75] Benjamin viewed history as having an ethical dimension, which he found lacking in Kant. Likewise, he was also critical of Kant adopting what is regarded as the perspective of the "natural sciences." Additionally Benjamin was critical of both Kant's and neo-Kantian epistemology. Now it has to be said that his own position was contradictory, complex and in the end unresolved. Clearly his claim that history could and did accommodate an ethics is at the very least contestable, as is Benjamin's belief that the development of historical knowledge could somehow be advanced by religious doctrine.[76]

Benjamin's second view on history and direction, as it was based on an organic history, a "natural history," was equally contradictory—not least because it failed to adequately deal with Kant's attributions of historical progress via the "cunning of nature." While one can find a scientistic inflection in Kant's characterization of the agency of nature it fundamentally turned on "violence" and "strife" being posited with an emancipatory *telos*.[77] However, and echoing Dilthey, Benjamin moved to a position wherein agency was lodged in a claimed objectified (nonreflective) form of historical consciousness carried by language—this in contrast to experience capable of exposing historical "truth." Thus while both thinkers evoked "nature" as having historical agency, by implication for Kant this agency was intrinsic, while Benjamin, as we are about to see, placed it within a process he thought was able to overcome subjectivism and historical thinking based on a transcendental capability. Yet at the same time he gave significance to art as a creative force, and within in it language—a view that was profoundly romantic. More than this, his thinking slated back to a relation to a theological *ur-history*[78] as grounded in exegesic knowledge from the Torah wherein "the word was truth" and interpretation thereof had the power of revelation. Here, as Beatrice Hanssen points out, Benjamin "persistently sought to integrate a Judaic history of revelation with a Greek notion of *phusis*."[79]

This concern with *phusis* takes us to the problematic of Benjamin's relation to "natural history," which again is replete with interest and confusion.[80] Effectively he acquired from Marxism a composite notion of "second nature" (what we now identify as the world-within-the-world that has been a product of human creation and that now constitutes our condition of dependence in the company of the biophysical). Added to this concern were arcane ideas and energies drawn from his engagement with Baroque dramatic culture, especially its "visionary habits" and "political-doctrinal emblem-code";[81] and ideas he accepted and imported, after initial rejections, from Dilthey's "life philosophy" (which grounded history in anthropology). In doing this he accepted much of Dilthey's thesis as it centered on a kind of decisionism, and the promotion of the idea, of natural law (although he departed from Dilthey's scientific inflection).

Surprisingly Benjamin did not make a connection with the biological semiotics of Jakob von Uexkull and the reconfiguration of the perception of nature by Ernst Haeckel—whose work just before and after the turn of the century had made serious contributions in Germany to transforming how nature was to be understood. These thinkers' exposure of the temporality of natural systems simply did not arrive to challenge Benjamin's more eccentric and questionable, but nonetheless interesting, pluralist views on the plural characterization on nature, time and change.[82] Rather what Benjamin meant when evoking "natural history" was "the mutual imbrication of nature and history, for they equally converged in the moment of transience that befell both." Such thinking elevates a temporal process (wherein "all that is" decays (nature) but in passing leaves a trace (history)).

The historicity of the natural world and history do not exist in a binary relation, in so far as the ecological processes of natural systems increasingly have been, and are, transformed via human worldly interventions as they constituted a "second nature." In this respect the ontological designing of "man and nature" changed the course of "nature" as an evolutionary cyclic process (and in so doing effected a rupture in the historicity of the natural world) while establishing an originary moment able to be named as "history." What came out of this moment was the event of the transformation of the "being-of-beings"; and the agent able to narrate this event retrospectively. Thus the arrival of "the human," as an intervention in the historicity of the *ontic*, and the arrival of the potential to create "history" were all of the same anthropocentrically configured moment. Benjamin walked in the shoes of Marx when he asserted in the *German Ideology* that there were two histories—the history of nature and the history of man. Marx was incorrect on two counts. Man, as animal, is not outside, not other than "nature" (although the perverter of it, and thus of itself); and nothing has "a history" without it being rendered as such, therefore there is no "history" without "man" as its fabricator.[83]

For Benjamin to talk of the "logic of decay" was to think with the trace of Hegel's idea of "reason in nature" and to manifest a materialized nihilism that negates "the new," continually returning as the same to decay. At its most basic what we see is complexity being layered upon two flawed premises: the first premise was undone by Darwin (nature as meaningless— nature has no design, reason, or history—it just is, as process); the second is undone by the recognition that what anthropocentric being brings to presence is a supplement to "what is"—which is to say all history and representation is logocentric ("what is" is made present and otherwise by naming). Whereas Benjamin, from his deep intellectual relation to Jewish theological writing, would have it that the word is truth and truth is God, an engagement with the historicity of anthropos suggests the word is "man."

Discussions of "our" origins have moved on from both Benjamin's concern with the formation of history and the limits of the human, as it equally has from Heidegger's notions of the relation between "world," the human and the animal. An interrogation of the formative and transformative agency of language, the symbolic, technology and design – certainly over the last half century by the likes of André Leroi-Gourhan, Jacques Derrida, Giorgio Agamben, Bruno Latour, and Bernard Stiegler – has changed the frame of the debate on origins.[84] Likewise, the fall of science as history, and the exposure of the limits of science's post-Darwinian biological account of what we are and our origins as "human beings," have shifted the ground of such questioning. And then, from an anti-Eurocentric perspective there has been the undercutting of Enlightenment and post-Enlightenment concepts of human being and history anchored in categories of human freedom and teleology.

Essentially while Benjamin sought to displace an Enlightenment centering of the human subject (and thus humanism) as the basis for historical inquiry—this through his understanding of "natural history" reconfiguring "origins"—he actually failed to reach the point of nonorigin in the unbroken transitional process of the animal to the human animal. In this respect, his theological *habitus* (a being within sacred history) blocked him seeing the emergence of the human animal out of the meaningless of both creation and a pre-hominoid symbolic existence. Ironically, he was trapped in time—a time wherein religious knowledge was deemed to be the primary ground of experience and the source of a projected future (a salvation from decay).[85]

Why was Benjamin so important? Benjamin scholars would provide a long list of what he opened into thought which, it would be claimed, transcends questions of what he got right or wrong. But in the end what has to be most valued was his thinking across the grain. He repositioned how "things" could be seen in time, be it as they carried traces of the past or as they marked the presence of the future in the moment of "now." In so doing, in an age becoming ever more chronophobic and acting *now* upon the future, his agenda has more in common with Nietzsche and Heidegger than an address to their differences suggests.

Michel Foucault

At its most blatant Foucault's position could be called "history against history"—that is history against the form of extant historical narratives and the practices of historians. He viewed the work of historians as largely evading history.[86]

If there is one text that succinctly exposits this position it is the essay he published in France in 1971 that appeared in translation in English as

"Nietzsche, genealogy, history" in 1977.[87] This position interlocks with Nietzsche's suprahistorical stance (in *On the Advantages and Disadvantages of History for Life*). Foucault questioned and challenged the forms of history; contested how time was viewed, considered how subjective experience of the past counters its displacement; and reacted against history destined toward completion and as articulated to an objective position and transcendentalism.[88] What resulted from this critical action was that for Foucault history, as "history," no longer existed with any authority. As such, it couldn't be reduced to be about any one "historical thing."[89]

Foucault describes genealogy, as method, as a patiently meticulous uncovering of the detail of "entangled and confused" copied and written over "parchments."[90] Genealogy looks for origin outside of how origins are cast as foundational. It looks for what is found along pathways of difference outside regimes of order, but in the corporeal realm of being.[91] It equally looks for what emerges out of forms of force and power.[92] After Nietzsche, genealogy contests the nature of history that thereafter becomes "action with a purpose" intended not to discover the roots of our identity, and our metaphysical foundations, but to dissipate them.[93] Thereafter, it sets out to collect that which cannot be gathered by the methods of historical practice. In part it does this via a close engagement with the objects engaged. Against the confusion created by the historians ordering of "history," what Foucault makes clear in "Of genealogy" is that it . . .

returns to the three modalities of history Nietzsche recognized in 1874. It returns to them in spite of the objections that Nietzsche raised in the name of the affirmative and creative powers of life. But they are metamorphosed: the veneration of monuments becomes parody; the respect for the ancient continuities becomes systematic dislocation; the critique of the injustices of the past by a truth held by men in the present becomes the destruction of the man who maintains knowledge by the injustice proper to the will to knowledge.[94]

Genealogy then is a searching for events outside any sense of closure, a searching in unlikely places. In their discovery these events demand detailed address in their relational complexity. In so doing the "facts" of an event are seen as products of the means of its classification. All genealogical interpretations of events are transformative of "conditions of experience and knowing."[95]

Universal notions of human nature fall at the feet of genealogy, for the very totalized discourse of "the human" cannot survive its scrutiny. By implication what evolves in the Darwinian sense has been an animal not a human. The reality of the differences in the ways of life of a fragmented humanity are covered over by the discourse of humanism, it "makes it clear that our ability to share such conditions with others is, at best, limited."[96] Roth's statement here is both insightful and understated. The reality of difference in actually is a "world of difference" in which the human is imposed and resisted—world history not only fails to recognize this situation but conspires to conceal it. It is totally counter to how Foucault understood and engaged history, for "effective history" works against the proximity that metaphysics creates and that "shortens its vision to those things nearest to it."[97] Equally his mode of investigating the past ruptured all relations to neat and comfortable history by exposing its discontinuities.[98]

Foucault characterizes a primary historical concern with how human beings are made subjects.[99] His study of power, which became a major preoccupation, is directly linked and subordinate to this concern as it relates to those modes of objectification that employ forms of distributed power to form subjects.[100] Here, he foregrounds three types of inquiry: the sciences across the entirety of their practices; what he called "dividing practices" (as they designate the sick, mad, the sane, criminal etc.); and the auto-produced self (subjects of sexuality).[101] All of these areas of inquiry center on discourses that exercise power—they are not dependent on gaining power from elsewhere.[102] As such they constitute practices and define their own (nonintrinsic) truths. In doing this they demonstrate that power is always dispersed and in flux—while it always strives to exercise control, it equally is always reactive to resistance. It follows that discourses are deemed to be more than purely linguistic—Foucault sees them as materialities and within discourses words act as things. Obviously, here language is not merely seen as communication and the deliverer of transparent meaning—the reverse—it is viewed as opaque.[103]

In these contexts Foucault asked what constituted the nature of power, and answered relationally: it is not just posited in and with "partners, individuals or collectives" but "in the way certain actions modify others."[104] Power was of course also bonded to knowledge: "power and knowledge directly imply one another; that there is no power relation without the correlative constitution of a field of knowledge, nor any knowledge that does not presuppose and constitute at the same time power relations."[105]

Fundamentally Foucault's approach to the historical could now be called posthumanist in that it refused an anthropological basis of inquiry (history as the history of human beings) as a condition of historical possibility.[106] As this, it railed against cultural totalities and rigorously pursued grounded historical knowledge.

Derrida in the company of Marx

Jacques Derrida's position towards history is perhaps best understood through two moments. The first was a 1963 essay "Cogito and the history of madness," which was a response to Foucault's massive *History of Madness* of 1961 (published in abridged form in English as *Madness and Civilisation* in 1967).[107]

Derrida's engagement with Foucault was contradictory; he honored and challenged his former teacher and in some ways quietly abused him (which was not the volume that Foucault heard). While the most critical of Derrida's comments were directed at how Foucault configured the relation between madness and reason, they also parted on how the relations between historicity and authors were posed. This difference centered on the claim that authors can transcend historical determinism, and on the issue of appropriation as either justifiable or transgressive. However, as noted by Peter Fenves, Derrida did set out to undercut Foucault's historical project by suggesting his argument depended on history, the very practice that his former mentor had set out to undermine.[108]

Moment two arrived thirty years later at a conference on the future of Marxism at the University of California, Riverside. The lectures Derrida gave (there were two) were published in the following year (1994). In these lectures Marx's thought arrived as both the past and the future. The book *Specters of Marx: The State of the Debt, the Work of Mourning & the New International* was edited and introduce by Bernd Magnus and Stephen Cullenberg.[109]

In his 1978 reading of Nietzsche, Bernd Magnus drew our attention to the idea of "Chronophobia"—the fear of time and the illusion of permanence.[110] Just over a decade after the publication of Magnus' book the Berlin Wall fell, and with it the end of a seemingly linked series of fears: of a nuclear war between the West and the USSR; of totalitarianism as an eternality; and more generally of the future bonded to the past.

At this moment it appeared as if communism had turned to dust and Marxism was now in the dustbin of history. In truth communism, endowed with the spirit of Marxism, had died in 1927 with the birth of totalitarianism at the hand of Joseph Stalin. As for the ideas of, "that glorious, sacred, accursed but still clandestine immigrant" Karl Marx, and counter to claims to the contrary, they have retained both a certain presence and imminence. Marxism continues to send a message very much like the content of the famous cable Mark Twain dispatched when his obituary was mistakenly published, "The reports of my death are greatly exaggerated." Capital retains a fear of Marxism in the form of a fear of the ghost of Marx.

It was against this backdrop that the "Wither Marxism" conference unfolded and Derrida's exposition focused on the significance of Marx in relation to worldly change and the responsibility that arrives with the recognition that "time is out of joint." Here he echoes the ghost of Hamlet (Act 1, Scene V):

> The time is out of joint; O cursed spite,
> That ever I was born to set it right!
> Nay, come, let's go together.[111]

In our age that "time is out of joint" is registered by multiple levels of worldly dislocation, becoming ever more pronounced as "time" passes away. Global unsettlement deepens, and with it fear both felt and unconscious. Capital is failing (while visible in a situated sense in the crises of Europe, post the global financial crisis of the first decade of the 21st century), more profoundly as it rests with the structural contradiction of an ideology of continual growth starting to be seen as en route to hitting the reality of:

- the finitude of planetary resources;
- the anthropocentric damage caused to a now revenging climate;
- the instability in prospect from an increasing inability to feed a growing global population;
- increasing dangers from conflict over natural resources (especially water); and
- asymmetrical war becoming a permanent feature of everyday life of ever more people in ever more parts of the world.

The fears of the world going badly, as listed, that reverberates through Derrida's text now touches this present moment of unsettlement. His fear is an old fear of time, a fear linked to (rather than of) the ghost of Marx, and a new fear of the future. Such fears then are what we have to confront as we find ourselves at a historical turn. Not only is this moment one wherein the past will get recast as its relation to the future is realigned but one where the future will start to look ever more finite for us (our species). Time is not merely out of joint, it is actually being diminished (for our collective being) by the collective defuturing of actions—actions in which capital is, and has been, deeply implicated. The question is not if we will survive or not, but rather in what numbers, how and with what consequences.

Our past actions now haunt the future, and thus, recognize it or not, this means we are all haunted.

To be haunted by Marx is to be haunted by a vision, a promise that lingers: "whether they wish it or know it or not, all men and women, all over the earth, are today to a certain extent the heirs of Marx and Marxism."[112] Against this backdrop, mourning for millions of people is not for the loss of Marxism but for what it failed to accomplish.[113] As Derrida made clear, the ghost of Marx is not at rest—the promise, which is of emancipation, remains to be kept. But now the focus widens, and we ask: emancipation from what? Is it from something far more than just a "world going badly" wherein time is out of joint? The answer is yes.

What was promised by Marxism was a "break with myth, religion, and the nationalist 'mystique'" "to establish 'a new concept of the human, of society, economy, nation, several concepts of the state and of its disappearance."[114] Here is the promise of a Utopia, "hope" from which we cannot escape. The debt, the ideas, and the remnants of the Marxist dream remain and haunt. But they are of the past, resonating from the world (of the West) that has gone. The debt to be paid now is one to the future, a debt created by a shattering of possibility that was the essence of sustainability. The problem to be faced is not so much about what has to be destroyed (including the nationalist "mystique," the extant form of the nation state and a defuturing economy) but how to do so, and then what to create in the void. Here history and utopias have no agency.

Derrida gives an account of this condition of things "going badly" pointing out that central to it for him is both (a) loss of viewpoint and (b) a fracturing of a sense of a *telos* (itself a loss of any directional ordering of history).[115] One can frame this view via Nietzsche's notion of nihilism, for we go badly in a "world" within which an inequitable populace is polarized between a loss of agency and a condition of anomie, unable to see "the crisis" while living it.

In saying "time is out of joint" Derrida equally places "the world" out of joint—for if time is disjointed likewise so is the world. But neither time nor world can be taken as singular: both are plural. Thinking, speaking, writing as if there were one world, one time, one mode of being of "human" or for that matter, one culture, is to be disjoined. Yet for all the theory and rhetoric centered on difference, the singular constantly overwhelms the plural.

Obviously a great deal of the historically located detail of Marx's analysis has fallen away (not least his philosophy of history). What remains of the spirit of Marx, what Derrida rightly affirmed, and what is underscored here, was his power of critique (of and beyond capital). "We" thus are haunted not just by the afterlife of this ability but how it stands against a contemporary lack of criticality (including of capital, technology, science, currently existing politics, acquisitive modes of being, the hegemony of entertainment, instrumentalized education, and global inequity as they all fuel unsustainable ontologies and defuturing action). The "world" goes badly because we humans (unevenly) have made it so, this mostly unwittingly by our own creations—for Derrida it is wearing out and being worn down.[116] But it is more.

De facto the condition we are trying to grasp here divides between four configurations:

- individually recordable empirical conditions (economic, environmental etc.);

- unspoken and unengaged relational connections between these empirical conditions (like for example, economies, climate change, environmentally displaced people and conflict);

- anthropocentrically grounded chronophobic ontologies that are relationally disassociated ecologically, socially, economically and culturally, and

- conditionally uncritical populations whose mode of being-in-the-world prevents them from seeing crisis as it is indivisibly lodged both in themselves and their worlds.

From these perspectives we believe it worth bringing Derrida's twenty-year-old moment of "time being out of joint," viewed in a world going badly, together with contemporary global circumstances, this via working over Derrida's review of the ills of the "new world order."[117] But before doing this the very notion of a "new world order" needs to be brought into question: an action that Carl Schmitt prefigured.

Schmitt's "The *Nomos* of the Earth" was published in Germany 1950 (the English translation appearing in 2003 in the wake of the growing interest from both the left and the right in his work).[118] The central argument mounted by Schmitt was that the rule of *Jus Publicum Europaeum* (the rule of international relations by European law) had ended and is being replaced by the "*Grossraum*" (the division of the world into (large) spaces acting as "spheres of influence"). His view were strongly influenced by his reading of the US Monroe Doctrine of 1823 in which the US asserted its right to intervene in the affairs of Central and South America, thereby claiming the Americas as its "sphere of influence." The issues that Schmitt engaged have sparked considerable debate, especially because of the way many geopolitical developments seem to support his point of view (including the rise of the power of Asia and the decline of Europe).[119] From such a perspective, how one sees the "world" to be "out of joint" has shifted. Any notion that the world can be seen and be addressed as a geopolitical whole now seems as out of date—"the world" as a figures of geopolitical design(ations) is now increasingly "dis-jointed."

So now returning to Derrida's concerns, let's now ask: "for whom is 'the world' that is now disjointed 'out of joint'"? We answer: all those others for whom their world always goes badly. That is the all who live and work (or have no work) in a worn out (figuration of the) world that endlessly wears them out. Here is a world without care, be it a sweat shop in Asia or a multinational corporation investing in mega-regional development.[120] To support these views we will now work through issues of unemployment, homelessness, the free market, foreign debt, the arms trade, nuclear weapons, inter-ethnic wars, phantom states and international law from a current perspective, for these are the ten review points that Derrida's text addressed.

1   *Unemployment.* The global economic crisis that commenced in 2008 has clearly swelled the ranks of the unemployed, but because of the rapid growth of the global informal economy this worsening situation is far worse than Derrida acknowledged. In this context people work to survive from day to day, sometimes gaining work, sometimes not—this in contrast to a job with a wage and degree of

security (although ever more jobs in mainstream economies are causal). For example, in Africa 93 percent of all new jobs in cities are in the informal economy, while in rural sub-Saharan Africa 84 percent of all employed women work in this sector.[121] Echoing the issue of care, such people can work up to 18 hours a day, seven days a week, often in dangerous conditions and without any health, safety, or social provision—this just in order to be able to live, meeting the needs of "bare life."

2   *Homelessness.* This condition is ever expanding, and extends beyond the lack of a physical home. Increasingly it becomes the loss of a place of dwelling, a homeland, and a locus of belonging. Effectively climate change is already rendering some parts of the planet inhospitable, and will increasingly do so. The result: an ever-growing volume of climatically displaced people. This situation is projected to dramatically worsen over at least this century and potentially spark conflict with the prospect of tens of millions of displaced people crossing borders uninvited.

3   *Economic war.* Besides the ongoing ravages of un-free trade, Derrida complains about increasing resource conflicts (especially those implicating oil and water). This situation is again one that is getting worse as climate change bites deeper, as population pressures increase, and as geopolitical reconfiguration occurs. Moreover, flash points are arriving—the most recent is the opening up of the Northwest Passage through the Arctic. Enabled by climatic change warming melting sea ice, this mineral super-rich region is now being viewed as able to be exploited, and a number of nations aim to post claims do this. Russia created two army brigades to protect its interests, and deployed them in 2010, while the USA sent two nuclear submarines to the region in early 2011.[122]

4   *The "free market."* Derrida asks: "How is one to save one's own interests in a global market while claiming to protect one's 'social advantages' and so forth." There is no resolution to this contradiction: The market is flawed, not free. Moreover, there is a profound failure to grasp that common interests have to override one's own self interests (if one is privileged) for the sake of both the individual and the collective. The "free market" cannot deliver global equity—the modes of exploitation that Marx exposed have both continued (as the world's sweat shops evidence) and they have become extremely

sophisticated (as with digital manufacturing and its hidden production horrors in "newly industrializing nations"). The most dramatic example of the unfreedom of the free market is seen in the area of food—the problem is not that there is not enough food in the market but that people cannot afford to buy it. The media reported between 40 and 60 food riots globally in 2008. By 2011 food prices were much higher and had increased by 36 percent from August 2010—and these prices have been cited as one of the key reasons for the political destabilization of the Middle East.[123]

5   *Foreign debt.* The indebtedness of nations is far worse than at the time of Derrida's writing on the issue. European countries like Greece, Cyprus, Portugal, and Spain are economic basket cases –and the basket is getting bigger. The USA has deep economic problems and many poor nations are effectively economically dysfunctional. Ironically in an era of hegemonic capitalism, the global economic system, while still running, is a machine that is broken and currently lacking any means of repair. The ghost of Marx is watching from the wings. More fundamentally, the "nature" of global capitalism is entropic: continual growth via continuously increasing demand in a finite system can but end in systems failure—in the end no amount of technology and innovation can avoid this moment.

6   *The arms trade.* This trade remains a significant element of many of the world's leading economies. What has changed in the twenty years since Derrida addressed the issue is the continued destructive power of the technology and the extent to which information and robotics (including drones) have become major elements of weapons systems. Military technologies likewise increasingly infiltrate everyday life in the name of national security.[124]

7   *Nuclear weapons.* The threat of nuclear weapons now comes from two major sources: their use by politically volatile nations who already have them, or who are acquiring them; and the prospect that at some point a terrorist organization will obtain and use a nuclear weapon (a purchase from a rogue state, making a "dirty bomb," or an attack on a nuclear power station to "turn it critical"). The world ever becomes more dangerous as nuclear weapons continue to slowly proliferate and come into the hands of politically unstable nations, while equally remaining in the hands of nations committed to retaining their power and status.

8 *Inter-ethic wars.* Post 9/11 with conflicts like those in Iraq and Afghanistan, combined with the rise of the risk of conflict from climate change-induced population destabilization, the planning, conduct and thus nature of war is continually changing. Asymmetrical war is becoming the norm (with robotic war in the wings waiting its moment). This means, as I have already said, that the distinction between everyday life and conflict, the civilian and the military, constantly erodes. The Middle and Near East, Africa and East Asia remain actual and latent zones of such conflict. Rather than any escalation in inter-ethnic wars what is proliferating is the growing division and tension between the "West and the Rest" linked to a lack of resolution of longer-standing problems of conflict (like those between North and South Korea, Israel/Palestine, and Afghanistan/Pakistan). Added to this is a certain military expansionism of China as it significantly expands its navy and moves into the Pacific.

9 *Phantom states.* While Derrida addresses the power of the likes of drug cartels (in especially Mexico and Colombia) a new kind of danger is arriving—the potential combination of geoengineering and multinational corporations acting independently to intervene in the planetary atmospheric system. It is also the case that criminal organizations will increasingly fill the void as some small states fail and more widely as climate change bankrupts the economies of vulnerable nations.

10 *International law.* The failure of international law, and as registered the breakdown of the world order, continues unabated. Advanced technology in the form of cybercrime is adding to this problem, as are electronic and robotic technologies, mobilized via "a state of exception," and deployed without regard to borders or sovereignty.

Overall, and reiterating, the key historical factor that distinguishes the "now" from Derrida's 1993, is the impotence of geopolitics to deal with the scale of global problems that cluster around: climate change (many of these problems are not even being politically identified let alone engaged); "the world economic system"; food supply and security; and a cultural recoil from the West (as the speed of its decline increases and especially as the power of India and China grows). There is one more marker of difference between Derrida's moment and ours, and it is massive.

Derrida points to an implosion of Western representative democracy. For him politics had conceptually transmogrified "without anyone having really realized it." As he acknowledges, the media has played a major role in the production of such change—and ever more does so. That this politics has always been "distorted" and flawed is a long-time realization—not least by Derrida himself (cf. his "Call it a day for democracy" essay of 1992).[125] In this context, Derrida's Eurocentrism has not gone unnoticed.[126]

But what is increasingly becoming very clear is that, in the face of the unsustainable, democracy—of any stripe—is unable to deliver Sustainment. There are many reasons for this (as we have argued at length elsewhere) but at its simplest: people will not vote for the level of material change to ways of life that Sustainment, as process and project, actually demands.[127] Moreover, it is now evident that it is *the world of the West* that is historically out of joint. Its self-deception, its illusion of the politically projected image of "one world" (the product of modernity, and the sought economic goal of globalization)—a "vision" still carried by the United Nations—has fractured. In this fracturing the "truth" of its history has equally collapsed—"the event" of this fracturing has occurred (and is evident in numerous "humanitarian failures")—but what this fracturing means becomes increasingly ambiguous, and as Derrida knew well, all modes of temporal representation are always partly fictional.

The brute violence of colonialism, itself extended over five hundred years, was of an unparalleled global scale; this extending from genocide of the Americas, commenced in the fifteenth century enacted under "natural law," to ethnocide, and continual and ongoing epistemological colonialism. Notwithstanding what attainments of modernity can be claimed by the West, the wounds that it inflicted on the world's indigenous people's still fester and infuse so many contemporary global conflicts. Against this backdrop, as Walter Mignolo makes very clear, the process of decolonization has only just begun. This moment must not be confused with the postcolonialism (the exit of the political and military dominance of a colonial power replaced by arrival of "development" and induction into a globalizing economy).[128]

Time being out of joint goes well beyond Derrida's characterization, and in fact defines global historicality as framed by the rise and fall of the Enlightenment, as it intellectually empowered and sanctioned modernity, as that project repressed, failed to see and deliberately ignored "the rest." Its human, dehumanized and nonhuman forms increasingly return with a vengeance. This condition has already been named as the defuturing consequence of structural unsustainability—as it constituted not just all those systematic environmental problems produced by modern ontologies grounded in the unseeing and unthinking of anthropocentricity, but also in universalized cultural dysfunction as "humanism" dehumanized the collective "Other" (the colonized) by casting them outside "natural law"—as it defined human/nonhuman qualities (and thus not seeing or treating Others as truly human). Thus when Derrida "salutes" *the humanitarian* [his emphasis], and heralds the spirit of Marxism keeping faith with the spirit of the Enlightenment, and when he calls up deconstruction as the means to create a critique able to lead to a New Enlightenment, he not only exposes his conservatism but also a loss of perspective (in Nietzsche's sense of seeing history from the viewpoint of both the master and the slave).[129] Yes he well expresses outrage at the inequities of his moment, of the passing over of "the animal," but like the perspective of anti-foundationalism both it and he remained bonded to the very thing that was wished to be gone beyond.[130] Even so, one should not overlook (as many now do) Derrida's contribution to the exposure of so much that now can be recognized as being uncertain, undecided and indeterminate. Yet what is evident, and again should not be looked away from, is the uninterrupted passage toward the destruction of the plural human being. This destruction is not reducible to any particular historical moment, be it that the technology of destruction has moved from metal (the gun and the sword) to the mind (software and the industrialization of externalized memory). As such, the question of this destruction requires to be seen as not the same as the termination of "our" animality (that essential element of what "we" are).

In projecting forward from the spirit of Marxism, and while recognizing Marx as futural, Derrida failed to see the future traveling toward us. He did not travel with Benjamin's angel of history backing into the future, nor in the company of the slave—generalized as the body of the being of uneven development that still accompanies the "progress" of "the darker side of Modernity."[131]

Emancipatory history

Notwithstanding the considerable difference between all of these listed thinkers, what they have in common is an ability to break out of and into history. They affirm other ways of working with the historical and other understandings of historicity—freed from the strictures of the historian and the conventions of historical narrative. All in some way showed ways to displace history, challenge received foundations and philosophies of history, refuse grand narratives, establish a critical position, destabilize historically arrested temporality, render the historical subject problematic (or redundant) and confront their moment without simply reducing it to "a moment from which to interpret the past." They all shared the imperative of unlocking an ethics, not lodged in history but drawn from what confronting things past exposes, as they prefigure a future that, in part, determines the present. How Derrida places Marx in this frame powerfully makes the point when he says there will be "no future without Marx." He certainly did not mean that "Marxist ideology" and "dogma" will determine futures. Rather, to reemphasize, he evokes Marx's absolute acceptance of responsibility for what radical critique exposes. The spirit of Marx is therefore a spirit of unrestrained critical inquiry that recognizes that no problem can be solved unless it is seen in its total nakedness. Such inquiry stands before the specificities of a disjointed, fragmented and defuturing world-within-the-world of human fabrication. Rather than simply folding into a gestural call to "change the world," acting so informed means conjunctural engagements with "that which is futurally directive of the 'Being-of-beings.'"

Placing design in these disrupted domains of understanding history implies the shattering of the tropes of design history (and the illusions and unquestioned foundations they trade on). It also implies: the displacement of the historical object by its ontologically designing agency, recognizing how design practices are constituted and structured by specific discourses, and recognition that both the past and the future arrive in "the everlasting now."

Past and future: A question of imperatives

Emancipation, thought as "design transformed," offers a prospect of our self-transformation via the recognition and redirection of the ontological designing of what makes us what we are. The formation of worlds and beings-in-the-world are thus inextricably connected. Such radical redirection has the potential to counter the negation of futures that is intrinsic to neoliberalism, and to displace the deterministic legacy of historical materialism. The means to do this comes from an ontological materialism brought to the imperatives of our defuturing age of unsettlement, and to the advance of Sustainment as the process by which viable futures are secured. So qualified, emancipation does not arrive by, or rest with, the implementation of a political philosophy via a political regime. Rather it is a political project: a making, a work (to be done).

Action so understood cannot be based on a notion of historical universals—they no longer stand. The dream of monocultural modernity turned into a nightmare. Yet one ethical absolute has now arrived as unavoidable: it is articulated by the imperative of Sustainment *but* this can only be advanced as a "commonality in difference."[132] What this implies is a break with the idea of history predicated on a *telos* of beginnings and ends. Rather what a "commonality in difference" suggests is discontinuity, continuity and innovation based on the creation of conjuncturally varied assemblages according to situated conditions. This is to say that there can be variations in resources deployed, the speed of change, cultural practices, environmental and economic circumstances, knowledge and skill but with a common direction being worked toward.

Repositioning ethics

As indicated, the means to the creation of Sustainment, as both a futural project and process, can be formed and applied in difference. Clearly this does not imply one pathway, one culture, or one agenda. Fundamentally, what is essential to grasp is that we are in a global situation of deepening structural unsustainability, where the material demands of a still rapidly growing human population continually increase while at the same time the biophysical impacts of this population become ever more critical. Thus, in this situation of shrinking futures, there is an unavoidable message that is still a whisper but destined to become a roar: "without Sustainment we have nothing." The implications of realizing what this message means is "thrown beyond greatness" (*huperballo megethos*)—the meaning is currently beyond us. It defies instrumental reduction.

There is, however, one implication that begs comment here, which is to expose the opening into how Sustainment reconfigures ethics. At a superficial level ethics becomes a form of materialism whereby all that contributes to the advance of Sustainment is ethical, and all that negates it is not. But complexity starts to arrive once the causal agent arrives ("us"). Our actions framed by the need for such an ethics require that we understand ourselves as anthropocentric beings *that are aware of what we are* and accordingly accept responsibility for so being. The bridge linking "us and ethics" is provided by ontological design as it constitutes: things that act ethically; and us with a habitus from which the making of ethical things can emerge (this via education—a form of ontological design—of the subconscious).

The unsustainable cannot just be understood as the sum of all negative impacts that threaten human futures and the future of all that we depend upon (which by implication makes Sustainment an anthropocentric objective). Such threats go well beyond biophysical damage and enfold all forms of violence that harm being and negate "the time of life"—which for us is the extent of our finitude as delimited by our collective actions. Besides these threats coming from the present moment they also travel towards us as defuturing elements of a past that accumulate in a future containing "fragments of worlds that we once made" that will futurally decay, pollute, contaminate, die.

The historical question of future

The project of Sustainment is a project of historical inscription. While being an intellectual and practico-designing project of futuring it is equally about the creation, the "worlding," of a new historical foundation. As such it will aim to be selectively appropriative of the past, redirectively creative in the present, destructive of whatever forms of defuturing it can engage, and committed to thinking and action "in time" (by which is meant acting and thinking in the medium of time, and judiciously in the face of crises).

But one may ask: can it be discussed as if it exists? Yes, in a nascent form it does exist as an inchoate project. It has a history! As such it has: informed projects, been the topic of seminars, given direction to curricula, been an object of focus in the formation of a "change community"—all of this means the idea has been emancipated. It has taken on a life of its own. The critical question is: can it be given, or will it gather, significant and transformative momentum? One could say "time will tell," but it is not a matter of fate. Its history is to be made.

The concern of the making of Sustainment has to be the establishment of a developmental direction that is able to create futures with a future. To pose this intent is to invite the arrival of a myriad of problems that center on how to act futurally. Abstractly this means having a greater sense, and ability, to comprehend relational causality together with the formation of values that secure conditions of care materially inscribed in redirective practices, redirected modes of exchange and objects of desire. Concretely this all means learning by ontologically designed project by project (political, pedagogic, intellectual, cultural, social, economic, environmental, psychological) over time (the "work" of emancipation).

Those beings that we are (the human as plural) have constructed histories that, in part, have tried to tell "us" who we are and what we have done. However, in this setting fact and fiction merge with determinate consequences. History so formed, structurally fails to get to the essence of the key issues—the issues of the "who" and "the what" simply cannot be reached by history because the answers sought are encased in the ontology of "our" historicity—which is to say they exist neither in our plural identities nor in our recorded actions. Rather, on both counts, the imperative is to look to the historicity of what "we are" as it has remained the same. From this perspective it becomes possible to see that our very being has been predicated upon a negation. We are, and have been, more than just a "dangerous animal" for, and more essentially, we are world-makers (makers of our own world), but indivisibly we are equally unmakers who still continue to destroy the very ground of our dependence (that is called "the world").

We made ourselves out of our world-making. Beyond, and in relations with, those biological and social processes of our evolution, we are also a product of the ontological designing of our selves created by our appropriation of natural resources and their transformation (via the use of tools into forms of a world-within-the-world). This has not only been unceasing but has accelerated: the more of us there are, the more we take and the more we make. Bluntly: the essence of the unsustainable is that global collectivity we call "us," in action. All that is unsustainable comes from us as we destroy as we create, without ever really recognizing what we are doing. We call this "making." The "who" we are, then, are the makers and unmakers, and "the what" we have done in our unmaking is to progressively destroy what we most need (our conditions of dependence). So doing, "we" have effectively set ourselves on a path to auto-destruction. This is what we have (non)evolved toward, and this propensity is what has to be redirected (by design). In our condition of making, and of being made by what we bring into being (individually and in sum, materially and immaterially), we have to learn how to make a world-within-the-world other than it is, and our selves as other than we are—this in order to continue to be. How long do we have? Who knows? But let's say it cannot be more than a few hundred years (which, when measured against the tens of thousands of years our species has endured is but a speck of time). Three further points qualify these remarks:

- The more of us there are, and the more technologies we have created, the faster the rate of acceleration of destruction.

- It is not possible to engineer our selves out of this (ontological) situation.

- The environmentalist call to "save the planet" is totally misplaced. The planet while being damaged by us will recover in a transformed state (it has recovered from far more than our inherent destructiveness).

What demands to be understood is that none of this exposition is marginal to design history. Rather it is its very ground.

Now we will move to the problem of "our" developmental direction (in order to become the harbingers of Sustainment).

From what has already been made clear, Sustainment demands we change. But among all we do and create, how and what do we change? How do we break with our historical becoming? How to we gain a deep grasp of the historical and hold history in ruins at bay? There are a number of lessons and issues carried over from the past that indicate starting points. Over and above these, there is what we can employ from what we learn from the thinkers we have reviewed.

Preparation move 1: Sustainment as project and break

As an imperative, Sustainment is not merely a condition of an ongoing process to be created (a process that cannot be reified with any particular form), but one that can only be realized by being constituted as a project with a specific agenda that is based on a rupture with the *telos* of past world-making (that world that is made as the "world-within-the-world" of human fabrication) as it ontologically designs our mode of being-in-the-world at it most basic. Thus, what has to be broken is: how design is presented as history (so that it can be understood historically); and the practice of design as designing overdetermined by the client service relation (design/design practice "has" to be redesigned to serve Sustainment).

Currently, and dominantly in our induction into this world, we are induced into a condition of the unchecked production of destruction. Seldom, within this context, is the historicity of the "dialectic of sustainment" existentially acknowledged (which means overlooking that human beings learn to become makers, producers, creators without ever really learning that these actions destroy biologically, environmentally, culturally). This inherent trend of our being that was amplified by the arrival of productivism (out of the ancient world's conceptual notion of the atomic assemblage of the world becoming a model and possibility of adopted human action). Such thinking was fully realized as that knowledge that enabled industrial production to reach its zenith. However, the passage from a mode of thinking that drove a method of making continues and unceasingly turns all that was natural into artificial or hybrid matter.

Fundamentally, then, what is being identified to be at stake here is a futural redirection of the means of the creation of our very historicity, so that we may, to reassert, become other than we are. Against this backdrop the (plural) history that defines what we are, has to be contested. This does not reduce to a Jenkins-like question of whether we need history or not, but rather leads to *recognition that we need history as an object of critical overcoming, because it delivers signs and narratives indicating directional error*.[133] Without this mapping (which does not presume a simple claim that it is possible to "learn from history") it is just not possible to construct a new materialism of Sustainment (and therein a new designing/historical understanding of design); one that turns Marx on his head (who was haunted by the ghost of Hegel for his famous turning of him).

How does a directional rupture get made? Certainly they do not occur naturally.

There can be no expectation of revolution. It is not impossible that there might be a dramatic shift in the mode of production if there is a sufficiently large resource crisis (but it could equally drive innovation to produce even more dynamic capitalism, at least for a period). Even though the challenge is absolutely enormous, the strongest case rests with Sustainment as project. As an intellectual exercise it is not, and cannot be, orthodoxy. Rather, its only chance of arriving forcefully is as thinking able to be taken towards an unrestrained critical engagement with the inequitable status quo, and as a plural and vigorous response to a recognized necessity of paradigmatic "developmental change" (that is, change toward Sustainment). The only chance of this happening is if it comes from multiple traditions, both conceptual and instrumental, that are able to bring new discourse and institutions into existence—hence earlier comments on plural futures. Here, then, is a project of the measure of the Enlightenment, but one totally other than the Enlightenment's "will to power" and command (not least of the natural). Such a project cannot be constrained by the limits of reason. We have to comprehend that reason and modern rationality are merely the product of particular historical and Eurocentric conditions. This was one of Heidegger's main insights and, as such, is being seen as not only of increasing critical concern, but as an opening into thinking beyond reason.[134]

Preparation move 2: Prefiguring an ontological shift

A project of Sustainment is not going to come out of nowhere. It requires the creation of a change community, a new culture of thinking and acting, a new kind of education—all based on a critical politics and position toward rejected avant-gardism. We have explored this culture under the rubric of "a new culture of self-making and (un)learning"—a "*Neu Bildung*."[135] Building on existing critical thought, its agency would focus on "the deconstruction of education and the discovery of what to unlearn and learn" (here is the recognition that the unsustainable is something we learn to be, and that this learning has to be devalued and eliminated from education at every level—this process of the identification of what to destroy, preserve and create, rather than being new, is an inherent structural feature of the entire history of education). Equally, the task of bringing destruction into critical view (cultural, economic, social and environmental) is another major dimension of the agenda. What this exposes is the need to engage the borderland, formed in the afterlife of both modernity and colonialism, and starting to be examined by "border thinking."[136]

Out of this created perspective it becomes possible to approach destructions against destruction (no matter how hard it is, the defuturing structures and forces of the unsustainable have to be dealt with effectively, by design and ethically).

Implementation move 3: Enacting the ontological shift

Sustainment will not arrive, has no real power, if simply viewed as rhetoric or as an intellectual (academic) politics. It has to be constituted as discourses of transformation, which is to say it has to have an institutional ground and transformative practices (design remade and the "Urmadic University" being significant examples[137]). Breaking out of the limitations of "alternatives" and creating a counter "world-within-the-world" of the "world-within-the-world," has to be thought and projected into what will be growing spaces of dysfunction. All this slates back to a futuring (applied ontological materialism) wherein there is a re-directive remaking (that acknowledges the fundamental basis of ontological design whereby we were, and always are, very significantly made by a mode of making). Along with this is the activity of unlearning and relearning within a counter-worlding of de-investment in so many "desired things." Overcoming, overwhelming, the (human) animal—that "most dangerous of all animals"—who realizes or strives for the unbounded excess of "consuming" non-consumables, is unavoidable!

Back to the future

As already indicated, the future is not later than the past or in front of the present. There is nothing but now. "Temporality temporalizes itself as a future which makes present in the process of having been."[138]

> By the term "futural", we do not here have in view a "now" which has *not yet* become "actual" and which sometime *will be* for the first time. We have in view the coming [Kunft] in which *Dasein*, in its own most potentiality-for-Being, comes towards itself. Anticipation that makes *Dasein* authentically futural, and in such a way that the anticipation itself is possible only in so far as *Dasein*, as being, is always coming towards itself—that is to say, in so far as it is futural in its Being in general.[139]

Nihilism, as the loss of values and agency, as a face of defuturing, is equally a loss of the potential for a future; the loss of possibility. The commonplace notion of living for now is de facto nihilism underpinned by chronophobia.

> The future makes ontologically possible an entity which is such a way that it exists understandingly in the potentiality-for-Being. Projection is basically futural; it does not primarily grasp the projected possibility thematically just by having it in view, but throws itself into it as a possibility.[140]

Such understanding clearly cuts into how historical narratives are presented and what they claim, their hermeneutic basis and the way they insert an understanding of past, present, and future into the everyday. In this context great thinking can never be historically contained; the thoughts of Aristotle, Kant, Hegel etc., arrive from the past and the future, in so far as they travel towards and away from us—they are the past to be recovered, and the awaited and the to-be-discovered. Increasingly there is a contest over time and the future. What the agenda of a "*Neu Bildung*" goes to, is the destruction of that frame that projects the past as over, and the future as a void. The future is a daily site of contestation; it only exists for us (we own the idea) and is neither infinite nor a totality, for everything is passing in "a manifold and succession of nows as an extant sequence."[141] Our past is our unevenness coming back to us as our future *now* arrives.

2 ANOTHER HISTORY, ANOTHER DESIGNING

This essay is predominantly a case study of the "the Holocaust," an "event" in which design was deeply implicated, and whose horror overwhelmed its time and place.

But before approaching this case study one has to deal with how "the Holocaust" was (and is) made "history"—made a narrative/text that is, in fact, dislocated from the event. In so doing we need to ask: how do we deal with knowledge and truth, as they are contingent, perspectival and uncertain? This question in no way implies that *the event* did not take place; rather, it returns us to engage issues centered on the construction of *events* as historical narrative. To do this we will consider four interrelated critical figures: writing, narrative, reading and representation. To denaturalize the "event," as a literary configuration, the subject (as modern/human and proto-human/ancient) will be used to frame adopted points of view. Thus our primary concerns await this framing.

Seeing and the textual lens

The animal, in becoming human/animal, has no history. All that is known comes from interpretive readings of diverse palaeontological/ archaeological fragments—objects, bones, traces of cultivated and consumed grains, cave paintings, palaeo-anthropological evidence of migration patterns, and so on.

The some one hundred and fifty millennia of human nomadic life prior to human settlement are without knowable events in any detail. Nonetheless, palaeontological knowledge tells us something of the consequences of proto-human actions as they contributed to bringing the human into being. As explored at length elsewhere, "we" are essentially a product of a complex relation between biology, the social, artifice, and the symbolic.[1] With the arrival of human settlement around ten millennia ago, the events of our becoming started to be more discernable. Design, as an act of prefiguration, was a significant agent of our formation, this from the very distant moment when the animal acted to start to transform itself and its world.[2] The process of our becoming was a protracted event that awaited the creation of a text to transform historicity into a prehistorical historical narrative and (notwithstanding delusionist creationism) thereby rendered the mythological arcane. In this respect the past arrived to be ordered, seen and made legible. For example, the huge archaeological literature on Mesopotamia and the Near East as well as of India and China illustrate the point for, in part, the intent of its critical analysis was to bridge the silence between historicity and the historical.

Such literature grew especially from the mid-nineteenth-century onward. On Mesopotamia and the Near East, particular texts can stand for this era and for what its corpus of knowledge made possible. Three of these texts are: Leonard Wooley's *Excavations at Ur* (1930); Henri Frankfort's *The Birth of Civilisation in the Near East* (1951); and, representing the more recent past, Charles Keith Maisels' *The Near East: Archaeology in the "Cradle of Civilization"* (1998).[3] As for China, nothing surpasses the work of Joseph Needham, with his massive multi-volume project *Science and Civilisation in China*.[4]

The fact that history is always written in the culture of the present ensures an absolute disjuncture with a culture of the past. Added to this is the need to grasp that cultures are never coherent wholes. Rather they are (and increasingly so) a "circulation of fragments." People passing through from "the elsewhere" deposit into and appropriate from a culture—cultures live and change. Likewise, differences are also created out of divisions of wealth, knowledge, labor, systems of belief and so on.

One of the crucial observations to make about revisiting ancient knowledge (be it that it is mostly in the domain of the forgotten) is that it can be "excavated" to provide a basis from which to learn, not just things of the past but also for the future. Again knowledge from ancient China is a case in point. For instance, David Hall and Roger Ames drawing on it and the word *li* (pattern) write:

> In the absence of teleological guidance there is only an ongoing process of correlation and negotiation. One investigates *li* in order to

uncover patterns that relate things, and to discover the different resonances between things that make correlations and categorization possible. The nature of classification (*lei*) in this world is juxtaposed through some presumed similarity. As Needham has pointed out "things influence one another not by acts of mechanical causality, but by a kind of inductance."[5]

Bringing this kind of thinking to history, what is recognized is that ancient Chinese philosophy, based on thinking about correlative relations in contrast to a Western *telos*, exposes history as unfolding in difference in an "endless now" (as with Benjamin), as present always meets the past. Likewise, futural positions of understanding equally recognize that time is plural and that histories are not discrete.[6]

Reading, writing and speaking history

Keith Jenkins points out, as we have affirmed and as the Needham project made very clear, that history is always produced for "a someone" and, as such, is always positioned suasively with a specific direction.[7] Thus the "voice of history" is never my voice or yours but, reiterating, that of an "orator" with their own agenda, point of view, interests and objectives. As was made clear in the previous chapter, such writing always has effects— sometimes intended, sometimes large, mostly small, but dominantly unconsidered.[8] Moreover, Jenkins claims neither history nor historians can provide "any object/universal idea of direction, aim, purpose, meaning, truth, etc."—which is to say again that the "someone" is never independent of a particular regime of interests.[9] Moreover, by varied degree, historical narrative, "truth" and ideas always pass through an ethnocentric screen, with or without significant transformations of meaning. This is in large part because a story is read through the interpretative framework of particular cultures, and truth is not elemental to an object or text but something brought to it again by how a culture configures its understanding of it. Historians writing on the basis of "truth claims" (as they always do), while leaving their fictional fabrications unrecognized, are effectively, as Mark Poster tells us, acting with "real false consciousness."[10] Our position recasts this conclusion to say: to write on the historical is always to do so in the company of the undecidable. Notwithstanding the claims of science, cultural difference means there are no universally consensual truths (as is graphically illustrated by contested notions of creation).

Of course forms of "official history" project another view.

Western nations have a history of exercising their power over historical representation (the Western discipline of history being a product of the Enlightenment)—that, according Jenkins, stitches together a "knowable past" with an "understandable present" so as to create a "controlled future" in order to establish what Sande Cohen calls an "exclusion of new rival claimants to the future."[11] All of this prompts recall of one of the most famous lines of George Orwell from *Nineteen Eighty-Four*—"whomsoever controls the past controls the future." Here, then, is history recruited into the service of hegemonic power as a means of naturalizing the authority of the West. But, as Dominick LaCapra succinctly reiterates: history is a contested domain, wherein the legitimacy of the very category is contested. This long-standing observation is one that continually gets negated and clearly marks a significant level of limitation of the practice. Another limitation is to take the problematic rhetoric of history uncritically and thereafter to continually mobilize it in modes of "documentary" or "objectivist" address.[12] What, to reiterate, has been continually and often deliberately overlooked, is that all historical narratives are based on the linking of events by fictions (the bigger the gaps between events, the greater and more manifest the fictions).[13] As Jenkins well argues, the refusal to recognize the implication of history as fiction totally undercuts the epistemological claims and ground upon which history writing claims to stand.[14] As such it also, in part, goes to explain historians/history's general antagonism to those thinkers (like Michel Foucault) who theorize their historical practice.

In discussing issues of modern Chinese culture one cannot avoid the extent to which Chinese modernists waged "war on the past" from the mid-nineteenth-century to recent times. This disposition was of course not exclusive to China. Hostility toward history was, for example, significant in Europe prior to World War I (the example of this we gave in Chapter one being Italian Futurists, who embraced the war as a means to clear a path to the future—it was not without irony that leading figures of the movement died in the conflict). War thus was viewed as a weapon against the historical, and by implication against memory. The view was the new could not arrive unless the past was destroyed.[15]

The idealism of the historical within history presumes a conscious subject who acts futurally in the knowledge of the past. "It" believes it knows about the otherness of the other, about the past in its otherness. Yet in its hermeneutic identification with "an other" we again see once again an illusion produced. As Hans-Georg Gadamer first observed over fifty years ago, the subject who claims "historical consciousness" is itself a product of historical circumstances that effectively preclude this possibility. An independent view of "the past" simply does not exist.[16] This is especially the case because we now live in an even more highly mediated world that increasingly negates the possibility of anything like a definitive history. Increasingly life is lived in circumstances in which historically unknowing subjects are formed.[17] The shift out of history to "the event," a perceptual shift in some ways led by Michel Foucault, recognized this condition of limitation.

Counter to the abandonment of directional history are a number of salvational historical practices. There is, for example, the trend in history writing, noted by Caroline Bynum, for scholarship to gravitate towards the "collapse and deterioration" of both the object and narrative of history combined with attempt to reinstate continuity and a narrative by accounts of "the end."[18] Likewise, there is the kind of situated contextualism, described by Dominick LaCapra, which effectively partitions writing from a historical perspective with the claim of placing historical observation outside the discourse of history.[19]

Constantly what returns to history (the practice and its product) is contestation over its status, this when it is claimed to be an ordered and coherent discourse delivering truth and authority. Without this claim, as Jenkins points out, the notion of history having a definite object and mode of enquiry falls, and thereafter it is cast into the realm of rhetoric.[20] To say this is not new and does not actually resolve anything, as was evident in LaCapra's review of rhetoric and history in 1985.[21] However, as is clear from numerous sources, that which is taken to be history is a "narrative effect" that in turn constitutes what is deemed as "historical understanding." By implication, brute historical "facts" cannot in themselves be history. They have no voice outside of the narrative of their deployment.

Once history is acknowledged as a particular genre of narrative it is equally evident, and again widely recognized, that what is produced is from within this narrative, and its reading is the product of a creative act of interpretation. Thus, notwithstanding claims to truth and authority, again we note that history has no single point of view or independent meaning. This "fact" of history is so often masked by the "ficticity" manufactured by history writing as it appears to mobilize actual "historical facts." Layered over such writing is the power and ordering of fictions by historical metanarratives (the rise of empires, class struggle, modernity and so on). The crisis of history arrives out of these rhetorical relations in two respects.

First was the loss of historical authority, this once it was recognized that all historical representation is based on a position of bias out of which interpretation is created. The crisis of the loss of the authority of history also comes from a failure to recognize not only that history cannot escape pluralism or relativism but, above all, that it is purely a representational construct. While all cultures have a past, without this past being represented they have no history; however, "the past" (as event) and "the representation of it" are clearly not the same thing.[22] Second was the loss of the authority of master/metanarratives that gave the directional impetus to history— for example, the loss of the authority of the narratives of progress, the advance of human civilization, emancipation of the oppressed, and hegemonic modernity. Quite simply what died in the "postmodern moment," as prefigured by "the Holocaust," was the teleological idea that humanity was actually going somewhere; and an idealism that assured the future was destined to be better than the past.

While it has been recognized that historical representation was always the consequence of a relational assemblage—the pulling together of stories, events, information, detail, data—history fundamentally refused to embrace actual relationality as it was constituted by difference and the incommensurate. The propensity was always toward a "history of" that *made* sense of the past and so effectively rendered the actual historical complexity unrepresented. Historical narratives manufacture a sense of events that inherently do not actually *make* sense, for events are not sensible, they are always incoherent. It is against such a backdrop that Jenkins can say that now nobody really believes that meaning can be found anymore.[23] Yet the reverse is the case: while meaning can be and is recognized as not being able to be held and historically anchored, it continues to be unproblematically projected, sought and claimed by "the masses." So constructed, the simulacrum of meaning has agency, yet this is not to say it is constructively meaningful—de facto, meaning is contingent on the discourse in which it is situated, which may or may not be problematic.

Keith Jenkins claims we "can live without histories of either modernist or postmodernist kind."[24] He goes further than this, to say: "in the best of all possible worlds . . . we ought to live our finite lives in time 'but outside histories.'"[25] The former statement is ambiguous. It invites consideration of another kind of writing of the historical (as with a Foucault-inspired archeology or genealogy). The latter is far more problematic in so far as if all historical knowledge is banished, the significance of memory and received identity also go. Such thinking folds into chronophobia where a fear of time is legitimized and the illusion of permanence is reinforced. It likewise totally gives over to the industrialization of memory. A more appropriate stance is to accept history as an inadequate passage to the past; there are things of the past that, while always mediated by the present, beg critical engagement. In such a setting, the crisis of history invites to be embraced in a way that discards extant historical practice while advancing forms of critical inquiry of the past via plural modes of knowledge.

Rather than continue to deal with these issues in the abstract they will be worked through a very controversial and challenging object of historical account—"the Holocaust." Problems arrive immediately: use of the term "Holocaust" is contested and, likewise, the narratives that present it are all biased, not least those from the Jewish perspective. In terms of earlier remarks, what is absolutely essential to assert is the indivisible relation between historical accounts and memory.

What's in a name? "The Holocaust"—a case study

Not only has the "the Holocaust" been claimed to be the unrepresentable, not just because of the depths of inhumanity enacted within it, but also because its consequences were unable to be contained within any definable human measure. In this respect its collateral damage shattered any sense of a given human destiny, the idea of civilization and of the notion of humanity itself.

The event, "the Holocaust," has, since its first naming, been viewed as exceeding what befell its victims, for it is also recognized as a relational crisis of the West, and reason, history and design. The focus of what is to be done here will add no new knowledge concerning the event itself, with the exception of bringing design into the picture. In so doing what will be learnt is not simply how design was implicated in the historicality of the

"the Holocaust," but how the most powerful contributing function of design to it, was continued and amplified beyond the event.

Added to the challenges just outlined is the issue of the historical agency of design, as evident in prefiguration, intent, practice and product within, as and independent of events. Thinking all these relations will be brought to "the Holocaust." But let's be clear, the relation between actions that had design/designing intent and ongoing ontological designing consequences (from what had been designed and thereafter created) are extremely hard to adequately identify, comprehend and describe, yet without attempting to do this, the very processes of dehumanization in and beyond the very core of "the Holocaust" cannot be adequately attempted to be understood.

Design and the inhuman

Design in the context outlined cannot be understood without being appropriately grounded in the historical event in which it was embedded.

Before going any further there are a few qualifications to make. First, the account to be given of design will be partial. A full account of design's place in this "event" is impossible, for its role would have mostly escaped the intent and content of the archive. More than this, memories of design would have been limited because its forms and agency would mostly not have been seen as "design." And, even if there were relevant memories, they would now be lost in the passage of time and from death of those who owned them. So there is no position of overview. Whatever witnesses there were, their view will always be partial and, as implied, notwithstanding some key texts and images, the presence of design in the totality of all "Holocaust" documentation would have been insufficiently registered for its agency.

Next, it is important to recognize that "the Holocaust" sits within a Eurocentric frame of reference. As this, from one perspective, it shattered the humanist claim of Western civilization and the illusion of any essential progress in the essence of human beings toward evolutionarily inscribed perfectability. From another, it is defined against the silences within the partially documented histories of Western colonial genocidal actions. These actions reach back over five hundred years of Western colonial conquests on every continent, and have continued right up to the present. What a comparative view of such events demonstrates is that human life is not equally valued globally—racism not only underpins the act of genocide, it is also echoed in the differential worth of the lives of the exterminated.

As we now know, the inhumanity of human upon human that "the Holocaust" was deployed to epitomize, has not delivered the demise of such conduct. Inhumanity so enacted continues to travel from the past to the future and arrive in the present as a "the return of the same." Such "events" cannot be dismissed as merely aberrant. They are not just the product of the flaw in a particular culture, but rather mark the fact that humans as a species are not fully human. Moral condemnation is thus but nothing in the face of the precarious "nature" of (our) plural and insecure modes of humanity. Of course, what elevated the significance of "the Holocaust" was not simply the horror it manifested but, as has been pointed out many times and in various ways, that it occurred in the heartland of Western civilization. What were incinerated were not just millions of blameless human beings, but belief in an evolutionary process of continual, and progressive, advancement of human civilization. These beliefs were Eurocentric mythologies that simply looked away from the barbarism of centuries of Western colonialism, and avoided confronting the madness of World War I. So, while the human, civilization and progress represented certain figures of attainment, their dominant forms were illusory.

Just to take the example of "civilization"—as the West materialized and institutionalized its conspicuous symbols of civilization, it also acted with savagery and without constraint in exploiting people and resources. Consider, colonizers slaughtered about twenty-five million Mesoamericans from the sixteenth century onward. Equally we can register the post-Holocaust genocidal events of the twentieth century, including those in Cambodia, Rwanda, Darfur, Chechnya, Kosovo and Srebenica. And then there is the ongoing, horrendous and largely ignored conflict in the Democratic Republic of Congo where over five million people have died in war and from famine and disease. So, to reemphasize, it is inappropriate to present "the Holocaust" as a contained and aberrant event. It is not. So said, it still remains a certain "benchmark" of inhumanity, exposing the thinness of the line between being civilized and being dehumanized/dehumanizing in the very heartland of Western civilization.

In bringing design to the core, the essence, of "the Holocaust" the objective is to add a new frame of observation on both what was a "designing event" and design historically placed. To do this we will make a number of general remarks that position design, in a variety of forms, as a perspective to view three concentration/death camps: Dachau and Mauthausen work camp, Theresienstadt and Auschwitz. But before doing this, the relation between "the witness" and history need clarification.

History, ambiguity, event—who speaks, what can be spoken, silence

"The Holocaust"—etymologically understood (OED) as "a sacrifice wholly consumed by fire"—is a term that has evoked recoil from critical scholars. The term has actually acted to reduce perception of the complexity of the event reducing it to stereotypical characterizations.[26] It still remains difficult to make sense of "the Holocaust" in ways that keep it open to thought. For all his comments on history and historians, Jenkins assents that it is the role of the historian to "ensure" that this historical event "forever haunts us" as a "limit of history."[27] Certainly such a limit is an apt framing of the significance of "the Holocaust." As Dominick LaCapra has pointed out "'the Holocaust' may help us reconsider the requirements of historiography in general."[28] Certainly the intent here is to help expose the exclusion of design from its historical accounts and in so doing make explicit the challenge design poses to history, and history to design, thus furthering a critique of the "limits of design history."

What is clearly evident is that no images, facts/data, truth claims, narrative, theorized motives or rational analysis, whether taken alone or together, can make sense of it. "The Holocaust" as "event"—was/is not sensible. Causal accounts of it cannot stand upon the sensible, or adequately deal with the event as excess. As such it negates the ability to be represented yet, while so often designated as "the unrepresentable it has been continually subjected to representational practices."[29] In this context, one of the problems is the way in which the people who ran death camps have been (re)presented. For instance, a recent account has indicated that "most perpetrators of genocide were normal people," this in so far as nothing abnormal about them was picked up during "psychiatric screening."[30] As Hannah Arendt pointed out, and as Zygmunt Bauman later elaborated, monster(ou)s (people) were not born but made—this by the destruction of a fundamental and pre-human empathy: "animal pity."[31] Such people were normal people—be it that some were suffering from *Kriegsneurosen*[32]—who did abnormal things. One is now left with the question: can most normal people be made to do abnormal things?[33]

Design will now be brought to contribute to answering this question.

In its instrumental realization, "the Holocaust" was in significant part a product of design. As such it can be dominantly understood in three ways: as a designed organizational and management system; as a design system of mass production (of death, supported by specifically designed technologies); and as a designed architectural project.

Death camps themselves were partly prefigured organizationally and operationally—by the racist-inspired "euthanasia institutes" (the "insiders" name) that were created following an instruction by Adolf Hitler on September 1st, 1939. Here was a project of the most overt and crass form of designed social engineering. The "institutes" were publicly presented as charities providing "Institutional Care" or "Transport of the Sick," or were referenced anonymously with the chilling designation "T4." The activities of these "institutes"—of which there were four—was to rid the nation of *unwertes Leben* (unworthy lives), a task directed from an office in Berlin (at 4 Tiergartenstrasse—hence T4). The role of the institutes was legitimized by the Ministry of Interior's Department of National Hygiene (whose racial cleansing mission was to preserve "racial health") and by the Bureau for Enlightenment on Population Policy and Racial Welfare.[34]

The very names of these government bodies express a perversion of history, language and design function. As Zygmunt Bauman made clear: "*Unwertes Leben* remained the target all along. For the Nazi designers of the 'perfect society', the project they pursued and were determined to implement via social engineering at its most debased split human life into worthy and unworthy."[35] Thus, prior to the creation of death camps and the advent of gas chambers, attempts were made to rid the nation of the "insane and bodily impaired" while at the same time setting out to "breed a superior race through the organized fertilization of racially superior women by racially superior men."[36] Such thinking was underpinned by eugenic theory associated with Social Darwinism in the late nineteenth century and with the establishment of the international eugenics movement just prior to World War I.[37] It was also aided by another breeding practice: animal husbandry.[38] Such ideas, while taken to the extreme in Germany, were not regarded as unacceptable by large numbers of people in many "civilized" nations.

The management of the "destruction of European Jews" was conducted from SS (the Schutzstaffel—Hitler's "elite" guard) headquarters by a "Section of Administration and Economy," and as Bauman details it, was organized completely in line with Max Weber's description of a bureaucratic system, wherein objectives were carried out "without regard for persons."[39] Here then is a designed rational system appropriated and mobilized for totally irrational ends within which death was reduced to a mechanically directed routine act. Total compliance ruled within a system that excluded judgment and thought (compliance, it should be noted, has now become even more deeply entrenched in the structure of everyday life, not least in education in, and beyond, the West). Thus independent "judgment and thought" is further negated.[40] The omnipresence of compliance was and is one of the most significant, continuing and unrecognized features of "the Holocaust." This danger was, and is, at the core of the massive failure of "historical communication." "Instrumental rationality" was not only unable to prevent such abominations but was readily available to be called into service to advance it. Cuttingly, we find that most agents of genocide were not those gassing or shooting Jews (and others), but an army of bureaucrats writing memos, giving instructions, approving purchase orders, signing off on construction drawings, assigning troops to camps, authorizing medical activities and so on, to which others complied.[41] Likewise, the complicity of science and scientists was mostly left in the domain of the invisible.

As an underside of Western modernity, "the Holocaust" still exposes the negative face of the technical capability of bureaucratically organized technological society (as well as the underside of ontological design). Key to this "attainment" is *the removal of the decision to kill from the action of killing, with this act simply conducted by the compliance of actors ontologically designed to comply.* Of course the advancement of technology has continued to remove the decision-maker from the scene of the enactment of their decision so, while a factor in "the Holocaust," it has become ever more naturalized (as "systems function"), and thus more invisible. In fact, what the designers of especially weapons technology have now done is to abstract the victim and create forms representation that make the human invisible (like the target dot on the radar screen and the rise of "killer drones"). Accompanying this action is a language that equally removes any sense of human proximity (like the notion of collateral damage).

However, and more generally, what has been constant has been the deployment, in numerous forms, of organization and technology to increase the gap between the emotional bounds of the subject (and their feeling of being human), and reflection upon the subject who is to be the recipient of inhuman treatment. But, as the whole phenomenon of post-traumatic stress disorder indicated, repressed and displaced "feelings" are futural—they return to haunt.

While the compliant, and those who gave them orders, stood in the dock at the U.S. Nuremberg Military Tribunal, what was never exposed, tried and condemned was the designed system of compliance. As a result criminals and the criminal remained at large. Does this view imply that Western modernity and reason carry guilt? The answer is only partly no, because both have an underside: one that the "civilized" nations have been blind to. So one may well wonder if the bureaucrat and the technician of modern society are neutral actors in the face of what threatens? Certainly acting under instruction is a normative condition that carries a large ethical problematic that contemporary society chooses to overlook.

The design of concentration/death/work camps, and their facilities, arrived under the direction of architects. But to show the absolute degeneration of design rendered instrumental in the service of unreason, a brief comment will be made on a built structure designed by SS-Standartenfuehrer Paul Blobel, a qualified architect and mass murderer.

In 1942 Sonderkommando 1005 (also called Aktion 1005) was formed from concentration camps' prisoners to exhume mass graves and burn the bodies so as to destroy war crimes evidence. In March 1942 SS-Standartenführer Paul Blobel was placed in charge of this unit. The unit operated in Russia and Poland. One of Blobel's innovations was to design a pyramid structure using train rails upon which timber, and thereafter, bodies could be laid and burnt (a structure made famous in Herman Wouk's best seller *War and Remembrance* in 1978). Another one of Blobel's endeavors, for the same "cause," was a bone-crushing machine.[42]

The point of mentioning this example, and what such horrors evidence, is what Michel Foucault named as "biopower"—the reduction, direction and management of human being to "bare life." The genocide of "the Holocaust" marks a major moment of "history" as a document of applied biopower. As outlined by Sande Cohen (writing on Georgio Agamben): biopower is a force underscoring decisions whereby life is secured, taken away or sustained.[43]

Notwithstanding Blobel's structure, the point about design and "the Holocaust" is that it is not reducible to objects and structures, images or fashion (and yes one can call the look of the panamas of camp inmates "fashion") but rather that it was a designed relational phenomenon (with forms with absolute ontologically designing violent force). It did not occur or operate by accident—it was a product of intent, of planning that existed in the mind prior to its materialization.

Witnessing the witness

The fact of "the Holocaust event" is one thing; the truth of it is another.

The project of the destruction of evidence (the project of Sonderkommando 1005, and an obsession directed by the Nazi leadership) continued right up to the very last days of the war. Who knows exactly how many documents were destroyed to this end, for as Germany's defeat became inevitable the Nazi regime began to systematically destroy as much evidence as possible. For example, when the SS abandoned Auschwitz, most of the paperwork and the gas chamber buildings were burnt. Likewise, besides turning bodies to dust and ash, the Nazis destroyed other physical evidence, including the death camps of Treblinka, Sobibor, Belzec, and Chelmno. Other sites of atrocities were camouflaged as farms.

According to Primo Levi, what "the witness" tells us is that the ordinary "common prisoner" does not survive.[44] What enabled survival was not being ordinary, but being in some way privileged (as gained by stealth, luck or as nature's gift).

The witness is not the purveyor of facts or disinterested truth. Again Levi makes this clear, for they know that judgment is impossible: they exist in a grey zone wherein "victims become executioners and executioners become victims"—both are "ignoble."[45] They have a point of observation on "the inside or outside" and the only dialogue that is actually possible is that between each other.[46] Put plainly, and linked to the previous statement, survival demands doing what is necessary to survive and to do this erases any possibility of having any moral authority. Confirmation of this view comes from Zdenek Lederer who was deported from Prague in 1941, interned in Thereseinstadt and then deported to Osviecim (Auschwitz) death camp in 1944, and on returning to Prague in 1946 wrote a "witness account" about Thereseinstadt.[47]

As was clear from the remarks of so many survivors: "the 'survivors' vocation is to remember; he cannot not remember." The experience constituted a memory that overwhelmed all else that could possibly be remembered. What was actually remembered, borne witness to, was not necessarily what would have been expected. For: "If the survivor bears witness it is (sic) not to the gas chambers or to Auschwitz but to the Muselmann";[48] the being without humanity—the witness who, "if he speaks," can only speak "the impossibility of speaking." The absolute witness is thus seen in the becoming of what they end up being.

Dachau and Mauthausen work camp[49]

Dachau was the first "regular" concentration camp established by the Nazi government—in March 1933 at an abandoned munitions factory outside the city, some 16 kms northwest of Munich. It was created specifically for political prisoners. The first internees were communists, trade unionists, gypsies, homosexuals, habitual criminals and just a few Jews. There are no records of how many people died in the camp between 1933 and 1939.

In early 1937 the SS, using prisoner labor, demolished old factory buildings and built a larger complex. This was completed in 1938 and remained unchanged, with the exception of a crematorium with a gas chamber (which was added in 1942) until it was liberated in 1945. The camp consisted of thirty-two barrack blocks, including the infamous medical block, and a block created for clergy who had spoken out against Nazi rule. Evidence on the use of the gas chamber is not clear, but what is known is that sick or weak prisoners who were unable to work were sent to Hartheim (a euthanasia killing center near Linz and the Mauthausen concentration/work camp in Austria).

An estimated 200,000 prisoners died at the camp during Dachau's operation.

Dachau was an important facility beyond merely its detention function. It was where concentration camp guards were trained. Moreover, it was used as the operational design model upon which all death camps were based. Then, in 1944, it was made the center of a hub of around thirty labor camps in southern Germany (these camps were serviced by about 30,000 prisoners, of whom an approximate 28,000 were worked to death).

Dachau's notorious reputation in large part came from the medical experimentation conducted there—it was in fact a key part of a network of such activity. These experiments were conducted mainly for the Luffwaffe and the Institute for Aviation. Human beings were used in these experiments as if they were mice or rats. For high-altitude trials prisoners were put in low-pressure chambers to establish at what altitude parachutes could be used; likewise in hypothermia experiments the exposure to cold was taken to the point of death, as were tests on drinking seawater. Additionally there were many experimental tests on drugs for infectious diseases that prisoners had been infected with.

In 1938 Heinrich Himmler, Reichsführer of the SS, (and the military commander who, more than any other, directed "the Holocaust") gave orders for hundreds of prisoners from Dachau to be sent to Mauthausen that, as said, was near Linz—to build a labor camp for the Wiener Graben stone quarry. As Evelyn Le Chene made graphically clear, Mauthausen was designated as a "category three camp."[50] What this meant was that the return of prisoners "was not desired" and that the quarry should be managed with the objective of "extermination by work." As the camp grew it was divided into five sub-camps. If not enough prisoners died the SS guards helped things along by, for example, stripping prisoners naked in a yard on very cold winter days then spraying them with water and then letting them freeze to death. By 1942 there were almost fifty camps in the Mauthausen system.

The quarries had the highest mortality rate of all labor camps. Jews, in advanced states of malnutrition, were sent to them to work and die. The means to kill them was simple: the carrying of large rocks from the quarry floor up the 186 steps to the quarry top.

So here we have the barbaric treatment of human beings sentenced to death by work. Such "people" were reduced to bare life, and this life, their life, was given absolutely no value, not even the value of an animal. Yet the process was directed by a finely tuned design regime directed by a specific and "grand" design objective.

As Michael Allen poignantly observes: the design regime of the SS Economic Administration Main Office (Wirtschaftsverwaltungshauptamt, referred to as the WVHA) brought "modern management methods" (which were, as Himmler made clear, inspired by Henry Ford[51]) to direct slave labor, and did so "with the same basic structures as any modern organisation in the West."[52] Thus there was an absolute disconnect between the design of the bureaucratic system and the actions it facilitated. Managers simply managed, as "ordinary men doing an ordinary job." Process was therefore completely dislocated from the inhuman social relations of production. Here is the power of instrumentalism as it exposes the general, fundamental and ongoing disjuncture between reason and technological rationalism—this genie remains out of the bottle.

But what was it all for? Why such a demand for stone? As we shall see in a moment, the answers to these questions place architectural design center stage.

Architects played a crucial role in the technical design of concentration/death camps.[53] More generally, architecture occupied a special place in the Nazi spectacle and vision. Hitler, who exposed his views on architecture in his book *Mein Kampf* in 1925, spoke of himself, and was spoken of, as the architect and builder of the nation. He saw himself as the builder of the Thousand-year Reich and, of course, as the conceptual driver of the New Berlin (dubbed *Germania* and in which the evidence of the architecture of Jewish owned business—finance houses and department stores—would be completely destroyed). His manic vision, as Jeffery Herf details at length, was to reinstate a mythologized Greek past, by technological means, in the present.[54] This vision, with Hitler at its head as its symbolic architect, was supported by Albert Speer, with his passion for Delphic architecture. The 1939 full-length portrait of Hitler by Fritz Erler marked how he wished to be viewed, which was as the great builder. To signify this, at Hitler's feet we see the tools of the stonecutter and stonemason.

There were twenty-eight monumental buildings built by the Nazis, as symbolic figures of spectacle. The two most overtly expressive—the Nuremburg Zeppelinfeld Party Rally Grounds and the New Reich Chancellery (with its hall over a mile in length)—were designed by Albert Speer. These buildings existed to be seen, not used—they were monumental in a literal sense. Writing on them, and on Hitler, years later while in prison Speer said: "These monuments were an assertion of his claims to world domination long before he dared to voice any such intention even to his closest associates."[55] They were equally projected as epitomizing the sacrifice of labor for the value of a higher ideal, whereby mankind, as Walter Benjamin put it, "can experience its own destruction as an aesthetic pleasure."[56] Yet as monuments they "represented" something far removed from pleasure of any kind.

Hubert Schrader writing in 1937 suggested these buildings of the Third Reich were in fact simply elements of the overall aesthetic regime, within which members of civil and military society figured and were subordinated as part of a totality of order gathered by architecture and expressed in stone.[57] Schrader's suggestion begs two comments.

First the Nazi "overall aesthetic regime" needs greater emphasis as a "total design phenomena" in which everything was designed and had its place within the whole: uniforms, military insignia, the applied aesthetic of aircraft, ships and transport and armored vehicles, the symbolic spectacle of military events, bodies types, buildings, postage stamps, stationery, camps, autobahns, music, signage and so on. This all folded into a vision culled in part from a Greek past and brought to the future of German society as an enframing: a materialized ideological stamping aimed at total determination.

Second, as seen via the horror of Mauthausen (which had the highest mortality rate of all work camps[58]), what was expressed in that stone destined for the construction of the monumental architectural structures of the regime, was in actuality a manifestation of the triumph of a perverted order brought into service by absolute unreason. For those who carried the stone, all that the buildings symbolized was an extreme of inhumanity, a complete lack of value for their lives and their imminent death. The buildings built with these lives, as unremunerated costs, were unread markers of a rendered invisibility—the invisibility of lives consumed by pain. Lives lacking even the smallest amount of "aesthetic pleasure," that were reduced to a diminished existence and a heartless death. It is not without considerable irony that we read Speer's view of these buildings as "stone witnesses to history" (his words expose that contradiction which is history).[59]

Comparable with the brutality of the quarries was the creation of underground tunnels as bomb-proof factories—again this was an activity that cost the lives of thousands of prisoners, who were likewise worked to death.[60]

Work camps and slave labor also have to be seen as integral to the design of the labor process of Nazi wartime production. Labor represented a massive organizational challenge directed by the WVHA. Slave labor accounted for 25 percent of the total national labor force (many slave workers were imported from occupied countries, but some 700,000 were drawn from concentration camps).[61] The objective driving the entire process was to "match allied production tank for tank, plane for plane"; a goal that, once America entered the war, would never be met.

In the autumn of 1945, during Nuremberg trial of Dr Guido Schmidt (a politician and Nazi collaborator), evidence was presented that drew on a confession of SS Standartenfuehrer Franz Ziereis, the commander of the Mauthausen Work Camp. Ziereis had been shot and seriously wounded while trying to escape capture by American troops. In the presence of a number of official witnesses he made a confession—and died almost immediately after making it. He confessed to camp inmates being gassed, murdered by freezing, injected with benzene, and being starved to death, subjected to brain operations, worked to death, shot while being used as live targets on the camp rifle range, and blown-up in mines.[62]

In contrast to these remarks, one can contemplate the apology offered by Albert Speer who believed, when Hitler's architect, that he was simply an "unpolitical" functionary. However, on February 8, 1942, his world changed—he was appointed Armaments Minister. He wrote:

After two and a half years, in spite of the beginning of heavy bombing we raised our entire armaments production from an average index of 98 for the year 1941 to a summit of 322 in July 1944. During the same period the labor force expanded by only about 30%.[63]

What Speer failed to say was that a good deal of this labor was slave and forced. Rather he claimed that the performance mostly rested with "thousands of technicians with special achievements."[64] However, Speer did write something on slave labor employed on the V2 rocket project, and it is illuminating. He clashed with Himmler—whose agenda was for the SS to have complete control of all camp labor, not least for it to be able to make as much money as possible. The clash was over the management of slave labor and the ill-treatment of prisoners, not because of humanitarian concerns, but because Speer understood that if the prisoners were weak they would not be productive. While feeling guilt, he actually said: "the sight of suffering people influenced only my emotions, but not my conduct."[65]

Insightfully, an article appeared in the British newspaper *The Observer* on April 9, 1944 which said Speer was more important than any of the Nazi leadership, including Hitler, because he was "a classless bright young man without background, with no original aim other than to make his way in the world and no other means than his technical and managerial ability."[66] He was a pure technocrat and as such a precursor to that new instrumental ruling class that secures the continuity of the culture of compliance that they are produced by and foster. Yet in contradiction we read him saying in his memoirs (written during his twenty years as the sole inmate of Spandau Prison, Berlin) "the more technological the world becomes, the more essential will be the demand for *individual freedom and the self awareness of the individual human being as a counterpoise to technology.*"[67]

On considering Theresienstadt

This camp was unlike any other concentration camp. Whereas all camps had to be designed at the level of accommodation, facilities, security and so on, Theresienstadt became designed as an object of strategic representation—which is to say its function and appearance became a figure of aesthetic management.

We are going to look at the camp in two ways: first as it has been described historically; second as presented by one of its inmates, the already mentioned Zdenek Lederer, who spent almost three years there. To frame these observations Lederer sets the scene:[68]

> The structure of Theresienstadt was different from other German concentration camps. There was an ample measure of self-administration, and even a semblance of normal cultural life. To define the character of the community in Theresienstadt is an extremely difficult task. Some of its features were reminiscent of ancient slavery, and others of modern totalitarianism, while certain features cannot be clearly defined. It is, however, possible to discern three characteristics:
>
> A. Abnormal and pathological elements in the social structure of Theresienstadt
> B. Structural anomalies not existing in any other type of society
> C. Characteristics shared by Theresienstadt with other communities.

What A suggested was a kind of psychosis based on fear of deportation, depression, and life with a false hope of security; B was simply life in the double world of a ghetto that was equally a concentration camp, and C was the common experience of many people from different European cultures as they lived under the boot of German fascism.

An outline historical view of the camp

Theresienstadt was a ghetto-concentration camp some 60 kilometers north of Prague. It was created from the town of Terezin—a fortress city (with a large and small fort) established in the late-eighteenth-century as protection against invading Prussian armies.[69]

Five months after the Nazi invasion of Czechoslovakia the Jewish population of Terezin were subjected to restrictions, a year later the Gestapo set up a prison in the small fortress. By November 1941 the whole population had been evacuated and the town/fortress had become Teresienstadt, the ghetto/concentration camp. On November 24 the first group of 342 young men arrived; transported to the camp to undertake the conversion works, they were to be part of an eventual construction army of 1,300 Jewish men.[70] The camp was designated as "privileged" and as such it was made a "showplace."[71] As this, it accommodated Jews deemed important, including well-known writers, artists, and musicians. The appearance created was that "kulture" was respected and taken seriously by the Germans, thus these gifted artist, writers and musicians were given the freedom to produce and make "bold statements." But this freedom amounted to little, for all these people were fated to die.

The manufacture of appearances was also used to deceive Swedish representatives of the International Red Cross, who paid a visit on June 23, 1944.[72] Streets were cleaned, buildings were painted, turf was laid, park benches were installed, a sports field was made, a children's playground was created, monuments were erected, a hut was signed as "boy scouts hall," there was the smell of baking bread and a cart delivering vegetables was seen on the street. Notwithstanding the face of this fantasy, the people were coerced into silence. The design of fear can and did take many forms.

The Red Cross visitors were taken on a tour, including to the billet of Dutch Jews that had been enlarged, furnished, fitted with curtains and given a window box. The ploy of what became known as "the Embellishment" worked (or at least the visitors allowed themselves to be fooled).[73] The Nazis made a film of the visit and regarded the whole exercise as an outstanding propaganda success.

What the Red Cross did not see was that the ghetto/concentration camp, based on a town of 7,000 residents, was now accommodating a transient population of between 35,000 and 60,000 men, women and children—the result, besides overcrowding was poor sanitation, lack of power and contaminated water, plus huge numbers of vermin. Combined with a lack of food and medicines the death rate was very high. To deal with this a crematorium was built and was able to dispose of almost 200 corpses per day. Notwithstanding passing appearances, the ghetto/camp was a place of horror. To cite just one example: Nelly Toll tells us that some 15,000 children entered it, but only 100 survived.[74]

The actual reality of Theresienstadt was that it was a "transport clearing station" delivering Jews, rounded up in many European countries, to extermination camps in groups between 1,000 and 5,000 on a regular basis. Its constructed appearance was to mask this function, as well as to make this exercise as easy to manage as possible.

Lederer's view of Theresienstadt is nuanced and reveals its many contradictions. For example, he exposes the class structure of the ghetto. There was a ruling class of Jews who received significant privileges; there was a Jewish middle class who practiced a variety of specific trades; and then there was a class of menial workers. At the same time the Nazis could remove privileges in an instant and deport a person to a death camp in the east, at a whim. Lederer tells us that within this insecure setting, relationships were forged or ended, sexual life continued (but without a great deal of privacy), and in conditions of insecurity and oppression, a word, a sign, a look all could assume great importance.[75] He also gives us a picture of the more overtly brutal side of the ghetto/camp.

The River Ohre divided the small fortress from the large fortress (the ghetto). It was where people of the ghetto who were found guilty of a crime were sent to be punished—effectively this amounted to a death sentence carried out by an "SS Murder Command." Again, as part of the psychology of the designed representational strategy employed, appearances of a "normal life" could be constructed while at the same time the figure of terror (the small fortress) was constantly present as a signifier of fear to control the population. As such we see, at least in part, how it was possible for the Nazis to gain the compliance of the population for the Red Cross "Embellishment" deception.

The creation of the illusion, by the SS, of a concentration camp made to look like a Jewish ghetto with its own semi-autonomous administration, needs to be understood not only as a general condition of Theresienstadt (taken to a higher level during the embellishment). More fundamentally, it should be seen as a very substantial design project: one that established a convincing everyday-look that masked the actual fiction of place. This was not just a matter of constructing an image of the environment of a ghetto, but equally of the forcing of Jews to set up the appearance of the rule of law and of a civil society where the population enjoyed the freedom of full civil rights.[76]

The Jewish Camp Administration (JCA) was created on December 4, 1941, which was the same day that the second "construction command" arrived. The JCA was made responsible for the management of the construction works of the town within the large fortress as it was transformed into a Jewish ghetto, but with the addition of ten barrack blocks (which included the SS headquarters and billets, police billets, a bakery, and a delousing station—later a rail terminus was added).[77] It also directed the operations that constituted the elements of the fake civil society:

- The Security Service, formed from the two hundred-strong "Ghetto Guard" (which was reformed and renamed as the "Guard for the maintenance of order); the Fire Guard (who were also medical orderlies); Air Raid Wardens; and auxiliary technical staff.

- The Central Registry, which kept all records (including of new arrival and mortality rates) and served notices to people to be transported.

- The JCA Bank that, besides providing the Ghetto with a currency they could spend internally, also provided the guards and administrators with money to pocket. All money sent from family, friends and well-wishers to inmates was converted into the worthless Bank-invented currency, while that which had been sent was reallocated to those in charge.

In addition to these elements there were a number of specific departments created,[78]

- The Economic Department—which ran the food stores, managed materials depots, and production facilities, engineering, which included everything from plumbing to watch repairs; woodworking which, for instance, made the bunks for inmate billets; a paper and cardboard workshop making boxes for ashes of the dead; a clothing and footwear repair workshop that also made bandages; plus a laundry and bakery.

- The Labor Department that supplied male and female labor for all ghetto works from manual to office.

- A Finance Department that was just a pure fiction.

- A Youth Welfare Department that had token activities but mostly worked to undermine the Nazi's ban on education and to improve children's nutrition.

- The Health Department that tried to deal with the poor environmental health conditions of the ghetto, as well as the old and infirm (some 32,647 people died of diseases during the three plus years the ghetto/camp existed[79]).

By early 1942 the fiction had materialized. The JCA was running the illusory functional life of the ghetto, but under strict directions of the headquarters staffed by the SS—who were of course the real power of the camp (organizationally, the SS were under the direction of the Camp Commander, and included a Special Security Service Unit divided into three bureaus: administration, economic and security). The design objective of this "constructed everyday" was, as indicated, to give the impression that the Jews were leading a "normal life" and were being well treated. For instance, shops were opened to sell clothes, footwear, children's toys, and books (the one shop that was actually valued as a means to improve life[80]). However, all these goods were in fact acquired by being confiscated from newly arrived Jews at the camp. Goods purchased were paid for with a special "doggy-money" issued by the JCA Bank. Likewise, all workers' wages were paid in this bogus money. Thus the system simply allowed people to buy back what in effect they already collectively owned.[81]

The JCA was a controversial body—it justified its collaboration with the SS on the basis that its actions improved the quality of life of the people (by distributing food, and by improving accommodation, sanitation and the water supply, as well as by maintaining law and order). It was made up of a Council of Elders supported by a Central Secretariat with three sections: applications, complaints and transport. The first sections were token, but transport was not. Its function was to assist in the deporting of huge numbers of people (prisoners) to work and to death camps.[82] However, on the basis of his own experience, Lederer claims this level compromise by the JCA was unavoidable: the leaders had no option. Any form of defiance would have led to the ghetto simply becoming a camp like the others.[83] Clearly we are in no position to judge between collaboration, reluctant compliance or defiance. The basic view was that any form of resistance would be met with violence.

Making moral judgments of a reign *of* terror is one thing, making such judgments *in* it is clearly another.

The last "selection" to be exterminated at Auschwitz was from Theresienstadt—it arrived on October 30, 1944. A month later Himmler ordered the demolition of the camps gas chambers and the crematorium (another and unsuccessful attempt to erase evidence).[84] Between September and October 1944 some 18,000 young and middle-aged men were deported to death camps. The camp administration did this because the Nazis feared a repeat of a Warsaw-type uprising (that started in April 1943). This uprising had lasted two months and was not defeated until the entire ghetto was leveled to the ground. Hopelessly confronted by a powerful military force that bombed, shelled and attacked with tanks, the lightly armed men, women and children fought in the certain knowledge of death—an act of resistance that Jewish history has claimed for all Jews.[85]

Albert Speer provided a telling comment on this catastrophe after hearing Hitler talk about the devastation, remembering Hitler saying of the City of Warsaw that "it was the most beautiful in Europe."[86]

Auschwitz: Writing after the surplus of the excess

What more can be said about Auschwitz?

In that there is little or nothing more to say about what happened at Auschwitz than what has already been said in many media, in no way obstructs the necessity of going on reflecting, feeling and speaking—it is not just that memory demands this voice, so does the historical understanding of design. Where, then, is the dividing line between a critical confrontation with self-deception carried out in the "civilizing" claim of Western culture and what Sande Cohen once called the blossoming of Holocaust studies in academia?[87] Who knows? Who is in a position to judge? Finding the answer can be but passed to the reader.

Auschwitz was that exception that redefined the normal. As this it has normalized human degradation not by being the exception that could not be repeated—but as "an act that rendered poetry impossible." But for so many what happened has now passed over into banality. What died, what is not mourned, what "the young" fail to recognize, was that the illusion of civilization and transcendental culture as "our" destiny did not survive. The word "civilization" is now out of fashion and an almost empty signifier. Death and destruction have become banal and, for the many, frequently only command a few moments of televisual attention. In contrast, for a minority such events warrant a little thought, a short conversation and sometimes the donation of a few dollars. Yet the procession of horrific events that continues to unfold as elemental to modern life confronts us with our absolute loss of agency, imposes our complete nihilism. While Hannah Arendt could say of concentration camps: "Something happened there to which we cannot reconcile ourselves. None of us ever can," the reality is that "humanity" always moves on, the Jews included.[88] More than this, as Bauman pointed out: first, as a historical event "the Holocaust" changed very little, unlike the invention of "the wheel," "the French Revolution, or the 'discovery' of America; second, as subsequent history has revealed, our still evident human flaws, together with the (still increasing) power of instrumental bureaucratic systems, suggest there is nothing in contemporary 'civilized' society to indicate that such events cannot happen again."[89] Stridently, and with emphasis, he says: "*we live in a type of society that made 'the Holocaust' possible, and that contains nothing which could stop 'the Holocaust' happening again.*"[90]

So while, as indicated, it is possible to identify many ways to address "the Holocaust," including grasping it as a designed phenomenon, the overwhelming design observation and lesson is futural, and goes to what should command design focus. Unquestionable it was a "command system" of compliance inscribed in the altogether instrumentalized systems of the operation of everyday working life. While in the past these systems of instrumental reason were mobilized by the ideological fever of German fascism, in the present they arrive by a quieter, but nonetheless equally powerful, means: education in the service of the economic status quo. From tenets of political correctness to a naturalized induction into economic functionalism, compliance to this status quo has become elemental to educational institutions and workplace culture.

It is in this setting that one can start to contemplate the need for another kind of designing—one that is able to start to design out the dehumanizing instrumentalism of educational and work practices as they have been articulated anthropocentrically—this to reinforce forms of self-interest (compliance-to-consume to the maximum which, with ambition and effort, can be realized). Clearly this is an enormously hard thing to do, but openings into the task exist.[91] Without deflecting from acknowledging this designing as key and almost totally unrecognized, the design lessons of "the Holocaust" and a few more design observations on Auschwitz beg to be made.

One can characterize the whole design regime of Auschwitz as "design for death." On writing about the "extermination camps" Paul Jaskot remarks that:

> architects played a crucial role. But the architectural considerations were not aesthetically driven but rather technologically based. Construction of buildings was functionally determined in terms of [the] massive and complex process of organizing the deaths of millions of people.[92]

In 1941 architect Hans Stosberg was appointed to oversee the expansion of Auschwitz. The vision he was to realize was to increase the size of the camp around a pavilion plan with several large roll-call areas to accommodate the expected large numbers, as well as developing the IG Farben chemical plant for which the camp was to supply labor (but by the end of the year the policy shifted from forced labor to mass extermination).[93] Additionally, there was the aim of turning the ancient town of Auschwitz into an ideal German settlement.

The design regime of Auschwitz was totally in line with our overarching observations on the primacy of the designing power of the functional elements of the bureaucratic system. As said, it was directive of, and reactive to, an everyday and continuous flow of orders, memos, requisitions, materials, transport, capital, administrators and, above all, bodies. In this context architecture and technology completely fused. So framed, Auschwitz has been characterized as "a mundane extension of a modern factory," but rather than producing goods it was "manufacturing" death by "in-line" methods.[94] Once running it was merely a matter of servicing the death-machine with the bodies it had been designed to demand. Besides the size of the gas chambers, the furnaces of the camp crematorium were the main determinant of the death flow where, as Agamben puts it "people did not die, rather corpses were produced."[95]

The furnaces of the camp were the result of design and development to specific design and technological requirements. These were addressed by a firm of famous blast furnace makers—Topf and Sons—they saw this technology as a new market to take advantage of, which they did until mid-1944. By that time they had supplied numerous camps with incinerators, and the elevators to "feed" them. With a capacity of 20,000 corpses Auschwitz alone incinerated more than one million human beings.[96]

Agamben formulates the lesson of Auschwitz thus: *The human being is the one who can survive the human being.*[97] He directed the signification of this statement to the *Muselmann*—the inhuman capacity to survive the human. The word *Muselmann* literally means "Muslim," and was said to have originated at Auschwitz (and claimed to have based on the kneeing position of the weak who could not stand looking like a Muslim at prayer). Sadly, events in the Middle East over past decades have recoded the term with tragic irony.

The *Muselmann* is the living dead, the human made inhuman, that "grey" area of being between life and death—a residual being when the human no longer is present.[98] As such they become the ultimate reduction of biopolitics and a figure that haunts the present as much as the past, in what Agamben names as "the catastrophe of the subject."[99] We live in a world of such subjects, they have many names, the "they" are among us. We still treat them as they ever were. Where I live many can be found behind razor wire in detention centers. Their crime: trying to survive.

3 DESIGN IN THE MAELSTROM OF TIME

We have not set out to resolve the relation between design and history as an imperative of design history. Rather we have sought to argue that to understand the historical and futural agency of design the complexity of both design and history need to be exposed and articulated. We have also set out to show that there is a need to far better understand the directional power gathered and exercised under the rubric of design because it is deeply implicated in the creation and resolution of many problems that threaten viable human futures. In fact, in the omnipresent condition of global structural unsustainability we only have a future by means of Sustainment delivered by design. Clearly this means there is lot at stake in the way perceptions of design are constructed and mobilized, in and beyond extant communities of interest in design. However, for the importance of design to be recognized, focus on it has to be widened to diverse constituencies to expose the extent of its worldly connections.

In the spirit of this approach, this part of the book is a contribution to unsettling design as "it" is present as an active agent in "the unfolding age of unsettlement."

World and the question of world history

The planet is an object of matter in space and time, whereas "world" is an idea. As such it is a human construction that gathers materialities, structures, designated systems, symbolic forms and meaning into a representational projection that has constituted a regime of seeing and the seen. So configured "world" is created in cultural difference and as such can never be simply a geographic figure: it cannot be reduced to a singular entity that "just is." Rather "world" is always a nonreducible, plural and culturally fabricated entity. Moreover, how the ontic (the "all that is") is understood by a particular cosmology changes how "world" is viewed and characterized.

Within the fragmented discipline of history divisions have opened up between history based on grand world narratives of, for instance, nations, states, political movements, classes, cultures, wars, revolutions, *and* those histories aiming to disclose the everyday experience of specific people(s) in their particular conditions of existence. But in both cases the fundamental problems of the historian's proximity are exposed. These problems are epistemological and center on the relation between: (i) an adopted theory of knowledge, (ii) the position of observation in relation to the subjects observed, and (iii) the issue of, and claims to, authenticity. All of these problems were starkly made evident earlier when looking at the issues of the witness in the context of "the Holocaust." Against this backdrop, we are reminded that history is never just a history of an event, but equally a history for a particular constituency (who may or may not have directive power over how the event is described or accounted for).

As we have shown, history, as event narrativized, is never created randomly: it is always the product of intent. However presented, the past always arrives as partial, as incomplete. There is always the untold, the missing, and the unfulfilled. Likewise, when Nietzsche's relation to history was examined it was evident just how frequently it is disjuncturally posed (as narrative) against the historical (event). To recognize this in practice requires working from a declared interpretative position that configures its relation and intent to very specific, rather than general, historical claims and discourses. Here, then, we have the ground that enabled Michel Foucault's mobilization of the historical against history. In this context it is important to register the extent to which historians have so often simply fallen into line with a dominant habitus of the practice, with its force of metanarrative. Consider, for instance, how accounts of the rise and development of the West so often overlooked, obscured, or simply forgot that so much of the scientific knowledge this process deployed to create "advancement" emanated from Asia, the Near and Middle East. At the same time, not only did these planetary regions get designated as backward, uncivilized and "underdeveloped," but "the darker side of modernity" (the horror of coloniality) was ignored.

Quite clearly historical narratives—from plural worlds (rather than from "the world")—are deeply implicated in how change and progress have been represented and understood. At the same time narratives have arrived that have contested and critically interrogated these accounts. In this respect history has been a site of conflict characterized in a variety of ways ("culture wars"; colonialist vs decolonialist; "traditionalism vs post-structuralism" and "humanism vs post-humanism/anti-humanism"). What thus has to be continually emphasized is that the creation and use of history is profoundly ideological (politically). And again it should be emphasized that "world history" is never from or of "the world" but rather is always of a place and a position—it is always, in some form, situated and so biased. As we can understand from Martin Heidegger, while our being in place (*dasein*) and the being of things are both "world-historical," in so far as they are of "a world," they do not gain their significance because of this, but rather because they are encountered in "the world" of a specific place.[1] Thus the world-historical/world history has no voice, notwithstanding what is spoken (ethnocentrically) in its name. One of the best known of these voices is William H. McNeill—a promoter of world history for around fifty years and the author of one of the most cited papers on it—"The changing shape of world history" first presented at the History and Theory World History Conference, Wesleyan University, Connecticut in 1994.

McNeill's rhetorical position adopts romantic idealism at it most generalized: consider—"human ingenuity and inventiveness" will win through and enlarge "the scope of human life," and while risks "may be greater than ever before" the "possibilities are correspondingly vast."[2] As for historians, he tells us they are "faithful guardians of every level of human collective identity."[3] Everything reads like a feel-good high-school history textbook of distant decades. There is no sense of the machinations in history, its theory, methods and practice or the near demise, in the company of literature and philosophy, within the degeneration of the university over the past forty years and more. Thus "world history" is out of joint, step and focus. It is frankly naïve. The "we" it assumes us to be is totalized and designated as "fully human," claimed to have "introduced" cultural evolution, and positioned as if "our" collective acts of worldly negation were offset, and so balanced by, creative and affirmative actions.[4] As a position it is an affront to cultural difference. The actual complexity of plural human existence and worlds of such difference is thus completely displaced by the hyperreductionism of an evolutionary *telos* wherein all strangers unite in "the family of man."[5]

Yet, not withstanding the uncritical void into which McNeill's writing falls, it has acquired influence.[6] In particular, "world history" has been taken seriously in conservative quarters.[7] It is as if the critique of its progenitors—from Herodotus to Hegel, Diderot, Marx, Spengler, Toynbee, et al.—and of their "master narratives"—had never taken place.[8] Yet it is the very relation between historical discourse and a critical engagement with the present that enables the possibility of historical understandings of the future (be it with or without "history" exercised by "historians") to be advanced. This is so, essentially, because so many actions of the past and present throw much of the past into the future, thereby ensuring "we" travel towards the past as it travels towards us (climate change is one clear and extreme example of this propensity).[9]

Notwithstanding substantial critique, there are historians still producing "world history" (including of design) that negate the nature of events in time as well as their essential difference. *Theory*—especially via critique delivered by Marxism, structuralism and post-structuralism—has shattered the legitimacy of this practice and exposed the flaw of its propensity toward both universal totalization and generalization.

There is no overarching "world" viewpoint from which to describe "the world"—to adopt such a perspective is an act of ethnocentric violence intrinsic to Eurocentrism. This is not to apportion "blame" to individuals for such thinking; the practices it supports are structurally part of a widespread "education in error" of formal and informal education. Moreover, the projection of such a view of "the world" continues to have global agency and remains elemental to the cultural face of globalization. Again we note that any mode of design history asserting or constructing an overall global historical narrative is complicit in the construction of the illusion and negation of difference. No matter how inclusive it claims to be, it constitutes a pluralism that trades on fabricated equivalences, imposing a particular construction of design as if it were universally historically articulated. This is to say that while all people, all cultures, design, no one culture can legitimately claim (and speak with) the authority to impose its understanding of phenomenal forms of design as categories and classification on "the rest." In so doing difference is reduced to the sign but the very relational complexity of design is erased both phenomenologically and culturally.

Design historians of course do not set out to erase difference as a malicious act. They do so because they have not theoretically grasped the ontological agency of design (as the active "life" of the "world of things" in difference) in the plural constitution of human becoming. This is equally to say that they negate the complexity of design as it is implicated in multiple practices that extend the world-within-the-world (created by design as it constantly transforms "the given world," and in so doing ending demarcations between the natural and artificial). More than this, there has also been a growing inability, or refusal, by design historians to comprehend the globalizing and instrumental function of technology, posited with and by design, in the service of hegemonic capitalism.

Here we note that as technologies have proliferated, especially cognitive extending technologies, the actual critical bite of the philosophy of technology has declined.[10] Quite simply, as technology expands the reach of mind, a comprehension of what it actually is and ontologically designs diminishes. Unlike the long-standing comprehensive inquiry into first nature (the biophysical), exploration of the second nature fusing with it (the technological world of dependence) remains massively underdeveloped. The issue is not a question of overcoming technology, any more than it is a question of overcoming nature (for as implied technology has become naturalized as another nature formative of our nature). Rather, in common with biophysical nature, technology begs to be understood so its dangers maybe avoided.

An historical understanding of design can and should be a major contributor to the creation of knowledge of naturalized technology (operationally, politically, economically, culturally and psychologically) in worlds of difference. Design history, as it is, gets nowhere remotely near to being able to do this. But this is its challenge, this is the project— one that rips design history from its comfort zone so it may gain actual agency in the essential (and in the end unavoidable) task of the creation of Sustainment.

The world of modernity

The effects of the five centuries of the "project" of modernity not only has shaped the economic, geopolitical, cultural, psychosocial forms and institutional structures of the everyday everywhere on Earth, but its consequences will continue to travel toward us from the future for an incalculable time. The formation and deformation of nations as foundations of conflict, global inequity, the epistemological colonialism that continues under the banner of Eurocentrism (of which "world history" is just one example)—these are but three instances of endowed problems.

Modernity names the making and global export of the hegemonic power of the West. The process overwhelmed all other developmental directions (including non-European modes of Enlightenment) as well as, via its indivisible colonial "darker side," being a force of genocidal, ethnocidal and ecocidal destruction. No matter what positive attainments of modernity can be claimed to be, they do not offset the price paid in human lives and suffering, nor the damage done to the environments of life's dependence. In particular, and notwithstanding the claims of humanism carried by modernization theory, we note that racism was implicit in modernity, and reconfigured "the world" territorially, geopolitically and culturally. At its most basic, and in many cases, what the formation of the nation state did was to force ethnically diverse societies into a monocultural national structure. The result, ethnic cleansing and genocide on a vast scale from the nineteenth century to the present, not least in Africa. Moreover, as Zygmunt Bauman observes: "racism is unthinkable without the advancement of modern science, modern technology and modern forms of state power. As such, racism is strictly a modern product. Modernity made racism possible."[11] Put another way: racism as now understood required (a now discredited) theory of race (that earlier modes of discrimination and persecution lacked). Likewise, modernity equally legitimized an extension of the means to control nature by science—which meant that it was inherently anthropocentric. In the claim of the rule of modern man over nature and Others, expressed through anthropocentrism, technology and racism, one has an explicit and demonstrable content that affirms that modernity begets numerous modes of violence.

In contrast to the actuality of the underside of modernity, it has been dominantly mischaracterized as an expression of the attainments of Western civilization (with claims whereby humanity displaced barbarism, reason overcame ignorance, objectivity won out over prejudice, progress over degeneration, truth over superstition, science over magic and rationality over passion).[12] So presented, to be Western and modern was to be civilized. But for the West "the Holocaust" shattered and exposed the reality of civilization as illusory, with barbarism being ever just beneath the surface of its appearance (the rest had always known this). As a result a whole cluster of Eurocentrically universally projected binary oppositional differences dissolved: humanity and barbarism, reason and ignorance, objectivity and prejudice, progress and degeneration, truth and superstition, science and magic, rationality and passion all were exposed as able to fold into each other.

So often what modernized civilizations managed to do was to design their violence out of sight, ship it to the elsewhere, treat problems as clinical and thereafter technologically de-severed (which is what instrumentalism actually does). Yet, as the repressed, it returns—as exemplified by counter-globalizing terrorism as a political weapon of recoil and negation in the late modern world. The other and linked major "attainment" of Western civilization is to exercise violence through it becoming applied simply via a State bureaucratic system enabling "good people" to do evil things, "kind people" to perform acts of cruelty, and "reason" being applied to create a means of global mass destruction.[13] While "the Holocaust" was the extreme example of this ability, and while this does not mean that modernity and "the Holocaust" can be conflated, it does expose a real and ongoing danger wherein the feared, and measures to deal with it, cojoin in the "national security state." Moreover, the biopolitical character of "the Holocaust" (where human beings were reduced to, and treated as, merely organic entities of "bare life") has become a generalized mode of conduct in dealing with displaced people, the abject and the dangerous. What of their history? Certainly it can be written about, but what chance does it have to be written from?

"The enemy" can become designated as an administrative act, and management systems deployed to direct its engagement. Such action also registers an advancement of the means whereby conflict is removed from public scrutiny, and increasingly posited within a management regime of executive control. The war in Afghanistan is a case in point—it continued largely without public interest or passion. It simply ran on behind a wall of media management as "a systems-managed event" enabling continuity without progress. It is no wild claim to say that for the vast majority of people it took place without rhyme or reason." It made no sense, and the explanations given for it (not least the "war on terror") were hollow. The drift now occurring from conventional to asymmetrical warfare makes this approach even more pervasive, for the less visible the enemy becomes, the easier it is to abstract and dehumanize "it." Moreover, because of the geographic dispersal of "the enemy," systems of intelligence and surveillance treat everywhere as danger zones, with the result that all space is becoming militarized. Moreover, as technological life becomes "normality," living in "totally observed conditions"—where everyone is under electronic scrutiny—is naturalized and so taken as given. This means that in a civilized society violence is deemed acceptable if it is elsewhere, managed and is felt not to encroach on everyday life. But at the same time "soft violence" is omnipresent. The riot, the bomb, the uprising, constantly reveal the provisionality of what appears to be normal, and the threat of such activity legitimizes a militarized condition as normality.

In truth, civilization is a mask that covers its absence, with "civil society" having become a representational trope to be strategically deployed. The fact is that not only have "we" never been civilized enough, but the very notion of civilization itself has now become a conceit, a simulacrum.[14] Against this backdrop of appearances, where does design fit? The direct and naked answer is: everywhere as a means of concealment, for as meta-design it hides "the animal that we are," the "defuturing" of the created worlds of our inhabitation, our pacification through the nihilism of hegemonic entertainment.

So contextualized, the history of the designed, a history becoming ever more critically important, is completely at odds with design history.

Design resides in the domain of danger. Design is always an act of will and, as such, is an imposition by a "someone" on a "something or somewhere." At the extreme, it has been mobilized historically in the service of the "total design" of a society (be it communist, fascist or capitalist). At worst this has meant that those who did not fit the idealized model were exterminated, or put out of sight in camps, and at best it unleashed utopian dreams that empowered the acceleration of the unsustainable. Design history has at times superficially touched on the danger of design, but has looked away, always falling back into its comfort zone of historical and worldly disassociation. Always refusing to engage the sheer historical force and pervasiveness of design, its plural forms and continual presence as a complexity beyond representational possibility.

While the presence and historical significance of design can never be fully explicated, it is equally the case that in order to try to more adequately understand the world of human fabrication it is essential that the effort to better understand design historically be made.

The time after the modern

While agreeing with Bruno Latour that fundamentally the modern has never arrived (which is to say that the project of modernity did not actually succeed in establishing a modern world able to bring a fully modernized human being into existence[15]) the failure of modernity still remains understated. And although postmodernity, which is not a teleological moment after modernity, registered a critical engagement with this failure, it itself failed. It neither exposed modernity's colonial underside nor the defuturing momentum it generated. Yet as has been recognized, postmodern theory did expose that the foundation of knowledge upon which history stood was flawed. That it is now in ruins is something the vast bulk of historians, with "world historians" at the fore, appear not to have noticed.[16]

One of the major features of the loss of the authority of history's epistemological base has been a wider recognition of the breakdown of a linear model of time. This we have recognized, but to reiterate: the past is no longer simply prior to the present but is equally in front of it. Moreover, there has to be a future for a past to be possible. So framed, our being is a moment of both the departure and the arrival of time, wherein every moment of our "continuous now" enfolds time's loss and becoming. As the remembered, and as the forgotten, our past travels with us. While having determinate consequences, this does not mean we can make sense of it, or that any real correspondence exists between events and how we represent them, even to ourselves. Meanwhile, in the worlds around us, the past is constantly being thrown into the future in ways that prefigure what occurs in the present. Designed things are very much implicated in this process.

So much of the material fabric of the world we have already created, and its accompanying problems, directs our future life. For instance, our cities, homes, industries, infrastructural systems, institutions, our damaged climate and reduced biological diversity are of our future and delimit so much of our present. Thus the future is to be imagined as an obstacle course with all we have deposited in it. Faced with the obstructions littering this course we have to learn to find a way. This means recognizing that our actions in the present determine our finitudinal limit (not least through what we cast into the future—the more damage we do to that which sustains us, and all we depend upon, the less time we have as a species). The reverse also applies. Crucially, what begs to be understood is that the future is not that which has to be completed, but rather that which must be secured against all that would negate it.

Thinking time and event is something that most of us recoil from doing. There is a reason for this—we are "chronophobes."[17] As already made clear, we are frightened by time and entertain an illusion of the permanence of that which is actually transitory. All things move in time, be it with dramatically different dynamics. Design is one of those practices that can be directive of the time of things, but dominantly it does this superficially (not least via the designation of an object's "design life"). It could and should be otherwise—designing in time has to become a major preoccupation of the designer. They need to know how much time to inscribe into the things they design—a consideration that needs to be more than simply the determination of worldly duration. In this respect performativity becomes more important than design life, which implies things have to be seen as process rather than object, and as cause rather than effect. How to do this is a massively important and challenging learning exercise for designing to become affirmatively futural and, in so doing, rupture, through the power of ontological design, the subject–object binary.

Ethics: An opening and an ending

So often ethics has traveled with the claim that it is informed and supported by history. Clearly because of the shifting ground of the nature and integrity of the field of history, the relation between history and ethics (itself always problematic) cannot be claimed as stable or resolved. Ethics is in no position to speak for history. As Keith Jenkins points out— "History has always been ethically/politically/*ideologically driven and governed*, and ethics has never escaped historicity."[18] But, as he goes on to say, this relation has never gone beyond the pragmatic, the aleatory, the contingent. Yet Jenkins affirms Richard Rorty's position—that the certain is never absolute or available—however, and notwithstanding this, "belief can still regulate action, can be still be worth dying for" be it that it rests on nothing but "contingent historical circumstances."[19]

Because the history/ethics relation cannot be resolved, Jenkins makes a strange and unwarranted move—he calls us to "forget ethics."[20] But of course ethics is not fixed: its form is contestable. Moreover, it is not a matter of certainty versus belief, but rather the adoption of values in the face of imperatives that are far less pluralistic and relative than the notion of "contingent historical circumstances." In this context we will assert an absolute: *without Sustainment we have nothing.* This is to say without the continuity of all we depend upon we, and many other species, will not survive as a viable life-form. It follows that Sustainment, the process and the project, is an imperative in response to the unsustainable as it is manifest by diverse and substantial empirical evidence, as presented by various intersecting discourses. It is therefore not unreasonable to deem Sustainment as a value that can underscore a materialist ethics, totally independent of a culturally relativist morality. In this respect "Sustainment" is an ontological condition prior to all politico-cultural difference. It is a fundamental need that is only essential if such need is posited with this value as such. Which is to say, first of all, that in a Darwinian world of meaninglessness there are no intrinsic values but nonetheless life hangs on a thread of given value. And second, the value of Sustainment is not recognized as a fundamentally essential value by all, for there is a huge constituency who have invested all they value in the unsustainable. In this setting, ethics as Sustainment materialized (Sustainment given form as an ontological force of making time, of having a future) under the rule of democracy, therefore becomes a matter of choice. But it can be forcefully argued that if humanity is to have a future, is to be sustained, then such choice has to be displaced by a new political imaginary and ideology—one in which the value of Sustainment rules.

So, rather than forgetting ethics, what we have done is to abandon a humanist ethics in favor of the post-humanism of Sustainment—for Sustainment, while generated out of an anthropocentric imperative (our species survival), recognizes that "we" cannot survive as an autopoietic entity. Rather we can only survive in the midst of biological and cultural ecology of dependences that we still only have a partial picture of. This limited understanding is not merely circumscribed by the complexity of the "biological world" but also by the naturalization of technology and by the power of social ecologies.

At their worst, such social ecologies have an ability to take caring human beings and turn them into "inhumane agents of defuturing." Controversially, the famous experiment by psychologist Stanley Milgram at Yale in 1974 exposed this capability.[21] What he set out to show was that perfectly "normal" people, who abhor dishonesty, cruelty and violence, can be induced to behave with complete inhumanity by becoming part of a regime where compliance to order displaces individual critical reflection and judgment. So viewed, the horror of German Fascism has nothing to do with say the intrinsic flaws of a particular "race" but, as was indicated, reflected a capacity able to construct monstrous conduct in all people. Citing Milgram, and in engaging fascism, Bauman makes the point powerfully that *"inhumanity is a matter of social relationships"*—this as they become "rationalized and technologically perfected."[22] Increasingly technology abstracted the proximal space between the social actor within an authoritative regime, and the social actor acted upon by it. In this context, and put simply, the less contact with "a victim" the greater the propensity to act with cruelty. Technology thus can, and does, make conventional ethical judgments become more marginal (killing people using drones, programmed to seek and find a target, clearly makes this point).

What these observations expose returns us to the limits of history, the future and the materialization of ethics.

Effectively a historical examination of the relation between bureaucratic systems, technology and authoritative regimes reveal a "designing in time" that posit dangers in the future arriving in the present. So said, and revisiting Jenkins' evocation for us to "forget ethics," the pressing need is for the ethics/history couplet to be abandoned and replaced by a configuration of ethics, Sustainment and futural historical inquiry. Such action is counter to the ongoing concern of Jenkins, and many others over many years, with "human emancipation"—justice has to be broken as a purely human construct. Human beings can never be free while acting just on the basis of their anthropocentric self-interest. There has to be an acknowledgement, and a giving over, to the web of dependencies of "the being of our being." By implication then, justice cannot be attained as just a human concern, because we remain equally an animal among animals, life amid life. This is not external to the idea of justice to plants and animals; it is to say that ethical conduct enfolds our conduct toward all livings things of which we (in our being-in-being) are elemental. To recognize this is to place the ethical and futural human (the agent of Sustainment) in a position of opposition to the moral-ethical power claimed by the state, its mobilization of technology and the ethical-juristic claim of law as sovereign. Bluntly, if ethics is materially grounded in Sustainment, all that negates this end, all that negates becoming futural (including the state, technology and the law as currently constituted), is unethical.

The position just outlined removes any relation between ethics and free choice. While individuals, as actors in a variety of worlds, may choose or not to advance Sustainment, all actions that negate "the potential for it to be" are still nonetheless unethical. The unsustainable, as animated via defuturing practices, has drawn this line. Just as Carl Schmitt made the friend/enemy distinction absolutely explicit, so the ethical distinction between the unsustainable/Sustainment begs to be viewed as just as unambiguous. Currently ethics evades us: we may desire and strive to be ethical but its realization is out of reach. Ethics so cast becomes directive of the agenda of ethico-political action—it becomes that *to be kept in mind* and worked towards. It is a radical decisionism that flies in the face of the pluralistic radical decisionism espoused by Hayden White, which Jenkins supports.[23]

"What is decided" is that in coming to recognize the omnipotence of the unsustainable there is an essential and total change in the frame of reference of ethics that reframes the question of "what we are and do." Rather than diminishing the significance of human conduct, such a change makes it all the more important. So rather than "making of the past what you will" the creation of a "future with a future" filters how "the past" is viewed, because it can help expose what futures and what defutures. In other words the postmodern axiom of undecidability is stood on its head. Thus while a good deal of the unsustainable and the sustain-able may remain unknown, undecidable, the radical decision is to make Sustainment the ethical imperative. Numerous decisions therefore flow from this decision. But the key issue is not that truth and certainty are claimed but rather that an ethico-politics has been adopted that negates a pluralistic meta-reading of historical events. For example, the actual events of a war may well be open to being made of "what we will" but war itself is firmly placed in the certainty of the unsustainable as it destroys lives, families, environments, ecologies and potentialities. War may be unavoidable, and may be waged as efficaciously as possible to delimit loss of life and material and environmental value, but still it cannot be claimed as ethical. War is never "contained" – it always destroys more than the evil of "the evil enemy." So while war might be pragmatically justified as a "just war" (where an ethical end is claimed to be justified by the deployment of unethical, unsustainable, means) it remains expedient and actions taken in no way displace its unsustainable and unethical character (and the fact that victory is not just winning the conflict).

At base, while our actions are shrouded in uncertainty what is certain is that unless human beings learn to act futurally, in conditions of deepening and proliferating defuturing, then our ability to survive as a species will be compromised or even fundamentally threatened. Of course what is left open in this statement is the form that such futuring may take (an issue that has been dealt with at length elsewhere[24]). What in large part obstructs taking futuring action is our chronophobic condition—the fear of time—as it sits in the wider condition of fear that marks so much of the nihilism of late-modern life. Here is the fear of the being who is unplaced, a being without meaning or agency who is complicit with the rule of the status quo because they see and know no other way. Yet the real danger to which this being is exposed—a falling into the abyss by simply doing what they are told—goes unrecognized and thus unspoken.

NOTES

Introduction

1 These views are summarized at length by Leo Strauss in his notes on *The Concept of the Political* (trans J. Harvey Lomax), in Carl Schmitt, *The Concept of the Political* (trans. George Schwab), Chicago: University of Chicago Press, 1996, pp. 100–101.

2 On the forms of design history in the early stages of its emergence, see the review in Tony Fry, *Design History Australia*, Sydney: Hale and Iremonger, 1988, pp. 21–54.

3 Siegfried Giedon, *Mechanization Takes Command*, New York: Norton, 1948.

4 Jean-François Lyotard, *The Postmodern Condition* (trans Geoff Bennington and Brian Massumi), Manchester: Manchester University Press, 1984). The text was initially published in France in 1979.

5 See for example Walter Mignolo, *The Darker Side of the Renaissance*, Ann Arbor: Michigan Univerity Press, 1995.

6 On the discussion of history as forgetting see Charles R. Bamburg, *Heidegger, Dilthey, and the Crisis of Historicism*, New York: Cornell University Press, 1995, p. 259.

7 While "we" exist in the biophysical world "we" also exist in the environments that we have constructed that are of such a scale and transformative force to be "worlds-within-the world"—these worlds mutually transform each other.

8 The debate between Fran Hannah, Tim Putnam, "Taking stock in design history," *Block*, 3, 1980 pp. 25–6 and Tony Fry (sic) "Design history: a debate?" *Block*, 5, 1981, pp. 14–18, was an example of this contestation.

9 Tony Fry, *Becoming Human by Design*, Oxford: Berg, 2012 specifically presents a post-evolutionary explanation of design as a causal factor in our becoming human beings.

10 See Walter Mignolo, *The Darker Side of Western Modernity*, Durham: Duke University Press, 2011, p. xi.

11 On the discussion of history as forgetting see Bamburg, *Heidegger, Dilthey*, pp. 270–73.

12 Bamburg, *Heidegger, Dilthey*, pp. 259–60.

13 See Nelson Maldonado-Torres, *Against War*, Durham: Duke University Press, 2008, p. 216.

14 See, for example, Anthony Giddens, *The Consequences of Modernity*, Stanford: Stanford University Press, 1990; and Jürgen Habermas, *The Philosophical Discourse of Modernity* (trans. Frederick Lawrence),

Cambridge: MIT Press, [1985] 1987. Enrique Dussel's best know work is *Philosophy of Liberation* (trans. Aquilina Martinez and Christine Morkovsky), New York: Orbis Books, 1985.

15 Michel Haar, *Heidegger and the Essence of Man* (trans. William McNeill), New York: SUNY University Press, 1993, p. 145.

16 Emmanuel Levinas, *Otherwise than Being or Beyond Essence* (trans Alfonso Lingus), Dordrecht: Kluwer Academic Publishers, 1981, p. 128.

17 On the industrialization of memory see especially Bernard Stiegler, *Time and Technics, 2: Disorientation* (trans. Stephen Barker), Stanford: Stanford University Press, 2009, pp. 97–187.

18 See Michel Foucault, *Language, Counter-Memory, Practice* (trans. Donald F. Bouchard and Sherry Simon), New York: Cornell University Press, 1977, pp. 139–65.

19 Keith Jenkins, *At the Limits of History*, London: Routledge, 2009, p. 234.

20 See, for example, Jacques Derrida, "Racism's last words," *Critical Inquiry*, Autumn, 1985, pp. 290–99.

21 On this notion see Martin Heidegger, drawing on the chorus of Antigone of Sophocles, in *An Introduction to Metaphysics* (trans. Ralph Manheim), New Haven: Yale University Press, 1958, pp. 147–50.

22 Hans-Georg Gadamer, *Truth and Method* (trans. Joel Weinsheimer and Donald G. Marshall), New York: Crossroads, 1990, p. 259.

23 We note "The term 'colonial' has a specific meaning in decolonial thinking. It refers not to the Roman Empire's understnding of colony as a polity built or ruled by imperial order but to the modern meaning of 'colonial' as a 'conquered and managed territory' linked to the process of European colonization grounded in destroying the existing social order and imposing one responding to the neeeds and habitus of the conquerous." Madina V. Tlostanova and Walter Mignolo, *Learning to Unlearn*, Columbus: The Ohio State University Press, 2012, p. 17.

24 The "idea of natural history" as a theory of history was announced by Adorno in a lecture to the Kant Society in Frankfurt in 1932—cited by Jenkins, *At the Limits of History*, p. 13.

25 See Fry, *Becoming Human*.

26 This is a claim Gadamer makes in *Truth and Method*, p. 357.

27 This investigation was part of Husserl's massive project of the critique of *The Crisis of European Sciences and Transcendental Phenomenology* which was not published in full until sixteen years after his death in 1938.

28 Martin Heidegger, *Hegel's Concept of Experience* (trans. not acknowledged) San Francisco: Harper and Row, 1989, pp. 113–14.

29 See Gadamer, *Truth and Method*, p. 355.

30 Much of this material was prompted by the publication of Bill Readings, *The University in Ruins*, Cambridge: Harvard University Press, 1996.

31 Iain D. Thomson, *Heidegger on Ontotheology*, Cambridge: Cambridge University Press, 2005, pp. 157–62.

32 Martin Heidegger, *Being and Time*, translated by John Macquarrie and Edward Robinson, Oxford: Basil Blackwell, 1962, p. 186.

33 Thomson, *Heidegger on Ontotheology*, p.152.

34 Thomson, *Heidegger on Ontotheology*, p. 151.

35 Thomson, *Heidegger on Ontotheology*, p. 147.

36 Thomson, *Heidegger on Ontotheology*, p. 147.

37 Thomson, *Heidegger on Ontotheology*, p. 147.

38 As Walter Mignolo outlines, between the years 1500–2000 (the year of the publication of the book in which he made this statement) "Western civilisation established a system of knowledge that asserted an authority out of which the dominant construction of human history was written—the ongoing agency of this authority is the very ground of 'epistemological colonialism.'" *Local Histories/Global Designs*, Princeton: Princeton University Press, 2000, p. x.

39 Thomson, *Heidegger on Ontotheology*, p. 143.

40 Thomson, *Heidegger on Ontotheology*, p. 143.

41 Martin Heidegger, "The age of the world picture," in *The Question Concerning Technology and Other Essays* (trans. William Lovett), New York: Harper and Row, 1977, p. 116.

42 See Fry, *Becoming Human*, Part 1 and 2 in relation to the account of the relation of the "stone, animal and man" in Martin Heidegger, *Fundamental Concepts of Metaphysics* (trans. William McNeill and Nicholas Walker), Bloomington: Indiana University Press, 1995, pp. 185–212.

43 This view of observation draws on Niklas Luhmann's chapter on the observation of observation in *Ecological Communication* (trans. John Bednarz), Chicago: Chicago University Press, 1989 and Cary Wolfe's placement of his thinking in *Critical Environments*, Minneapolis: University of Minnesota Press, 1998, pp. 41–86.

44 The excavation of history as habitus was, in large part, the project of Michel Foucault—this meant exposing the structuring substrata of what "history" projects as historical knowledge.

45 The Universidad Intercultural Amawtay Wasi—A university for intercultural understanding of and for the indigenous people of Ecuador is a good example—see Madina V. Tlostanova and Walter D. Mignolo, *Learning to Unlearn*, Columbus: Ohio University Press, 2012, pp. 225–35.

46 Thomson, *Heidegger on Ontotheology*, p. 101.

47 Thomson, *Heidegger on Ontotheology*, pp. 162–5.

48 Thomson, *Heidegger on Ontotheology*, p. 162.

49 A great deal of this thinking goes to how the idea an practice of a *Neu Bildung*—a new culture of self-making and (un)learning—as has been elaborated elsewhere as a recognition of the need to take responsibility for our becoming technological as it is extended by our impositional nature (our anthropocentrism). As such, counter knowledge in this practice can be brought to redirecting what "we" design and make toward the delivery of structural "care" within the frame of an advance of "Sustainment" (as a post-democratic decolonizing politics based on a revitalization of the idea of the common good). Beyond this notion, a new kind of university is now a subject of discussion in the contexts of thinking the university in crisis already mentioned.

50 The already cited Amawtay Wasi university for intercultural understanding being a case in point. Tlostanova and Mignolo, *Learning to Unlearn*.

1. Rememberings and dismemberings

1 Mark Poster, *A New Kind of History*, London: Blackwell, 1985, p. 75.

2 Bambach, *Heidegger, Dilthey*, p. 200.

3 Bambach, *Heidegger, Dilthey*, p. 200.

4 Cited in Bambach, *Heidegger, Dilthey*, p. 243.

5 Bambach, *Heidegger, Dilthey*, p. 243.

6 Our remarks here draw on Hans-Georg Gadamer's account of Dilthey and problems of historicism in *Truth and Method* (trans. Joel Weinsheimer and Donald G. Marshall), New York: Crossroads, 1990, pp. 218–42; and Martin Heidegger's engagement with his thinking in *Being and Time* (trans. John Macquarrie and Edward Robinson), London: Blackwell, 1962, pp. 397–404.

7 Dilthey's method here was first outlined in his *Introduction to Historical Knowledge*, Princeton: Princeton University Press, 1991.

8 What Dilthey actually tried to do was to establish and retain an epistemological position that asserted experience was, and could be, made available to scientific inquiry. What resulted was a flawed notion that equates with a kind of "scientific subjectivism" in which historical subject of experience could undertake objective observation.

9 Heidegger, *Being and Time*, pp. 377, 397–404.

10 See Gadamer's discussion in *Truth and Method*, pp. 242–64.

11 Mark Sinclair, "Nietzsche and the problem of history," *Richmond Journal of Philosophy*, 8 (Winter 2004), p. 2.

12 Sinclair, "Nietzsche and the problem of history," citing Nietzsche.

13 Jenkins debate with Michael Coleman, see Keith Jenkins, *At the Limits of History*, London: Routledge, 2009, p, 142.

14 Heidegger, *Being and Time*, p. 395.

15 For a discussion of Weil's *Logique de la philosophie*—which was his major work and centered on experience an history, see Michael Roth, *Knowing and History*, New York: Cornell University Press, 1988, pp. 149–86.

16 Bambach, *Heidegger, Dilthey*, p. 245.

17 See Tony Fry "Time," in his *A New Design Philosophy: An Introduction to Defuturing*, Sydney: UNSW Press, 1999, pp. 206–12.

18 The key moment of this time was World War I where troops from Africa, the Middle East and Asia were drawn out of their own time and into the uniform time of the coordinated European war machine.

19 The relation between social, economic and cultural colonialism and "epistemological colonialism" is dealt with at length in Walter D. Mignolo, *The Darker Side of Western Modernity*, Durham: Duke Univeristy Press, 2011, pp. 77–118.

20 Bambach, *Heidegger, Dilthey*, p. 259.

21 Bambach, *Heidegger, Dilthey*, p. 259.

22 Defuturing is presented at length and in relation to design in Fry, *A New Design Philosophy*.

23 Roth, *Knowing and History*, pp. 77–8.

24 Francis Fukayama, *The End of History and the Last Man*, New York: Free Press, 1992.

25 On the limits of democracy in the face of the unsustainable see Tony Fry. *Design as Politics*, Oxford: Berg, 2011.

26 Alexandre Kojève was perhaps the most important of the twentieth-century French Neo-Hegalians. Roth, *Knowing and History*, pp. 83–4.

27 Jenkins *At the Limits of History*, p. 7. For a comprehensive critical review of Keith Jenkins oeuvre (including *At the Limits of History*) in relation his work, his critics and supporters see, Dr Alexander Macfie, review of *Keith Jenkins Retrospective*, review no. 1266), http://www.history.ac.uk/reviews/review/1266. Accessed May 30, 2013.

28 Macfie, *Keith Jenkins Retrospective*, p. 13.

29 Macfie, *Keith Jenkins Retrospective*, p. 15.

30 Many of these thinkers are cited and their positions reviewed by Jenkins in *At the Limits of History*.

31 Gadamer, *Truth and Method*, p. 261.

32 These remarks are informed by, but modify, those made by Heidegger, see *Being and Time*, p. 403.

33 Heidegger, *Being and Time*, H 379. See also Gadamer, *Truth and Method*, p. 257.

34 Gadamer, *Truth and Method*, p. 257.

35 Heidegger, *Being and Time*, p. 20.

36 Heidegger, *Being and Time*, p. 20.

37 Heidegger, *Being and Time*, p. 20.

38 Heidegger, *Being and Time*, p. 375.

39 Theodor Adorno *Negative Dialectics* (trans. E.B. Ashton), London: Routledge, 1973, pp. 358–60.

40 Heidegger, *Being and Time*, p. 14.

41 See Warwick Mules, Heidegger, nature, philosophy, art as poietic event', Transitions, Issue 21, 2012. http://www.transformationsjournal.org/journal/issue_21/article_06.shtml

42 Tony Fry, *Design* and *Becoming Human*, Oxford: Berg, 2012.

43 Friedrich Nietzsche, *The Use and Abuse of History* (trans. Adrian Collins), New York: Bobbs-Merrill, 1949. This was reprinted as *On the Advantages and Disadvantages of History for Life* (trans. Peter Preuss), Indianapolis: Hackett Publishing, 1980. A revised edition was published in 2010 (trans. Ian Johnston) by Vancouver Island University, Nanaimo, Canada.

44 This view was expressed by Hayden White in *Topic of Discourse*, Baltimore: Johns Hopkins University Press, 1978, p. 32. In view of his foreword to Jenkins anti-history *At the Limits of History* (see n.9) on wonders if his view on Nietzsche still holds.

45 Sinclair "Nietzsche and the problem of history," *Richmond Journal of Philosophy*, 8 (2004) (PDF version), p. 3.

46 Sande Cohen, *History out of Joint*, Baltimore: Johns Hopkins University Press, 2006, p. 22.

47 Sinclair, "Nietzsche and the problem of history," p. 1.

48 Nietzsche, *On the Advantages and Disadvantages*, p.10.

49 Nietzsche, *On the Advantages and Disadvantages*, p. 11.

50 Nietzsche, *On the Advantages and Disadvantages*, p. 12.

51 Nietzsche, *On the Advantages and Disadvantages*, p. 14.

52 Nietzsche, *On the Advantages and Disadvantages*, p. 14.

53 Nietzsche, *On the Advantages and Disadvantages*, p. 50.

54 Biology had arrived as a named science at the start of the nineteenth century, Darwin's ideas (which were known to Nietzsche and problematically engaged by him) were being promoted in Europe by Georg Seidlitz (1840–1917)—who was Jakob von Uexkull's teacher—and were competing in Germany with those of Karl von Baer (1792–1876). Biologist Ernst Haeckel (1834–1919) had named the study of biological system "ecology" in 1866.

55 Nietzsche, *On the Advantages and Disadvantages*, p. 15.

56 Nietzsche, *On the Advantages and Disadvantages*, p. 15.

57 Nietzsche, *On the Advantages and Disadvantages*, p. 17.

58 Nietzsche, *On the Advantages and Disadvantages*, p. 17.

59 Nietzsche, *On the Advantages and Disadvantages*, pp. 18–19.

60 Nietzsche, *On the Advantages and Disadvantages*, p. 37.

61 Friedrich Nietzsche, *The Will to Power* (trans. Walter Kaufmann and R.J. Hollingdale), New York: Vintage, 1968, pp. 40–84.

62 David Farrell Krell, "Introduction," in Martin Heidegger *Nietzsche Vol. 1* (trans. David Farrell Krell), New York: Harper Collins, 1991, p. xxvii.

63 Farrell Krell, *Nietzsche Vol. 4* (trans Frank A. Capuzzi), p. 53.

64 Heidegger, *Being and Time*, p. 379.

65 Heidegger, *Being and Time*, H 380. Architecture is a case in point as it is always the present passed.

66 Heidegger, *Being and Time*, p. 20—a being's past it should be noted also constitutes, in part or whole, its future.

67 Heidegger, *Being and Time*, p. 379.

68 Heidegger, *Being and Time*, p. 388.

69 Heidegger, *Being and Time*, p. 388.

70 Heidegger, *Being and Time*, p. 396.

71 Heidegger, *Being and Time*, p. 386.

72 See Fry, *Design* and *Becoming Human*, Parts 1 and 2.

73 Bambach, *Heidegger, Dilthey*, pp. 260–64.

74 This recoil was especially against Kant's "Idea for a universal history" (Beck 1784) and "Kant's theory of experience" (1871) Hermann Cohen (1885) *Kants Theorie der Erfahrung*, [*Kant's Theory of Experience*] Berlin: Dümmle has been the basis of all subsequent commentaries—see Scott Edgar, "Hermann Cohen," *The Stanford Encyclopedia of Philosophy* (Winter 2012 Edition), Edward N. Zalta (ed.), http://plato.stanford.edu/archives/win2012/entries/cohen/.

75 For a fully elaborated account see Beatrice Hanssen, *Walter Benjamin's Other History*, Berkeley: University of California Press, 2000.

76 Hanssen, *Walter Benjamin*, pp. 27–8.

77 See Immanuel Kant's "Forth thesis" in "Idea for a universal history," L.W. Beck (ed.), *Kant on History* (trans. L.W. Beck, R.E. Archer and E.L. Fackenheim), Indianapolis: Bobbs-Merrill. 1963, pp. 15–16. On Kant's "Teleology and the cunning of nature" see Yirmiahu Yovel, *Kant and the Philosophy of History*, Chapter 3, Princeton: Princeton University Press, 1980, pp. 125–57.

78 *Ur-History* is a concept grown out of *Urforms* as designated by Johann Wolfgang von Goethe. Goethe, through his contemplation of "abstract gardening," "discovered" the *"ur-plant"*—an ideal form that fused together the qualities of all plants past and future. His way of seeing the *"ur-plant"* centered on seeing it simultaneously in time and space. What he actually saw he named *"urphänomen,"* an archetype, which he sourced in a "pagan view of nature" and posited in "history." He believed he had revealed a convergence in time between the knower and the known. Likewise, *"urphänomen"* were also viewed as grounded in an ancient practice wherein *mimesis* was understood as able to evoke the presence of something that itself was absent. Finally, forms in general were deemed to be able to be seen as they were, are, and will be. Effectively *an idea of perception* was projected causally as directive of an actual mode of seeing.

Walter Benjamin, in what has been called his anthropological materialism, was influenced by both what now might be called Goethe's speculative realist ideas and by something far older. He brought Goethe's notion of *ur-forms* to thinking that he linked back to those *urtexts* embedded in the birth of the Jewish faith. He then projected this to what he had come to understand as the confluence of photography, cinema, technology and history in a composite moment of appearance.

What was actually present to be seen for Benjamin was never just the image of one represented moment, but a gathering in one moment of time of past, present and potential. This is most easily grasped through cinema wherein image, movement, time, and technology all converge and flow in a moment of fusion. Yet rather than trying to contain this understanding to any particular medium, what Benjamin did was to generalize it as a way of seeing everyday life, history, technology and change. In doing this he used the "ur" prefix attached to history (ur-history) to characterize how origin, history and phenomenal forms could all be viewed.

In some ways, echoing both Goethe on archetype and Plato on seeing, Benjamin recognized that the transformation of a form of thought was also a transformation of sight. However, the context of seeing was not taken to be neutral but subject to determinate forces—historical, economic and political. Here his thinking was inflected by his engagement with Marxism (especially his understanding of the relation between a mode of production and superstructural cultural forms, but without abandoning his mystical disposition as it was grounded in Hebrew *ur-texts*). Benjamin's mode of relationality brought everything associated with origins and futuring to the present moment of *ur-historical* interrogation. Not, however, as transparent figures but as clues to be found, deciphered and read. His thinking exposed that the materially present of a particular moment of history is a gathering buried in human (designed) artefacts or events. The revelation, or as Benjamin called it "rescue," of these objects or events he named as *Jetztzeit*—the act of exposing the "everlasting now." This has been likened to the *Nunc Stans* of Aquinas and obviously the *"Urphanomen"* of Goethe, but it equally resonates with the Nietzschean notion of eternal return.

For a full account of this complex progression see, Ashley Stewart Crane (Rev.), "The restoration of Israel: Ezekiel 36–39 in early Jewish interpretation," Ph.D. thesis, Murdoch University, 2006, p. 23; Eli Friedlander, "The measure of the contingent," *Boundary 2*, 35:3 (2000), pp. 20–22; Miriam Brata Hansen, "Room for play: Benjamin's gamble with cinema," *October*, 109, 2004, pp. 3–45; and Maria Zimmerman Brendel,"The everlasting now: Walter Benjamin's archive," *ArtUS*, March 1, 2007, pp. 54–60.

79 Hanssen, *Walter Benjamin*, p. 38.

80 Hanssen deals with this issue at length in her Chapter 3 on Benjamin's "turn to natural history", pp. 49–65.

81 George Stiener noted this in his introduction to John Osborne's translation of Benjamin's *The Origin of German Tragic Drama*, London: Verso, 1998, p. 12. The "*Trauerspiel*" was Benjamin's most esoteric work, written in 1925.

82 On this count and others, as Hanssen says, he was "idiosyncratic," especially in terms of how secularization impacted upon understandings of modernity and worldviews. Hanssen, *Walter Benjamin*, p. 53.

83 In the discussion of Hegel, Adorno, Marx and the character of history in relation to Benjamin's position Hanssen correctly reviews the added, but not problematic, complexity added by Heidegger. What is unresolved here, and more generally, is the reduction of an awareness of anthropocentrism as a perspective limit to humanism.

84 André Leroi-Gourhan's work on the prehistorical is seminal (see especially his *Gesture and Speech*, Cambridge: MIT Press, 1998 (first published in France in 1964), Jacques Derrida, *Of Grammatology* (trans. Gayatri Chakravorty Spivak), Baltimore: Johns Hopkins University Press, 1974 (first published in France in 1964), Georgio Agamben, *Homo Sacer* (trans. Daniel Heller-Roazen), Stanford: Stanford University Press, 1998 (first published in Italy in 1995), Bruno Latour, *We Have Never Been Modern* (trans. Catherine Porter), Cambridge: Harvard University Press, 1993 (first published in France in 1991), and Bernard Stiegler, *Technics and Time 1 – series 1* (trans. Richard Beardsworth and George Collins), Stanford: Stanford University Press 1998; *Technics and Time 2* (2009), *Technics and Time 3* (2011) (both trans. Stephen Barker), Stanford: Stanford University Press (published in France respectively in 1994, 1996, and 2001). On design see Fry, *Design* and *Becoming Human*.

85 His view of origins was also steeped in the thinking of his early career as in Walter Benjamin, *The Origin of German Tragic Drama* (trans. John Osborne), London: Verso, 1998, first published in Berlin in 1928.

86 Michel Foucault, *The Archaeology of Knowledge* (trans. A. M. Sheridan Smith), London: Tavistock Publications, 1985, p. 4.

87 See Paul Rabinow (ed.), *The Foucault Reader*, New York: Pantheon Books, 1984.

88 Cohen, *History out of Joint*, p. 25.

89 See Cary Wolfe, *What is Posthumanism?* Minneapolis: Minnesota University Press, 2010, p. 115, citing John Rajchman, *Michel Foucault*, New York: Columbia University Press, 1985, p. 55.

90 Rabinow, *The Foucault Reader*, p. 76.

91 Rabinow, *The Foucault Reader*, p. 78.

92 Rabinow, *The Foucault Reader*, p. 83.

93 Rabinow, *The Foucault Reader*, p. 95.

94 F. Nietzsche, *On the Use and Abuse of History for Life* (Vom Nutzen und Nachteil der Historie für das Leben), 1874.

95 Roth, *Knowing and History*, p. 209.

96 Roth, *Knowing and History*, p. 212.

97 Rabinow, *The Foucault Reader,* p. 89. We note here, as Hayden White points out, Foucault does not mean academic history when he evokes the term, rather he means "the fundamental mode of being of empiricities"—White, *Topic of Discourse*, p. 243. Yet as chair in history at the College de France until his death he was preoccupied with explorations of the past.

98 Poster, *A New Kind of History*, London: Polity Press, 1984, p. 74. Foucault discusses the complexity of discontinuity at length in his introduction to *The Archaeology of Knowledge*, pp. 3–17.

99 Michel Foucault, "Afterword: the subject of power," in Hubert L. Dreyfus and Paul Rabinow, *Michael Foucault: Beyond Structuralism and Hermeneutics*, Brighton: Harvester Press, 1986, pp. 208–26.

100 Foucault, "Afterword," pp. 208–09.

101 Foucault, "Afterword," pp. 208–09.

102 Poster, *A New Kind of History*, p. 87.

103 White, *Topic of Discourse*, p. 239.

104 White, *Topic of Discourse*, p. 219.

105 Michel Foucault, *Discipline and Punish* (trans. Alan Sheridan), Harmondsworth: Penguin Books, 1979, p. 27.

106 See Foucault, *The Archaeology of Knowledge*, pp. 15–16.

107 Derrida's essay was reproduced in the collection *Writing and Difference* (trans. Alan Bass), Chicago: Chicago University Press, 1978, pp. 31–63.

108 Peter Fenves in *Jacques Derrida and the Humanities* (ed. Tom Cohen), Cambridge: Cambridge University Press, 2001, pp. 273–5.

109 Jacques Derrida, *Specters of Marx*, London: Routledge, 1994 (the text was first published in France in 1993).

110 Bernd Magnus, *Nietzsche's Existent Imperative*, Bloomington: University of Indiana Press, 1978, pp. 191–5.

111 Hamlet, Act 1 Scene 5 in W. J. Craig (ed), *The Complete Works of William Shakespeare*, Oxford: The Clarendon Press, 1912.

112 Magnus, *Nietzsche's Existent Imperative*, p. 91.

113 Cohen, *History out of Joint*, p. 170.

114 Cohen, *History out of Joint*, p. 170.

115 Cohen, *History out of Joint*, p. 77.

116 Cohen, *History out of Joint*, pp. 77–8.

117 Cohen, *History out of Joint*, pp. 81–4.

118 Carl Schmitt, *The Nomos of the Earth* (trans. G.L. Ulmen), New York: Telos Press, 2006.

119 This debate is, for example, evidenced by the collection of essays edited by Stephen Legg, *Spatiality, Sovereignty, and Carl Schmitt*, New York: Routledge, 2011.

120 Mega-regions now are the largest and fastest global centres of wealth production that account for 60 percent of created wealth while accommodating only 14 percent of the global population. See www.asianinfrstructure.com/news/mega-regions/

121 UN Habitat, *State of the World's Cities 2010/2011*, London: Earthscan, 2008, see respectively p. 28 and p. 95.

122 The Artic is warming twice as fast as the rest of the planet, now its increasingly ice-free shipping lanes are inviting exploration of valuable deposits of fossil fuels, iron, diamonds, gold, and uranium. In 2007 a Russian submarine planted a flag on the sea floor beneath the North Pole; Canada and Denmark argue about the very small Hans Island, which is between Canada and Greenland; Russia and the USA have both staked claims in the area via military means. Juliana Hanle, "Bare new world" *Sierra Magazine*, September/October, 2011, at www.sierraclub.org/sierra/201109/grapple6.aspx

123 See FAO Food Index at www.fao.org/worldfoodsituation/wfs-home/foodpricesindex/en/

124 Drones (pilotless aircraft deployed as means of surveillance and targeted destruction) are now being deployed in countries, outside of war zones, as an instrument of state power to survey populations and to fight crime.

125 This essay appeared in Jacques Derrida, *The Other Heading* (trans. Pascale-Anne Brault and Michael Nass), Bloomington: Indiana University Press, 1992.

126 Cohen, *History out of Joint*, p. 2.

127 Fry, *Design as Politics*, pp. 109–69.

128 Mignolo, *The Darker Side of Western Modernity*, pp. 1–77.

129 Derrida, *Specters of Marx*, pp. 85–89.

130 Derrida, *Specters of Marx*, p. 85.

131 On Benjamin's angle of history see his "IX thesis on the philosophy of history," in *Illuminations* (ed. Hannah Arendt), London: Fontana, 1973, pp. 259–60. On the darker side of Western modernity see Mignolo, *The Darker Side of Western Modernity*.

132 To take a very simple illustration: while every one of us share a common need to be sustained by some form of nourishment, there is a massive diversity in the food we actually eat.

133 My emphasis.

134 See for example Hans Sluga, "Heidegger and the critique of reason," in *What's Left of Enlightenment*, Keith Michael Baker and Peter Hanns Reill (eds), Stanford: Stanford University Press, 2001, pp. 50–70.

135 See Fry, *Design as Politics*, pp. 187–209.

136 See note 14, Mignolo, *The Darker Side of Western Modernity*.

137 The Urmadic University (Ur the original, madic from nomadic = the first nomadic university) this is a project that started with a "hothouse" event in Brisbane in 2011, which led to another in Paris (2012), and Thessaloniki (2013)—each year the project has developed via its international network, projects and structure (see www.theodessey.org).

138 Heidegger, *Being and Time*, p. 350.

139 Heidegger, *Being and Time*, p. 325.

140 Heidegger, *Being and Time*, p. 336.

141 Martin Heidegger, *The Basic Problems of Phenomenology* (trans. Albert Hofstadter), Bloomington: Indiana University Press, 1988, p. 272.

2. Another history, another designing

1 Tony Fry, *Becoming Human by Design*, London: Berg, 2012.

2 The process is said to have started 2.3 million years ago, with our species—*Homo sapiens*—arriving some 160,000 years ago. Fry, *Becoming Human*, p. 8.

3 Leonard Wooley's *Excavations at Ur*, New York: Scribners, 1930—Wooley did a huge amount of work on this site during his excavations during the 1920s and 1930s. Henri Frankforts, *The Birth of Civilisation in the Near East*, London: Williams and Norgate, 1951—again this text represents a lifetime of work and several decades in the field; and representing the more recent past, Charles Maisels, *The Near East: Archaeology in the "Cradle of Civilization,"* London: Psychology Press, 1998.

4 Needham was sent to China by Winston Churchill in 1943 as a scientific counsellor in order to set up and direct an outpost on behalf of the Sino-British Co-operation Office established in 1942. In the face of China's

ongoing war with Japan, the aim of the mission was to strengthen bonds with the people of China—this by visiting learned institutions and also by auditing needs for books and laboratory equipment. Needham was an eminent biochemist who also acquired an extensive knowledge of China. Out of his work in China a vast process of documentation was created, and although Needham died in 1995 research continues via the institute he created. The first volume, "*Introductory Orientations*," was published in 1954 (currently there are twenty-seven, all published under the series title of *Science and Civilisation in China*).

What Needham's project did was to "discover," order and comment on many thousands of years of scientific development and practical innovation in China over a vast range of topic areas from physics, biology, astronomy and engineering to forestry, paper-making, philosophy and fisheries. Besides this project uncovering a huge amount of often hidden scientific and cultural material and associated empirical information that exposed the complexity, depth and extent of ancient Chinese knowledge it equally exposed two major situations: the first recasts how the West projects its intellectual history (during the Enlightenment, and without acknowledgement, much knowledge was appropriated from China by Jesuit priests. One well-known example is that of binary notation, which in 1698 was pointed out to Leibniz by the Jesuit missionary Joachim Bouvet—the idea appeared in a paper published by Leibniz the following year (see Tony Fry, *A New Design Philosophy*, Sydney: UNSW Press, 1999, p. 280, n. 7.); and second, the *Science and Civilisation in China* series remains an acclaimed and still extremely under-utilised resource that registers the impossibility of history (its mode of narrativization has been questioned, while as a massive translation project it has been commended, but it still remains a re-presented fragment of a forgotten and significantly erased past, but above all one has to recognize that the material is unavoidability transformed by all interpretation being vested in the contemporary. The entire modernization of China from the mid-nineteenth-century onward was dominated by a "war on the past" as it was deemed from the Qing Dynasty to Mao and beyond—the past was presented as a block to the future).

5 David Hall and Roger Ames, *Anticipating China*, New York: SUNY Press, 1995, p. 214—the note at the end of their text is to Joseph Needham *Science and Civilisation in China: History of Scientific Thought*, Volume 2, Cambridge: Cambridge University Press, Ch 13, pp. 280–81. They then cite Needhan (p. 281) who went on to say: "Things behave in particular ways not necessarily because of prior action or impulsions of other things, but because their position in the ever moving cyclical universe was such that they were endowed with intrinsic natures which made that behaviour inevitable for them. If they did not behave in these particular ways they would lose their relational position in the whole (which made them what they were), and turn into something other than themselves. They were thus partly in existential dependence upon the whole world organism." Following this Hall and Ames make clear (p. 268) that "world organism" has little in common with how this notion would be understood in the West—the notion actually means something more like "organization" on the basis that there is no final distinction between nature and human culture.

6 The key observation that illustrates the point comes from the relational and intercultural "history" of Western modernity and the Enlightenment as they rested upon the attainment of other and older cultures—the list of knowledge drawn upon from, for example Asia and the Near East, was immense: mathematics, the physical and biological sciences, technology, medicine, astronomy, agriculture, metallurgy, hydrology and more.

7 Jenkins, *At the Limits of History*, London: Routledge, 2009, p. 7.

8 Mark Poster "Foucault, Marxism and history," in *A New Kind of History*, London: Polity Press, 1984, p. 76.

9 Poster, *A New Kind of History*, p. 13.

10 Poster, *A New Kind of History*, Chapter 3.

11 Poster, *A New Kind of History*, p. 15.

12 Dominick LaCapra, *History and Criticism*, Ithaca: Cornell University Press, 1985, p. 17.

13 LaCapra, *History and Criticism*, p. 213.

14 Jenkins, *At the Limits of History*, p. 9.

15 To illustrate: the City of Coventry was the first city in Britain to have a planning department. Prior to World War II, under the influence of Le Corbusier, the modernist head of this department proposed that the center of the medieval city be demolished and replaced by a modern shopping precinct—this with no domestic architecture, and with the center surrounded by a circular ring road. The concept was rejected by the city council. During the war Coventry, as both an industrial and heritage city, was a major target for German bombers. A great deal of damage was done and the place became a national symbol of the "blitzkrieg." After the war the planning department took advantage of the situation. The result: bulldozers destroyed more of the City's historical buildings than were by bombs—thereafter, the modern city center was built.

16 Hans-Georg Gadamer, *Truth and Method* (trans. J. Weinsheimer and D. G. Marshall), New York: Crossroads, 1990, p. 360.

17 Jenkins, *At the Limits of History*, p. 5.

18 Caroline W. Bynum, "Perspectives, connections and objects: what's happening to history now," *Daedalus*, Winter 2009, pp. 80–81.

19 LaCapra, *History and its Limits*, p. 192.

20 Jenkins, *At the Limits of History*, p. 7.

21 Dominick LaCapra, *History & Criticism*, Ithaca: Cornell University Press, 1985, pp. 15–44.

22 Jenkins, *At the Limits of History*, pp. 5–10.

23 Jenkins, *At the Limits of History*, p. 4.

24 Jenkins, *At the Limits of History*, p. 15.

25 Jenkins, *At the Limits of History*, p. 16.

26 Its meaning is further exposited by Georgio Agamben in *Remnants of Auschwitz*, New York: Zone Books, 2008, p. 29.

27 Agamben, *Remnants*, p. 200.

28 Dominick LaCapra "Representing the holocaust: reflections on the historians' debate," in Saul Friedlander (ed.), *Probing the Limits of Representation: Nazism and the "Final Solution,"* Cambridge: Harvard University Press, 1992, p. 110.

29 Anton Kaes, "Holocaust and the end of history: postmodern historiography in cinema," in Saul Friedlander (ed.), *Probing the Limits of Representation: Nazism and the "Final Solution,"* Cambridge: Harvard University Press, 1992, p. 207.

30 Zygmunt Bauman, *Modernity and the Holocaust*, Ithica: Cornell University Press, 1989, p. 19.

31 Bauman, *Modernity and the Holocaust*, p. 20, see also n.25.

32 The German medical system noted a sharp rise in the number of *Kriegsneurosen* cases from 1942 onward. This was attributed to the reversal of German military gains in Russia and Europe, linked to a drop in German morale and a near collapse in the personnel replacement program. In particular, there were a significant number of neuroses cases involving German soldiers assigned to either extermination parties or concentration camps. Exposure to these environments, wherein human atrocities were common, imposed unbearable conditions on soldiers that led many to alcohol abuse, insanity, and suicide. See Hans Binneveld, *From Shell Shock to Combat Stress* (trans. John O'Kane), Amsterdam: Amsterdam University Press, 1997, p. 4.

33 Within a humanist frame of reference, history, not least the history of colonialism, suggests this indeed may well be the case.

34 See Bauman, *Modernity and the Holocaust*, pp. 68–9.

35 Bauman, *Modernity and the Holocaust*, pp. 69–70.

36 Bauman, *Modernity and the Holocaust*, p. 72.

37 The term "eugenics" was coined by Sir William Galton in 1883 and the First International Congress of Eugenics was held in London 1912. The movement was supported by many prominent figures including H. G. Wells, Winston Churchill, George Bernard Shaw, Theodore Roosevelt and John Maynard Keynes. See Lynn Richard, *Eugenics: A Reassessment*, New York: Praeger, 2001.

38 See Bauman, *Modernity and the Holocaust*, p. 113.

39 Bauman, *Modernity and the Holocaust*, p. 14.

40 Thus "judgement and thought" demand to be central to education at all levels and not least in design education.

41 Bauman, *Modernity and the Holocaust*, p. 24.

42 During the German invasion of the Soviet Union, SS-Standartenführer Paul Blobel commanded Sonderkommando 4a of Einsatzgruppen C—a mobile killing unit. Following Wehrmacht troops into the Ukraine (these mobile killing units were created to eliminate those people deemed "the unworthy." He also carried out a major massacre at Babi Yar (now Kiev). Blobel was sentenced to death at Nuremberg and hanged at Landsberg Prison in June 1951. In addition to his crimes against the dead some 60,000 deaths were attributable to him. There are many accounts of Blobel's deeds, see for example Richard L. Rubenstein and John K. Roth, *Approaches to Auschwitz*, Louisville: Westminster John Knox Press, 2003.

43 Cohen, *History Out of Joint*, p. 21.

44 Cited by Georgio Agamben, *Remnants of Auschwitz* (trans. Daniel Heiller-Roazen), New York: Zone Books, 2008, p. 33.

45 Agamben, *Remnants of Auschwitz*, p. 17.

46 Agamben, *Remnants of Auschwitz*, p. 35.

47 Zdenek Lederer, *Ghetto Theresienstad*, New York: Howard Fertig, 1983 (the book was completed in 1947 and first published in English in 1953).

48 Agamben, *Remnants of Auschwitz*, p. 164.

49 The overview of Dachau is drawn from *Holocaust Encyclopedia*: US Holocaust Museum http://www.ushmm.org/; Harold Marcuse, *Legacies of Dachau: the Uses and Abuses of a Concentration Camp 1933–2001*, Cambridge: Cambridge University Press, 2001; and Marcus J. Smith, *Dachau: the Harrowing of Hell*, New York: SUNY Press, 1995.

50 Evelyn Le Chene, *Mauthausen: the History of a Death Camp*, London: Methuen, 1971.

51 Michael Thad Allen, "From the business of genocide: the SS, slave labour, and the concentration camps," in Eric Katz, *Death by Design*, New York: Pearson Longman, 2006, p. 97.

52 Allen, "From the business of genocide," p. 99.

53 Paul B. Jaskot, "Architecture and the destruction of the European Jews," in Eric Katz, *Death by Design*, New York: Pearson Longman, 2006, p. 139.

54 Jeffery Herf, *Reactionary Modernism: Technology, Culture, and Politics in Weimar and the Third Reich*, Cambridge: Cambridge University Press, 1984.

55 Albert Speer, extract from "*Inside the Third Reich: Memoirs*" in Eric Katz, *Death by Design*, New York: Pearson Longman, 2006, p. 159.

56 Walter Benjamin, "The work of art in the age of mechanical reproduction," in *Illuminations* (ed. Hannah Arendt, trans. Harry Zohn), London: Fontana, 1973, p. 244.

57 Hubert Schrader, *Bauten des dritten Reiches*, Leipzig: Bibliographisches Institut, 1937, pp. 18–20 (English edition, 1939).

58 Jaskot, "Architure and the destruction of the European Jews," in Katz, *Death by Design*, p. 137.

59 Speer in Katz, *Death by Design*, p. 159.

60 Allen "From the business of genocide," p. 89.

61 Allen, "From the business of genocide," pp. 88–9.

62 Nuremburg trial record September 20, 1945 available at: http://www.nizkor.org/hweb/imt/tgmwc/tgmwc-16/tgmwc-16-154-02.shtml

63 Speer in Katz, *Death by Design*, p. 167.

64 Speer in Katz, *Death by Design*, p. 167.

65 Speer in Katz, *Death by Design*, p. 175.

66 The full extract is cited by Jack L. Sammons, Jr. from his "Rebellious ethics and Albert Speer," in Eric Katz, *Death by Design*, New York: Pearson Longman, 2006, p. 181.

67 Sammons, "Rebellious ethics and Albert Speer," p. 183.

68 Lederer, *Ghetto Theresienstad*, pp. 85–6.

69 Nelly Toll, *When Memory Speaks*, London: Praeger, 1998, p. 39.

70 Lederer, *Ghetto Theresienstad*, p. 14.

71 Toll, *When Memory Speaks*, p. 40. The Nazis set up designated "drafting rooms" where art materials were available and where artworks could be produced.

72 This account summarizes the entry on the visit in the *Holocaust Encyclopedia*: US Holocaust Museum, http://www.ushmm.org/

73 A full account is given by Lederer, *Ghetto Theresienstad*, pp. 88–121.

74 Toll, *When Memory Speaks*, pp. 41–2.

75 Lederer, *Ghetto Theresienstad*, p. 85.

76 Lederer, *Ghetto Theresienstad*, p. 57.

77 Lederer, *Ghetto Theresienstad*, p. 15.

78 Lederer, *Ghetto Theresienstad*, pp. 65–70.

79 Lederer, *Ghetto Theresienstad*, p. 265.

80 At some stage it was converted into a lending library. There was also another library in the Ghetto containing around 60,000 Hebrew books that had been gathered from libraries closed down by German occupying forces.

81 Lederer, *Ghetto Theresienstad*, pp. 52–3.

82 Lederer, *Ghetto Theresienstad*, pp. 52–3.

83 Lederer, *Ghetto Theresienstad*, pp. 57–9.

84 Franciszek Piper, "Design and development of the gas chambers and

crematoria in Auschwitz," in Eric Katz, *Death by Design*, New York: Pearson Longman, 2006, p. 26.

85 Of Poland's 3,250,000 Jews only 50,000 survived and most of them left the country.

86 Cited by Sammons, "Rebellious ethics and Albert Speer", p. 191.

87 Sande Cohen, *Historical Culture: On the Recoding of an Academic Discipline*, Berkeley: University of California Press, 1988, p. 175.

88 Cited by Agamben in *Remnants of Auschwitz*, p. 71.

89 Bauman, *Modernity and the Holocaust*, pp. 85–7.

90 Bauman, *Modernity and the Holocaust*, p. 88.

91 This challenge is partly met by "redirective practice." See Tony Fry, *Design Futuring*, Berg: Oxford, 2009; and *Design as Politics*, Berg: Oxford, 2011.

92 Jaskot, "Architure and the destruction of the European Jews," p. 139.

93 Jaskot, "Architure and the destruction of the European Jews," pp. 140–41.

94 Bauman, *Modernity and the Holocaust*, p. 8.

95 Agamben, *Remnants of Auschwitz*, p. 72.

96 A detailed account of this technology is given by Jean-Claude Pressac with Robert Jan Pelt "The machinery of mass murder at Auschwitz," in Eric Katz, *Death by Design*, New York: Pearson Longman, 2006, pp. 36–69.

97 Agamben, *Remnants of Auschwitz*, p. 133.

98 A German term widely used among concentration camp inmates to refer to prisoners who were near death due to exhaustion, starvation, or hopelessness. The word *Muselmann* literally means "Muslim." The Nazis running the camps considered the *Muselmanner* undesirable. Thus, during selections, these victims were the first to be sentenced to death. A person at this stage had no chance for survival; they would not live for more than a few days or weeks. See under entry in listing of terms at: Shoah Research Centre: http://www.yadvashem.org

99 Agamben, *Remnants of Auschwitz*, p. 148.

3. Design in the maelstrom of time

1 Heidegger, *Being and Time*, para 381/p. 433.

2 William H. McNeill, "The changing shape of world history," a paper originally presented at the History and Theory World History Conference, Chicago, March 25–26, 1994.

3 McNeill, "The changing shape of world history", p. 27.

4 McNeill, "The changing shape of world history", p. 28.

5 McNeill, "The changing shape of world history", p. 18.

6 William McNeill came to prominence in 1963 with his book *The Rise of the West: A History of the Human Community* (Chicago: University of Chicago Press, 1963), which won the 1964 U.S. National Book Award in History and Biography. In the twilight of his career he led the creation of *The Berkshire Encyclopedia of World History*. This multi-volume work was written by a team of 330 historians, archaeologists, anthropologists, sociologists, geographers and other experts from around the world, it was published in 2004.

7 In its loose language on, for example, the human "capacity to invent new ideas" and the agency of "contact with strangers" McNeill's rhetoric seems oblivious of contemporary critical thought and theories of change—*The Rise of the West*, pp. 10–13. In fact, McNeill is the arch-representative of the kink of thinking on history that Foucault recoiled against and, in its theoretical poverty, has precipitated the fragmentation of the discipline. De facto, the more history is appealed to, and characterized as a unified mass, the greater the recoil against it.

8 See for example Poster, *A New Kind of History*, p. 88; and in the same year LaCapra, *History & Criticism*, p. 25 was equally exposing the misplaced dream of historians to author a "total history."

9 Because of the long atmospheric life of CO_2, emissions made in the late Industrial Revolution are elemental to impacts that continually arrive in the present.

10 There are exceptions to this trend, must notably Bernard Stiegler—in particular, his three-volume work *Time and Technics* (1998–2004), Stanford: Stanford University Press.

11 Bauman, *Modernity and the Holocaust*, p. 61.

12 Bauman, *Modernity and the Holocaust*, p. 96.

13 Bauman, *Modernity and the Holocaust*, p. 153.

14 Bauman, *Modernity and the Holocaust*, p. 13.

15 Latour, *We Have Never Been Modern* (trans. Catherine Porter), Cambridge: Harvard University Press, 1993.

16 Jenkins, *At the Limits of History*, pp. 247–8.

17 This concept has been developed by Bernd Magnus from his reading of Nietzsche—see Magnus, *Nietzsche's Existential Imperative*, pp. 190–95.

18 Jenkins, *At the Limits of History*, p. 252.

19 Jenkins, *At the Limits of History*, p. 253.

20 Jenkins, *At the Limits of History*, p. 38.

21 Stanley Milgram, *Obedience to Authority: An Experimental View*, London: Tavistock, 1974.

22 Bauman, *Modernity and the Holocaust*, p. 154.

23 Jenkins, *At the Limits of History*, p. 249.

24 Tony Fry, *Design Futuring Sustainability, Ethics, and New Practice*, Oxford: Berg, 2009.

ESSAY TWO

HISTORY, DESIGN, FUTURES: CONTENDING WITH WHAT WE HAVE MADE

Clive Dilnot

Whoever wants nothing to do with the trajectory of history belongs all the more truly to it.

THEODOR ADORNO, "Why still philosophy?"

1 OUR HISTORY, OUR UNHAPPINESS

I

The structure of existence is undergoing a fundamental change

Thought in terms of how we can become adequate to "contending with what we have made," what follows is an incomplete meditation on the relation of history and the future—and on the interpolation of design as a moment, or better, perhaps, as a *capacity of acting*,[1] in relation to both. The transition we are now experiencing, to a world where the artificial (and no longer nature) constitutes the horizon, medium and determining conditions of our existence, changes the relation of all three terms in the title. That which was seen as distinct, even opposed, finds itself in dialectical relation. That which was delimited by norms (evaluative, professional, disciplinary) now rediscovers itself as open capability and even as thought. That which was certain—the future—disappears as such, or at the very least becomes that which we no longer know how to purposefully reach, except as the possibility, by no means remote, of a gradual slide into catastrophe and self-destruction.[2] Most paradoxically, that which, as "history," our epoch works towards obliterating in any meaningful sense, returns not just as "cause" but as the *very means of beginning to open again the future as possibility, that is as other than defuturing.*

By "history" is meant here therefore not only what is past but also what is to come. "History" means here future; the future that is determined, perhaps more than we think, by the past; but the future also as that which is—as the essay by Tony Fry in this book has already made clear—in *doubt*, and in doubt in the most profound sense. We stand at the edge not of "futuring" but of defuturing. In fact, to a large extent the future is *already* that which has gone from us, slipped beyond our capacity to grasp it. But even as the parallel evacuation of the past proceeds apace (their disappearance are dialectically related) history also stands as that form of *active* thinking of cause and consequence which, gives us a crucial degree of freedom to define the scope of our determination by it.[3]

"History," we immediately see, is here three things at once. It is at once *the* past (that which is determined and which in a real sense we cannot alter—*except* that we also receive this past through our conception of it, we essentially *construct* crucial elements of how the past coordinates our being and how we act to become)[4] and the *movement* of past(s) through the present into the future (as tendency, though without teleology or latent idealism).[5] But today, and most importantly, it also that form of *active* thinking of cause and consequence capable of changing our sense of the actuality of the world and its possibility. This means that acting—the manner in which we act in the world and especially that through which we are able to act to change the actuality of the world—now takes on a historical dimension that we almost certainly did not anticipate. That the onset of the artificial-as-world transforms primary relations of past, present and future, changes the relation of the former to the latter. Or more precisely, since the potential *lack* of our future is a historical product through and through, it might follow that is its obverse is similarly located—if today obscured—in history.[6]

The question of design in relation to history and the future is therefore the question of design thought *within* the processes of reestablishing a flow between the causative and consequential past, the present as the site through which we test, anticipatively, the relation of the actual and the possible, and the future as that which we must now cultivate into being. To be sure, since we are only now entering this epoch, there is little that is definitive that can be said. All reflections and speculations on teasing a humane future out of incipient disaster are necessarily tentative in the extreme. In any case, as we constantly discover to our cost, the world that is now passing, but which clings all the more tenaciously to thought, hobbles thought far more than practice—which in some ways is already, scarcely without knowing it, manifesting elements of what will be (though still as much, if not more, destructively, rather than as yet affirmatively).

Nonetheless, do we see, in some moments of practice, flashes of different modes of acting? And with respect to design, do we see instances that suggest roles for design capabilities in regard to this new historical situation that go beyond the trivial? Our situation is fraught with the possibility of crisis from which only private interest can benefit. The converse is that it is also suffused *objectively*, with possibilities we have not learned to recognize, nor generally yet dared to think in their implication. Our "crisis" (this word is over-used and perhaps should be retired, at least for a while) may yet turn upon and turn out to be a crisis of our incapacity to recognize our capacities. Possibility is now not what we think it is; nor, to repeat, do we in any manner *think* possibility well. To think possibility well we have to return to the notion of cause.

The necessity of history

"This hypothesis contains the suspicion that the structure of culture—*and therefore of existence itself*—is undergoing a fundamental change."[7] So opens Vilém Flusser's short book *The Philosophy of Photography*. This essay is motivated by a parallel suspicion. But it *reverses* Flusser's formulation. Today, it is not that that the structure of culture is undergoing a fundamental change and *therefore*, and consequently, so is that of existence. It is rather that the structure of existence is itself in transformation, and it is this that opens the *objective* possibility of different history, i.e., a different trajectory for the future. It is this that therefore also offers the *chance*—the word is used deliberately, nothing determinate is intended here—of a quite different structure and dynamic obtaining for human culture. That, after all, has to be the wager on which any hope of a hospitable future is based.

It will have seemed natural, given the period in which Flusser was writing (the 1970s) to lay stress as he did. By the side of "late capitalism" and exhausted liberal, social-democratic and Marxist politics, culture appeared to be the realm that promised possibility. But today the significant transformations are no longer confined, as was thought 40 years ago, to the realm of the culture industry or its equivalents. Today, the shift lies deeper, deeper even than the economic as it appears to us, even though the latter now determines everything. The change lies in the structure of the artificial. The latter is no longer confined to what we have previously called "artifice" or even "technology" in the older and now inadequate senses of the term, rather the artificial—thought in the expanded sense as including not only technical systems but also the entire realm of symbol production as well as the take up and processing of nature—now forms the totality of our existence.

It is in light of this that Flusser's basic hypothesis must be further re-drafted. It is not in fact (as Flusser thought) the "invention of technical images" that initiates the second "fundamental turning point in human culture"—these are at best symptoms of an apparatus in transformation—but the onset of the artificial as world. With this development, at once overarching as horizon and underpinning as condition, the nature of our history changes, and in fundamental ways. Time, disjunctive for us because we have been "broken" into the present, is no longer that which we can grasp with comfort. As the future eludes us we are left with an uncomfortable double conclusion: that the source of our unhappiness lies in how we stand, or fail to stand, to that history; and that it is history, "determinant" of the future, that we must think in order to have a future that is not also potentially catastrophic. The question for history in this case is not teleological but practical—how can a history, i.e., a future, be *brought into being* as a time of hospitality "towards all?"[8]

I see this as the central question that faces human culture as a whole. We are seeking, or we need to seek, to create the basis of another trajectory for our future. Given that we are today enmeshed in the artificial—and this is perhaps the *weakest* way of formulating this relation (the strongest would be to say that we are determined by, and perhaps already undone by the artificial)[9]—then that for which the artificial is its true subject matter (design) cannot escape this question and this task. But then in the relation between history, the future, design is already *internal*; there is no "and." To play off the structure of famous connexion that Heidegger previously established "Design and history are, each in its own way, inescapable for the future. The two, however, are also insufficient for the future so long as each busies itself with its own affairs in separation instead of listening to one another. They are able to listen if both—design and history—belong to the future."[10]

That design, the future and history, are today internally related produces the paradox (design) that of all things it is history that it now has to think. Design has to think history because design designs in the context of time. This is true, incidentally, even on a mundane level.

We now find ourselves in a situation where not only time has been eroded, but where, on the evidence of the nature of the things we build and construct, we are both incapable of designing in and for time,[11] and perhaps in fear of time. The fear of time is not just fear of the future, it is the fear of thinking time based on the sense that there has been an erasure, to put this in the language of tradition, of both "the ancestor's" and "those to come." Or more exactly, and better, we fear time because we sense that there has been an erasure of the flow between these moments; that there is a void in our acting and this void is time.

This has more and other implications than we care to admit. While we superficially so often associate freedom with the lifting of the weight of history—precisely so do the first shoots of proto-modernisms feel at the end of the 19th century, when the struggle appears to be that of sloughing off the "dead weight" of history—reflection shows that in this case history had already been "broken in two" by the irrevocable changes in the structure of culture that the onset of industrialization and industrial capitalism had both set in chain ("Is not to be modern to know clearly what cannot be started over again?").[12] The question in the 19th century was the inability of the century to live adequately in thought what it was busy manufacturing.[13] Our position is less different than we imagine. We manifest an equal inability to contend adequately in thought with all that we make.[14] The price we pay is not the "weight of history" but its opposite, the illusion of a certain "lightness of being" with respect to the future as project. Contemporary ideology, especially since the 1970s, has been happily deconstructing every affirmative model of history—save that of the infinite progress of accumulation and computing. But even here the "progress" is really simply more of the same so we find ourselves in a stasis, lacking an adequate "philosophy of history."

Of course, philosophies of history are today in bad repute. We are told repeatedly that such are both unnecessary and dangerous. They are dangerous, it is said, because they speak of human projects that are illusory ("progress") or which as myths of emancipation result in disaster ("socialism"). Yet disengaged from teleological aspirations they continue to be necessary. J. M. Bernstein's lapidary phrasing catches the necessity precisely: "Without a philosophy of history the present would be reduced to sheer actuality without potentiality, the principle of identity would be a blind fate forever ready to swallow non-identity, and the work of philosophy reduced to forever hinting at what eludes it."[15] Without some conception of the possible movement of history, some notion of a revelatory human project that pushes beyond what-is, then the actual, the given, the norm, "what-is," swallows what could-be.[16] Since "what-is" is for us the tendency towards catastrophe, then to accede to this would be to accede to the likelihood of disaster. It would be to collapse possibility and potentiality, both of which are opened in new ways in the artificial, and it would be to deny any other human project except the economic.[17]

We forget too easily that the "lack of history" in our times is a construction. The postmodern may have formed itself around the end of "grand narratives" but that was merely a story some told themselves to make intellectually palatable the fact that capital was busy disallowing any other conception of history.[18] But precisely because the economy today *poses* in this way—as a neutrality it does not manifest in actuality[19]— its contestation is necessary. Not only may we perish from it, but a moment that pretends that it has neither time nor history nor repetition ("this time is different")[20] can only be contested by becoming explicit again about history. To become explicit again about history parallels Sartre's inadequate, but still somewhat relevant, formulation that the aspiration of thought is to "give expression to the general movement of society."[21] However, since the latter, considered baldy, is without critical criteria, better perhaps is the injunction given in *Dialectic of Enlightenment:* that the "task to be accomplished is not the conservation of the past, but the redemption of hopes of the past."[22] But the hopes of the past are for the future. The redemption then is of the flow between what determines or appears to determine, and what is possible within the thinking and rethinking (the opening) of this "determination."

In either case the "movement" in question here, for us, is double. On one side it means thinking—and facing down—those modes of acting in which "what-is" is leading towards defuturing. On the other side are the openings offered through the fact of the coming-to-be of the world as essentially artificial. The first inversely,[23] the second affirmatively,[24] points to towards two principal tasks that this situation gives us—those, respectively, of creating a culture adequate to *bridging*[25] the present and the possibility of a humane future; and that of creating a new "doctrine of the subject," i.e., a subject adequate not only to the tasks of contending with what we have made, but also capable of developing the humane—as against the destructive—potential from within what the onset of the artificial-as-world opens for us.

*

Design, it should be noted, does not escape this demand. On the contrary, the question brings the issues of design's capabilities—and of design as the designing *of* and *for* capabilities—to the front burner. To reference the quotation from Badiou given above and contrary to ideology, design does not, like science, "possesses problems but . . . not a project." Rather, design is infinitely less a matter of "problem solving"[26] than is supposed. Conversely, it is always a matter of a "project," i.e., is ontological and addressed to the formation, the sustenance, of the subject.[27] Not for nothing does Elaine Scarry note, in her great study of the material making and unmaking of the person, that "achieving an understanding of political justice may require that we first arrive at an understanding of making and unmaking"[28]—a proposition that, if sustained, questions much of what we understand as both design and politics. To make, we might argue, is *necessarily* to have the project of justice in mind.

But design has a further internal stake in this question. The fact that it has a practical cast does not mean that that it simply takes off from what-is. On the contrary, design is ever the critical reworking of what-is in favor of what could be.[29] The attention here (when it is not caught up in private interests)[30] is at once to the subject—design, we can say, because as making it begins from the subject's need for mediation vis-à-vis the world, is essentially on the *side* of the subject—but also *towards* the potential and the possibilities opened up by artifice. Since artifice is not other than a moment of how, as humans we *have* to be[31] then the exploration of design, once we strip out the accretions and reductions it has been subjected to commercially, professionally and pedagogically, is nothing more, or less, than the exploration—which means the affirmative discovery—of the possible relations that subjects can have with the artificial.

But precisely because of this the task also becomes that creating a subject "adequate not only to the tasks of contending with what we have made, but also capable of developing the humane—as against the destructive—potential from within what the onset of the artificial-as-world opens for us." This task is not outside of design. To the contrary, precisely the onset of world-as-artificial/the artificial-as-world, emphasizes the demand, since it is now no longer possible to conceive of a subject adequate to engaging with—that is acting in *relation* to (and this word now takes on a sharper meaning)—this condition, who is not in some manner capable of "designing." Precisely this was anticipated, it should be noted, by Herbert Simon as early as 1968 when he ended the chapter "The Science of Design" in *The Sciences of the Artificial*, with the following paragraph:

> The proper study of mankind has been said to be man. But I have argued that people—at least in their intellective component—may be relatively simple, that most of the complexity of their behavior may be drawn from their environment, from their search for good designs. If I have made my case, then we can conclude that, in large part, the proper study of mankind is the science of design, not only as a professional component of a technical education but as a core discipline for every liberally educated person.[32]

What animated Simon even then was the question of how we could meet and deal adequately—i.e., nondestructively—with the potential of what the onset of the artificial-as-world opens for us.

Reopening towards the future

This last point is crucial. As we shall see below, a significant strand of our unhappiness arises because while we cannot yet think the artificial fully in its negative implications, so also we cannot think what might also be entailed affirmatively by it; we cannot think what the artificial might offer us as qualitatively other possibilities for how we might exist. Blinded by the status we have always given to nature as the source of our Real, we remain unable to think the artificial, except in negative or trivial, terms.[33] Yet if we are not "destined" to disaster then our only hope is an affirmative understanding of what the artificial makes possible. "Possible" does not mean here intitative extrapolation of what-is. In particular it does not mean the extrapolation of the technological or economic as-is. The possible: is *other* to Moore's law and *other* to the concept of infinite economic growth. It rather means what now becomes objectively possible for subjectivity as the qualitatively other. This possible—the possibility of doing things otherwise, of reconstituting subjective and objective relations, including those with natural systems—is the objective condition of a humane future. If this "other possibility" is *not* possible then qualitatively no other future is possible, and we are destined to what the extrapolation of what we have made leads us to. But to be able to think the objective possibility of another (hospitable) future—and to be able to design for it, to work actively and with political enthusiasm towards bringing in into existence—requires first that we can learn to grasp affirmatively the possibilities that the artificial-as-world now opens.

Yet simply to "think" the artificial—which will mean in actuality *making* the artificial, for there is no longer entirely the separate space of thought and this is one of the difficulties we now have to process[34]—may not be enough. That the victory of the market presents itself (in effect) as that which defines the "essence of what is" reminds us that these tasks demand their own metaphysic. Without alternate understandings (i.e., new interpretations) of what-is and of truth based on what is now emerging—the artificial creating a different basis of possibility—no move towards (for example) sustainment would be possible. It is unrealistic to imagine that anything like sustainment could be somehow established "on top of" our current axioms, or constructed on the basis of current interpretations and comprehensions of "what is" and of "truth." Today, the interpretation of what-is, and the comprehension of what truth can be, must *necessarily* be bound up with—that is must be adequate to—the nature and character of the world made artificial. The paradox that emerges is that a "metaphysics" of the artificial is no less a *necessary* basis for the mode of ethics through which a humane praxis *for* and *of* the artificial can be secured, than it is for the "certainties" that secure the drive to the impossible.

That which "drives the earth beyond its developed sphere of possibility": that which acts as the "guarantee of the stability of a constant form of using things up."[35] These lines, taken from Heidegger's most trenchant critique of metaphysics in its "technological" form, pierce to the heart of the unsustainability that we have created on this basis. They can serve as the inverted model of what it is that we require—which is, as we shall see, a metaphysic of the contingent and the possible; indeed, in a certain way, a "metaphysic" of design, or at least of the artificial. No teleology is involved here because the artificial possesses none. It merely—but this is understatement—opens possibility. Or rather, it puts possibility center stage as the essence of that with which we must deal, at once as danger and in the affirmative sense. To think the artificial in this way is to think the basis of a structural "metaphysic" in terms of possibility and contingency and it is to set in motion a different "unification" (meaning a different relation) of acting and becoming. To think the artificial and to think possibility in these ways is to think them through acceptance of the artificial and what it entails as the underlying condition of our time.

To think history—our history—is then to *think* the artificial as the realm of the possible, and it is to think the artificial as the ground of a "metaphysic" no less secure than that of nature subject to the procedures of scientific method and calculation. Of course, within it, the relation to certainty is inverted, but it is nonetheless a kind of certainty. Only within the *contingent* space of the artificial can we learn to become the subjects who depend upon it. The endemic contingency of the artificial is therefore paradoxically the only "certain" basis of the possibility of our becoming "(finally, perhaps)" human.[36]

If we bring this back to the level of design we can see that this means thinking the intersection of the capabilities of design in respect of negotiating history as a difficult possibility. This means to grasp history—our history to come—as itself a "wicked problem," or perhaps better as a "wicked possibility."[37] But in itself this is also to see that thinking here is not the abstract thinking of contemplation, nor can it stop at critical reflection. Thinking means here *intervention*; that is, it means *thinking* intervention or, more precisely, it means thinking *through* intervention. It means thinking how we conceive of what intervention—action—might be and it means thinking the knowledge embodied and exemplified in intervention, productive action.

The break with what we know as knowledge comes because intervention is an act, but "intervention" in the sense meant here, is not (quite) praxis in the traditional sense. It is this "not (quite) praxis" which gives the move from (roughly) technological will (which is also the will to accumulation) towards, we shall see, acting that is closer to designing.

To be sure, "according to current opinion, all of man's doing—that of the artist and the craftsman as well as that of the workman and the politician—is praxis, that is, manifestation of a will that produces a concrete effect."[38] But the problem of will—which means subjective projection, the exercise of the drive—is that it reaches its limit in action, remains enclosed in its own circle. As Agamben puts it, "it wants only itself through action ... it is not pro-ductive, and brings only itself into presence."[39] By contrast productive acting or poiesis, which operates in the space of possible becoming, does not exhaust itself in the act of willing but creates "something other than itself," it finds its limit outside itself. To think intervention in the artificial is therefore to focus not on praxis (on will or acting through will) but on production or poiesis—on that which *negotiates* with what is possible to bring into being.

Agamben summarizes the contrast in this way: "Central to praxis was the idea of the will that finds its immediate expression in an act, while, by contrast, central to poiesis was the experience of pro-duction into presence, the fact that something passed from nonbeing to being, from concealment into the full light of the work." And he adds, in some commentary useful for our purposes,

> the essential character of poiesis [is] not its aspect as a practical and voluntary process but its being a mode of truth understood as unveiling, ά-λήθεια. And it was precisely because of this essential proximity to truth that Aristotle, who repeatedly theorizes this distinction within man's "doing," tended to assign a higher position to poiesis than to praxis. According to Aristotle, the roots of praxis lay in the very condition of man as an *animal*, a living being: these roots were constituted by the very principle of motion (will, understood as the basic unit of craving, desire, and volition) that characterizes life.[40]

Poiesis is not situated in the dimensions of will but unveiling. Poiesis inhabits the space where the (asserted) certainty of praxis stops. The latter makes itself blind in order to act. Heidegger catches the point perfectly: "In the will to will technology (guarantee of stability) and the unconditional lack of reflection ('experience') first come to dominance."[41] Lack of reflection permits acting without consequence. By contrast, poiesis is acting in a state of reflection and measure. It occurs therefore "in a dimension in which the very structure of man's being-in-the-world and his relationship with truth and history are [put] at stake."[42] But precisely because these relations are at stake—i.e., put into question *as* question—so poiesis opens to "man his authentic temporal dimension . . . the space of his belonging to the world, only within which can he take the original measure of his dwelling on earth and find again his present truth in the unstoppable flow of linear time."[43] "Man on earth has a poetic status because it is poiesis that founds for him the original space of his world."[44]

Our historical position spans the transition from a historical period characterized by the all-but absolute domination of praxis towards one that opens the possibility of being characterized by something closer to poiesis in Agamben's sense. This is to see "intervention" then as belonging not (or not only) to praxis-as-will, but also, and perhaps in the end most characteristically, as poiesis or the unveiling of possibility.

To ask about design therefore "in relation to history" (the future) is to ask about that which, close to poiesis, but also close to technology in the wide Heideggerean sense (i.e., close to the "danger") is situated *within* what is today "most at stake" for us. Design inhabits the artificial as the potential of its self-consciousness. But it does so not only reflectively, as critique, thus outside of praxis, but as that which dares to proffer *poietic* intervention. Though trivialized beyond measure by those incapable of grasping the ontological implications of its capacities and acting—and this includes vast swathes of what call themselves the professions of designing, as well as, tragically, almost the entirety of the educational strata that sets these professionals going—the capacities of design proffer a space (one of the very few spaces in our culture it should be noted) in which, we are potentially able to establish once again a space through which we can attempt, in Agamben's terms, to take "the original measure of our dwelling on earth" and thus find again "our present truth in the unstoppable flow of linear time."

This gives a peculiar status to this inquiry. These terms, although in need of reformulation, open a different space of thinking and a different conception of acting. It also changes—or potentially changes—the position and status of both design and history/the future. We have said already, in relation to the onset of the artificial-as-world, that none of these concepts remain in their previously assigned positions. What intrigues, what then demands examination, is the relationship that then possibly emerges. This relationship, as we will see, objectively depends upon the possibilities opened by the artificial and on the way these possibilities offer resources for overcoming the powerful impulses towards destructiveness and catastrophe that are effectively wired into so much of what we inherit today—both as the norms of practice and action and as the determining concepts and categories that ensnare both practice and thought.

Agamben's formulation of poiesis, even in this truncated and essentially inadequate form, reveals it as a *necessary* mode of how, under the conditions of the artificial, we need to encounter the world. In striving against structural unsustainment (empowered in large part by a praxis run amok) and striving towards cultivating-into-being (into *becoming*) a humane world that is not redolent of human, social and economic catastrophe, then the recovery of the *poietic* stance, *not* as nostalgia but as the condition of genuinely moving forward into what could be, becomes essential.

> Only because in the poetic ... he experiences his being-in-the-world as his essential condition does a world open up for his action and his existence ... Only because he is capable of the most uncanny power, the power of pro-duction into presence, is he also capable of praxis, of willed and free activity. Only because he attains, in the poetic act, a more original temporal dimension is he a historical being, for whom, that is, at every instant his past and future are at stake.[45]

But poiesis is perhaps even more central than this. For poiesis is not a stance or a way of acting in the world that is somehow external to the act; it is not, shall we say, a *method*. It is rather a *gift*, but a gift that occurs in and through the act of making—or as Agamben prefers it, in and through "pro-duction," meaning precisely the activity of bringing-into-becoming, but now in the light of grasping, in and through this, our "belonging to the world." Pro-ducing conceived through (the gift of) poiesis creates work (pro-duction) capable bearing *as its gift* "the task of taking the original measure of man on earth." In such work, the simple continuity or the "given" of time, its *continuum* "is broken, and man recovers, between past and future, his present space,"[46] the space in which he can once again discover himself *in* time.

But in all of this we have a problem. It is precisely through understanding the character and context of our producing in this way that the way is offered to feel our way towards a *futural* understanding of producing. An immediate question for us then is: What blocks this mode of producing? Why then are we dislocated from poiesis? What maintains the effective domination or victory of praxis (will) over poiesis (mediation)? The answers to these questions link, strongly, to the question of the structures of domination and destructiveness that will be discussed below in §2. These questions are not disconnected to the issue of our historical unhappiness. Indeed it is by taking an excursus through the question of our unhappiness, its relation to our inability to deal adequately with history or the future, and its symptomatic expression in aspects of design, that we can gain more sense of the entanglement, for us, of the questions of design, history and futures.

II

The character of our unhappiness

On not being in history

Here is an image that we can scarcely recognize:

> For a society of this sort [a society fully capable of taking on board all that it has made and is making] history is not "a nightmare from which we are struggling to awake." We wake up, and we go about our daily affairs, free of the shadow of imminent apocalypse and secure in the objective knowledge that our activities as civilized beings are expanding our future options and improving our current situation. This is how we would interact with time if we human beings were really on top of our game.[47]

But we are not on top of our game. This is not—save as the deliberate disavowal of what-is—how we wake up or how we go about our daily affairs and it is especially not how we go about our affairs in the public realm. Our activities as a whole are not "expanding our future options and improving our current situation" and we are not "free of the shadow of imminent apocalypse," nor are we "secure in the objective knowledge that our activities as civilized beings" are working more for general betterment than they are in making unwitting contribution to future catastrophe. And so, in a deep sense, we are not happy. The connection to history and the future is essentially to the lack of both. It is their figured absence within practice and thought that is part, and not the part, of our unhappiness.

We are unhappy because in large part we confuse where our unhappiness lies. We confuse priorities and our needs. Take, for example, the manner in which today we act, and fail to act. We can describe this as a double inability. First, the inability to discontinue acting (compulsively) in ways we know will likely bring eventual unhappiness—if not on us then on our children. We can call this the (pathological) compulsion of the Drive.[48] Second, is our equal inability to act well, collectively, in respect of such global threats. Today, we have already become used to the fear of the future. What is more to be thought about is how this manifests in the paradoxical form, already hinted at, of the extraordinary inability to think generationally. A generation that cannot abide the risk of allowing its children to walk to school, is happily abandoning these same children (and in turn their children) to the all-but-certain difficulties of dealing, locally and globally, with the human, social and economic costs of climate change—difficulties that will provoke conflicts and dislocation on scales which will likely rival those of some of the most destructive moments of the past century.[49]

As an illustration, this condition is caught perfectly in the dissonance between two sentences in a recent pair of articles on climate change. The first, as almost the first sentence of the first article, notes "the extent of the consensus of climate scientists on the hypothesis of man-made warming." The second is the despairing title of the following piece: "Global inaction shows that the climate sceptics have already won."[50] "What makes the inaction more remarkable" the author adds

> is that we have been hearing so much hysteria about the dire consequences of piling up a big burden of public debt on our children and grandchildren. But all that is being bequeathed is financial claims of some people on other people. If the worst comes to the worst, a default will occur. Some people will be unhappy. But life will go on. Bequeathing a planet in climatic chaos is a rather bigger concern. There is nowhere else for people to go and no way to reset the planet's climate system. If we are to take a prudential view of public finances, we should surely take a prudential view of something irreversible and much costlier.

No surprise then that, collectively, we enter an age of unhappiness with the manner in which we act; an age defined by an unstable mixture of disavowal ("it won't really happen . . .") and Micawberism ("Something will turn up . . ."). Despite the opprobrium heaped on his head, we exist in something very close to Fukayama's *End of History*.[51] Our passivity *is* in a certain sense the End of History—just as there is something in the argument that a sense of history (of pasts and possibilities) is reopened by protest; that dissent is the moment when the past (the dynamics of cause) and future (the dynamics of consequence) reappear in the present, albeit if in a kind of truncated sense.

But for us, the absolute condition of the "necessity" of the global liberal economy—that which cannot be questioned—allows no space to assign its errancy. The closure of possibility is the simultaneous closure of history, now as null (or worse, as "heritage") and of the future—that which we no longer wish (dare) to prefigure, other than as technological extrapolation. But what closes allows no other opening. So restricted, we are caught in the present. We become increasingly unable to *see* historical continuity, or to see cause as passing from the past, through the present to the future, or consequence working back through the limits of now into the history that, unbeknown, prepared for it.[52]

Such hiatus in experience is not without psychological or political cost. It issues in what might be called "unromantic nihilism," the prosaic, but potentially disastrous, admixture of resignation in the face of what-is together with "a purely negative, if not destructive, will."[53] "Unromantic nihilism" is potentially catastrophic because it threatens to issue not just in a politics of resentment—though there is plenty of this around—but in the choice for total destruction, "its objective potential, rather than rise to reflections that will threaten its basic stratum."[54]

Symptoms of unhappiness in design and architecture

If we pull back for a minute from this largest and depressive—but nonetheless realistic view—we can also say that this present-without- history-and-without-future can be thought of as a kind wager on self-sufficiency, a bet that (somehow) sufficient understanding for our survival in the face of systemic adversity and challenges to the adequacies of our steering mechanisms can be generated, even guaranteed, out of the experience that arises from our positioning at this "edge" of history. Were it made fully conscious we could call it a wager on the possibility of discounting both past and future so that every scintilla of attention is focused on the moment, and it is out of this moment that a culture sufficient to carry us happily into the future can be created.

At least we might say this, if we did not know that it was not true. Yet in a certain way this wager becomes true through behavior, that is, it becomes true as failure. In effect we act as if this were the case. But when we look around we see that lack of history, lack of the future (meaning blindness to both) inhibits action in design no less than social action. Two symptoms of this—the absence of history in the recent understanding of design, and architecture's problem with its "lightness of being"—are sufficient to reveal the scale of the problem.

(i) First symptom: The absence of history in the understanding of design

When the study of design and its capabilities and its prospects emerged in its contemporary forms between the 1950s and 1980s it was axiomatic that at least one of its pillars, and by no means the least, was history. The sense of design as a historically specific practice—in terms of the forms it took, the mentalities that dominated it at any moment and even the capabilities foregrounded, was taken for granted not only in the history of design but also in earlier, seemingly more technical, studies of design methods. J. C. Jones's *Design Methods* (1970) only makes sense as *also* a work of history—or at least as a work informed by a sense of historical trajectory.[55] A not dissimilar understanding underlay the successive projects of Christopher Alexander—if now as in reaction to what he perceived as the historical logic of broken modernity which had become disengaged from the historical conditions of dwelling. From a different but comparable perspective this was also a period when any serious exhibition on design would axiomatically be thought of in terms of the lineage of its historical and social evolution—see for example the superb, and by the standards of today, astonishingly intelligent, catalogue that was produced by MOMA (Museum of Modern Art) for Emilio Ambasz's exhibition on Italian Design (*Italy: The New Domestic Landscape: Achievements Problems and of Italian Design, 1972*).

Part of the reason for the internalization of historical understanding was that this was a period when it was (rightly) felt impossible to distinguish design as we are now experiencing it, design in its modern professional and consumerist aspects, from specifically *capitalist* as well as wider industrial or technological developments. The common axiomatic of works as diverse as Manfredo Tafuri's *Architecture and Utopia: Design and Capitalist Development* of 1976,[56] the essays in Jean Baudrillard's still under-read little volume *For a Critique of the Political Economy of the Sign* dating from the 1960s,[57] or the case studies explored in Adrian Forty's *Objects of Desire* (published 1986)[58] was that the *depth* understanding of design (at least in the forms that it was manifesting in the late twentieth century) was impossible without being thought *simultaneously* within the perspectives of history and capitalism.

From radically different standpoints, each of these works—and this applies also to Jones and Alexander—understood design as a practice both revealed *and concealed* by this conjunction. Each understood that this dialectic is inescapable; that it would be naïvety of a high order to assume that in any practice that goes by the name "design" (whether self-attributed or assigned) design in its entirety is therefore revealed. Any *one* mode of practice of design is, at best, merely that; it has no necessary ontological priority.

This historical and *situated* understanding of design was capable of grasping that every mode of designing that becomes visible as such (i.e., becomes established as a procedure complete with its own methods, values and institutions) *reveals* certain aspects of the agency and capabilities of what we call design. But what reveals also conceals (sometimes consciously, think of the attempt to suppress what we might call social modernism by free-enterprise's "new urbanism"). In any set of shifting parameters of design practices, other modes, other possibilities of designing, other ways of practicing, conceiving, thinking the activity, disappear. Since we are implicated in history and cannot stand outside it, no ahistorical sense of design is wholly possible. What was comprehended here is that any *one* mode of practice of design—say, that which we receive and encounter today—is, at best, merely that; that it has no *necessary* ontological priority; what we attribute to design will inevitably be colored by the limitations and possibilities of the situations we inhabit.

Today, almost none of this depth understanding remains. History has all but disappeared from *thinking* design, and certainly from "design research"—which today acts as if it is in a permanent state of forgetfulness about what actually constitutes and forms "design" historically as we receive it (the forces, powers and relations determining it). There are reasons for this disappearance. Not least is the wider sense, post-1989, inculcated even within universities, of the "end of history". The rise of design in the universities is the second factor—particularly the quasi-objectification of design studies and specifically its aspiration, as "research" towards quasi-scientific or technical models of research. The creation of programs of design research has led to an emphasis, even in doctoral study, of work that is in general grounded less on the depth-understanding and articulation of design per se and more on the definition of (and superficial "solution" of) "design problems"—problems which are seen almost entirely without historical context. From this perspective, careful reflection upon design, reflection that would essentially require historical comprehension, has no necessity, it would merely complicate matters, "slow down" the attainment of the PhD—and add dimensions of thought to the research which, frankly, most doctorial supervisors in departments of design would find all but impossible to deal with. The result is that in the vast majority of design research the capabilities of design are understood *essentially* ahistorically.

But the cavalier disregard for how design is constituted and formed within historical circumstance by design research has its echo in the double disdain for the relation to practice and for *thinking* design analytically manifest by design history. The gradual ossification of the field as an academic discipline has stripped it of most of its claims to intellectual force. The reduction of history to trade and to versions of antiquarianism and collectorship—which come together in the museum show, now planned carefully in terms of the audiences "take away," but which is by no means the same thing as offering depth understanding of either history or of design—works to decry the necessity of historical understanding in reflection. What is worse is that in the same moment it gives research the perfect alibi to dispense with comprehending design in its historical and constitutive context.[59]

What replaces historical understanding is a triumphal mixture of myth and banality. Consider, for example, the opening paragraphs of the "Series Foreword" by the editors of a recent series of books on design thinking offered by a respectable American university press:

As professions go, design is relatively young. But the practice of design predates professions. In fact the practice of design—making things to serve a useful goal, making tools—predates the human race. Making tools is one of the attributes that made us human in the first place. Design in the most generic sense of the word, began 2.5 million years ago when Homo habilis manufactured the first tools. Human beings were designing well before we began to walk upright. Four hundred thousand years ago, we began to manufacture spears. By forty thousand years ago we had moved onto specialist tools. Urban design and architecture came along ten thousand years ago in Mesopotamia. Interior architecture and furniture probably emerged with them. It was another five thousand years before graphic design and typography got their start in Sumeria with the development of cuneiform. After that, things picked up speed.[60]

That this is neither scientifically nor hermeneutically sufficient is obvious to a moment's reflection. The view that the current manifestations of "Design" are the *natural* teleological outcomes of early hominid tool-making would be risible if, in this climate, it did not have many who will take it a face value—and happily conclude that the "end" of the proto-human and the human coming to consciousness through making and reflecting really is the design professions as we receive them today. But the model is not even historically accurate. As the metallurgist Cyril Stanley Smith never tired of pointing out, no warranty exists for the privilege given to tools as against what we would have to call today decoration or adornment or the making of weapons or symbol formation or the slowly emerging adaptation of nature.[61]

As history is rendered trite so too is understanding; historically banal, such triumphalist readings are at the same time naïve theoretically. The consequence of design being simultaneously extended to everything is that it is reduced to the manifestation of what it currently is. Worse, conflated with making per se it becomes all but impossible to identify what belongs specifically to it. The work of the intentional configuration of things for complex ends (which do not lend themselves without resistance to singular quasi-functional "explanations") is only obscured and made all but impossible to recover when history is flattened in this way.[62]

Conversely, the understanding of making, meaning the understanding of what making *makes* and in particular the relation between making and the making (and unmaking) of the subject is equally decimated when "design" is blandly assumed as a singular condition that subsumes the complex interior and mediatory work of the artifact. That formulations of this type can be accepted as the equivalent for adequate understanding speaks volumes concerning the conditions to which we are now succumbing. It tells us that in terms of the understanding of design we are in crisis.

No better however is the understanding of history; meaning no better is the understanding of design thought through history. Many, especially in practice, will presume this does not matter. Technology already seems "outside" of history, except in the sense of a continual accumulation of the *instantly* new that supersedes what has been (that which used to be the prerogative of fashion but which now extends into technology itself—a point already anticipated in the essay on the culture industry in *Dialectic of Enlightenment*).

Equally, no-one thinks of sustainment in terms of history. Yet just here is the real tension revealed. For it is hard to think of another threat to our being that is more rooted in history, *more* a product of our particular history. Unsustainment *is* our history; it is our historical *product*. It follows, though this goes against the grain, that sustainment (which is the simple name we give to the more complex project of creating a world hospitable to say ten billion persons) whether thought as an axiom of practice or as a realized condition to which we are required to aspire, is a project of history. Despite the fact that climate change is nothing other the accumulation of history—is the product of our history—there is a peculiar failure to comprehend not simply the history of unsustainment, but unsustainment *as* history. Design, which eschews the threat of disaster (except vicariously as design for disaster) and domesticates climate change as "thinking green" tries to make palatable what is not. It succeeds only in breeding an ethos of alibi and evasion. What is most germane to what we must understand and contend with—the history of the drives that in their structural and systemic consequence brought us to this point—is effectively obliterated even as it is ritually acknowledged, but thus scarcely comprehended. It is above all in relation to the question of sustainment that the discounting of history and the future—the discounting of the generational weave of the "ancestors and those to come"—becomes an effective discounting of design itself. Design has no purchase if it excludes the temporal. The formula, "Ontology is nothing other than the interpretation of our condition or situation, since Being is nothing apart from its 'event', which occurs when it historicizes itself and when we historicize ourselves,"[63] applies no less to design as a manifestation and externalization of being. Historicize here means "to mediate," not only as the subject vis-à-vis its environment but temporally, between inherited pasts and the futures to come.

Bauhaus design began as anticipation of the future brought into the present as one of its possibilities, as its teleological possibility, its inevitability—why, therefore, not welcome, configure it already into inception? But the closer modernization gets to realization— which, globally is very far away in the 1920s, so much so that it has only mythic reality, hence its compulsion and force in mind—so the gap between the future and design now closes. Design after 1945 becomes, increasingly, about now.[64] Its temporal view shrinks with that of culture, to the point where, by the turn of this century, it participates only in the now and can therefore only endlessly repeat without ever truly advancing in terms of understanding what it is doing. The proof of this is design research.

(ii) Second symptom: Architecture's unbearable lightness of being

If in design history is discounted, elsewhere it is displaced. "The gift of art is the most original gift" says Agamben, because it "allows man to attain his original status in history and time in his encounter with it."[65] But what is originally situated "in a more essential dimension" in which the work interrupts the "homogeneity of profane time" and opens us—throws us—back into what can be felt perceptually as a more original time (time which contains the infinite space of reflection on being) cannot be maintained.

Two impulses shatter this "concrete space of the work." The most immediately obvious, the one that most defines our time, is the detachment that comes from the aesthetic standpoint: "When the work of art is instead offered for aesthetic enjoyment and its formal aspect is appreciated and analysed . . . the origin that gives itself in the work of art and remains reserved in it"[66] ceases to be visible. The impulse to "free the work" from its dependence on the Mythic context, loses the original *ek-stasis* but substitutes for this the play of form and thus displaces ecstasy in favor of contemplative detachment. This detachment however, which is translated into aesthetics, and later into ideologies of professional autonomy, erases the prior understanding, "the engagement that keeps man in the truth and grants to his dwelling on earth its original status").[67]

"Aesthetics, then," says Agamben, "is unable to think of art according to its proper statute, and so long as man is prisoner of an aesthetic perspective, the essence of art remains closed to him."

Aesthetics cannot think this essence because it is in itself displacement (it is precisely as a series of *displacements* that we can best grasp Kant's *Critique of Judgment*). Aesthetics cannot think this because it loses, as the work itself loses, even deliberately, the original experience. Thus both "the engagement that keeps him in the truth and grants to his dwelling on earth its original status" and "the space in which once man's action and the world found their reality in the image of the divine, in which man's dwelling on earth used to take its diametrical measurement"[68] disappears, both in actuality and in thought. This is the victory of modern aesthetics, and it is, as we know, comprehensive.

In design, this is seen nowhere more sharply than in contemporary building. Architecture in the present is more configuratively emancipated—or at least is permitted a greater degree of formal play—than at any time in the recent past. Seemingly (if not in truth) unhampered by necessity, it appears to have achieved an enviable condition of weightlessness and artless freedom, one that belies the necessity of anything that might tie down the formal imagination.

Yet outside of Italo Calvino—who famously placed lightness as the first of the virtues for our millennium[69]—others have been less sure. As the title of his most well-known work suggests, *The Unbearable Lightness of Being* is Milan Kundera's understanding of lightness not as a virtue but a threat, not a freeing but its opposite, "a terrifying burden not to be borne another instant." In his novels Kundera's central characters constantly discover that that which holds out the promise of levitating us above the weight of the world (acts subtracted of all relations) turn out to lead to versions of hell. Once our acts have lost all reference, then the true horror is not the heaviness of the deed, but "the absence of weight" in everything we do.[70]

If we look no further than at the contrasting fates of Daniel Libeskind in Berlin (1989—the Jewish Museum) and Daniel Libeskind in New York (the Freedom Tower) we can see that this notion of a lightness of emancipated formal play is somewhat illusory. Where it matters—in 98 percent of building—the rubric of economics (or what comes to the same thing, convention) holds. Formal invention is sanctioned in almost exact proportion to the social, economic and political inconsequentially of the project.[71] Today, it often announces n othing more than "culture" in the high sense: all opera houses are sensational in aspect, all new museums dramatic in their exterior (the latter precisely in order to mask the paucity of contents within). Meanwhile the median quality of the built world, as with the physical environment in general, shrivels in line with the more general destitution of the public domain.

In any case, what is vaunted and presented as dramatic formal invention is often nothing other than a mixture of what technical software now permits and the projection of the ego-without-judgment, encouraged by those who see spectacle as a source of additional rents—why else would an architect of Renzo Piano's sometime intelligence and sensitivity connect himself to the banality of the Shard, for example?[72] Once, however, it runs against the former's limits and the latter's insistence on added value, imagination in this tenor has nowhere else to go. Lacking a deeper ethic, and without the succour of building to draw upon, it retreats rapidly into sensation.[73]

Outside of architecture, the public is growing as tired of gesture without substance as it is with instrumental maximization of floor plans dressed up as the "spirit of the age." The Bund remains the most genuinely modern moment in Shanghai. The rest convinces no-one; we merely agree to make use of what we are provided with, and grow immune to the oscillation between the scenography and instrumentalism (as the experience when, directed to the bathrooms in such buildings, one is suddenly propelled outside the fantasy of the restaurant and one encounters in the back corridor the unscripted utilitarianism of the toilets, the latter, one concludes, slightly less hard-faced than the former). All this suggests, not an excess of invention but its lack. And it points, as well, both to underlying fragility in the contemporary bubble of architecture, and a visible cleavage in building and making— first, between the vaunted "creativity" of representational software and the realities of the act of building; second between architecture conceived as the "free exercise" of art and poetry or poetics conceived as "the very name of man's doing."

We can trace here the inimical effects of a division of labor that might once have held significance (the struggle to create an autonomous profession and discipline) but which now tends to condemn architecture to a caricature of its origins. Paid for by marginality, on the one side architectural poetics is traduced by economics (which mocks it for not being able to supply the same mathematical ratios and certainties that the latter can now offer to manage for everything but the economy itself) while on the other formal invention traverses (and trumps) the contexts of building. But although architecture in these modes sails beyond the contexts of building—any of the other "prosaic" contents that might ground its act other than in whim or force—because it cannot identify with these and therefore cannot take them into itself, it empties itself of all content.[74] It loses its ontological bearings, and with it cultural resonance beyond the superficial attempt to awe.[75]

Thus just as today we sense that in art the ultimate truth of the work that is given to us is really nothing other than an insistent demonstration of the ability of "the free subjectivity of the artistic principle" to operate independent of, and in the absence of, content, so the same condition spreads to building and architecture comes close to what Agamben tells us that art already is—"a self-annihilating nothing."[76] Precisely because so much of this work *is* nothing, deserving of little but contempt, it might be thought scarcely to matter. The reverse however is the case.

Artistic subjectivity without content is the pure force of negation that everywhere and at all times affirms only itself as absolute freedom that mirrors itself in pure self-consciousness. And, just as every content goes under in it, so . . . the concrete space of the work disappears in it, the space in which . . . man's dwelling on earth used to take its diametrical measurement.[77]

The point then is that the collapse of the ability to measure—or to think "dwelling" except in ways that hand it to the theologians—is the collapse of being able to think, well, our inhabitation of the world.[78] Yet the notion of actively—i.e., operatively, *transitively*—"building a world for man's dwelling on earth" captures the ontological dimension of poiesis *not* as nostalgia but as the prefigurative and the propositional and thus as the *discovery* of what might be possible within the open of what, qualitatively, the future can be.[79]

Rescuing measure, rescuing the future

In an age where we are told that the *qualitative* transformation of the world is impossible; that anything other than the extrapolation of what, politically, economically and technologically—*is*, cannot be considered, it is necessary to insist on how radical as well as necessary is the proposition of poiesis as that action which offers the discovery of what may be possible for the future. Of course we permit action-as-*will*, especially in the form of the drive (to which we are almost pathologically addicted).[80] But will is always *within* the logic of what is already dominant, even if it is the will to realize what is most extreme,[81] and even if it is self-destructive in its consequences. What is forbidden then is not will, but, in effect, any conception (and any practice) of the fundamental *reconfiguration*, the qualitative transformation,[82] of what-is—particularly, but by no means only, in the economic and political sphere. What purely formal possibility represses, therefore and often viciously, is production as the revealing into presence or becoming of the possible *actuality* of the substantive qualitatively other—a revealing which, because it is revealing directly of our potential status on earth, cannot be untied from ontological, political and ethical reflection of who and how we are and might be.[83] Formalism, therefore, is *the effective repression of the exploration of what is qualitatively possible*—that today we require in order to stave off destitution and to induce at least the possibility of a hospitable world. In this respect, the loss of poiesis in the strong Agambean sense—which is also the loss of dwelling, the loss of "the concrete space of the work" and the loss of the sense of "production into ethical presence"—is serious, above all in respect to the public realm, which acts as the bellwether indicator of how practice thinks about the social present and its possible futures.

Let me give two instances.

The first is the direct reproduction of the third of Gui Bonsiepe's "Virtues of Design." It is quoted here both for its prescience (it was drafted more 20 years ago, but is today more true than ever) and because it points to the kind of concrete content so eschewed by the architecture of spectacle.

Virtue 3 – Public Domain: The Netherlands possesses a great tradition in civic virtues that manifests itself in the care for the public domain.

A foreigner visiting the Netherlands is struck by the attention given to detail in such simple everyday objects as an address label for post parcels or a timetable for trains. Moreover he is struck by the apparent *Selbstverstandlichkeit* with which caring for the public domain is taken for granted and considered one of the noble tasks and outright obligations of public administration. This care for details and quality of public service is a result of a political commitment that might be traced back to the civic history of the Netherlands. Certainly it is not the result of a single short-term action, but rather the outcome of a steady practice rooted in the political body of Dutch society. Politics is the domain in which the members of a society decide in what kind of society they want to live. Politics therefore goes far beyond political parties. Care for the public domain, though a profoundly political commitment is at the same time trans-political insofar it exceeds—or better should exceed—the interests of the government in turn.

As the third design virtue in the future I would like to see maintained the Concern for the Public Domain, and this all the more so when registering the almost delirious onslaught on everything public that seems to be a generalized credo of the dominant economic paradigm. One does well to recall that the socially devastating effects of unrestricted private interests have to be counterbalanced by public interests in any society that claims to be called democratic and that deserves that label. The tendency towards Third-Worldization even of richer economies, with a programmatic binary system of a small group of haves and a majority of excluded have-nots, is a phenomenon that casts shadows on the future and raises some doubts about the reason in the brains of the people that find utter wisdom and desirability in such a delacerating scheme of social organisation.[84]

The second tells a small story.

There is a bridge in Miami, on Northwest 27th Avenue. At its opening in 1939, after its expansion in 1938–9 as part of the New Deal, H. A. Wortham, regional director of the Public Works Administration, dedicated the newly inaugurated bridge "to the construction of good for mankind." An artist comments, in relation to a contemporary exhibit that utilizes some surviving fragments of the bridge,

> this simple phrasing … served to convert an act of labor (i.e. construction) and a product of labor (i.e. a bridge) into philosophical

and moral precepts. The structure itself now stands as a monument to that moment in time when good design and public works were equated with the general welfare of a people, a society, and a nation itself.[85]

Though it is easy to mock, Wortham's phrase nonetheless conveys a respect for and an interest in the public domain, in its future, and in what we can only call the "sovereignty of the good"[86] that is today sorely lacking. Disavowal of what is at best implied here misses the point that it is precisely in the *attempt* to make this kind of extraordinary translation—of matter into ethics through space and technics—that architecture potentially lives as other than superficiality. Architecture on this reading should therefore be something like the discovery of hitherto unknown or unforeseen possibilities for conditions of dwelling. Poetics enters this process, via design not as formalism but as agency of transformation and transmutation.[87]

The term *discovery* in this context is significant. Architecture tends, almost endemically, to be constantly reductive of discovery to formal invention and to seek to own it wholly in these terms. In his short work *The Art of the Novel* Milan Kundera recovers discovery as ethics; that the work of the novel is to protect against the "forgetting of being." Kundera insists that this task is to be undertaken *not* by remembering or recalling this-or-that moment of existent being, but by *discovering* new forms or ways of being and acting: "the sole raison d'être of a novel is to discover what only the novel can discover. A novel that does not discover a hitherto unknown segment of existence is immoral. Knowledge is the novel's only morality."[88] And Kundera adds, later in the same book: "a novel examines not reality but existence. And existence is not what has occurred; existence is the realm of human possibilities, everything that man can become, everything that he's capable of. Novelists draw up *the map of existence* by discovering this or that human possibility."[89]

In Kundera's understanding, the poetics of discovery is thus irredeemably an ethical act. What are discovered, what are revealed, are substantive constitutive possibilities of existence. If we translate them into the language of building, this means hitherto unknown or unforeseen possibilities for conditions of dwelling. Discovery in this sense seems very close to the speculative and exploratory structure of design. To link this back to the engagement with Agamben's insights we can say that the essential character of the work undertaken in these modes is not praxis thought as will, but poiesis understood as a process or mode of *unveiling*.[90] The work unveils what is possible, and it does so through the complex inventive configurative negotiation with the circumstances that bears upon it. That poiesis is located here (and not in the mere immediate expression of an act as in praxis or will) means that the act of unveiling that produces the work situates it in a very particular dimension of being, very close to what Agamben earlier called the space of our "authentic temporal dimension"; the "dimension in which the very structure of man's being-in-the-world and his relation with truth and history are at stake."[91] It is because the work (potentially) opens this dimension that poiesis or the poetic can also be that which gives the measure.

Measure in this qualitative and political sense is the very essence of the work of thinking futurally. It is, after all, in the name of *measureless* necessity that social transformation is declared impossible. Put another way, the "certainty" of what-is as to its necessity, occurs in part, perhaps in very large part, through how it resists measure—not least by forcing the change that does occur into substitutions that bolster its own force. Measuring is here a breaking of the "holding hostage" that errant power achieves. Politics is the act of giving visible measure to, and thus taking a distance on, the "errant, unassignable, invisible excess" of immeasurable necessity—whether this is of the State (as in classical political theory) or more generally as the unsustainability of the global liberal economy. Looked at from this viewpoint, "What-is" can therefore be seen not just as existence but as the "measureless enslavement of … the situation"[92] by what assigns itself power and necessity. By contrast, to grasp the situation in the sense of grasping it in terms of the possibility of change—the very essence of design's work—is therefore to give measure to the situation. To put this slightly differently, design which takes the measure of both the forces and the potential of the situation with a view to their transformation ("changing existing situations to preferred ones") is axiomatically a matter of qualitative measure and on this plane is not dissimilar to politics. This means that design's essential activity is twofold: at once intervention (change) and measure. The depth of the former is directly linked to the depth of the latter. Unhindered from what in times limits it in formal and subaltern ways, design can be understood as a transformational measuring of the conditions and character of our existence—as this is measured, in turn, through the mediating situations that determine how we are able to be.[93]

Thought in these terms, Agamben's phrasing, takes on additional resonance. To adapt his words: "By opening these dimensions of work, the space of design thought in this way opens for us the space of us belonging to the world."

*

We cannot think where we are, we cannot think the transformations that have led us here, we cannot think futurally within frames of thought and practice that eclipse time, if we continue to try to think design only within the corpus and limits of the present, or that of architecture within a scope of practice that seeks to reduce itself to the "lightness" of formal relations evacuated of substantive context.

These symptoms, respectively of generational collapse and the loss of history and of the destructive displacements of the temporal by the formal, indicate the range of the task now given us, the scale of which is given in some lines in the final paragraphs of Agamben's chapter, "The original structure of the work of art."

It is worth quoting these in full; first, because they indicate again what is truly at stake; second, because Agamben's own formulation reveals the limits of art but also both gives the hint towards the place from where we might be able to undo the destructive logic at work here.

> This original structure of the work of art is now obscured. At the extreme point of its metaphysical destiny, art, now a nihilistic power, a "self-annihilating nothing," wanders in the desert of *terra aesthetica* and eternally circles the split that cuts through it. Its alienation is the fundamental alienation, since it points to the alienation of nothing less than ... very space of his world, in which and only in which he can find himself as man and as being capable of action and knowledge. If this is true, when man has lost his poetic status he cannot simply reconstruct his measure elsewhere: "it may be that any other salvation than that which comes from *where the* danger is, is still within non-safety *[Unheil]*."[94]

If salvation must arise from "*where the* danger is" then the task of salvation originates in that which partakes equally of danger and salvation. What partakes in this way is the artificial. The artificial is both the site—the condition—of our being and the possibility of both catastrophe (let us say, of a potential cascade of disasters) and of our "overcoming" of destructiveness (which would in fact never be such). What must now be examined is what the artificial opens towards, at once objectively and *for us*, and the ways in which, in so opening, it perhaps provides us with some crucial resources towards overcoming catastrophe. Everything in regard to the future, depends upon this.

2 THE ARTIFICIAL AND WHAT IT OPENS TOWARDS

I

Thinking the artificial

All societies have a sense of the future. Ours, largely, does not. This immediately suggests the peculiarity of our situation. The break with the previous century in this respect is decisive. Modernity is defined by the creation of the future as compensation for the loss of the organic continuity with the past. After 1900 to design is to design *for* the future, it is to bring the future into being as a contemporary possibility. Politics "worthy of the name" is little different. There too the vision that motivates is on behalf of a future that can be made better than the past. The slogan "from the existing to the preferred situation" becomes a generalized credo. Yet the most memorable cultural statement of the last forty years, The Sex Pistols "No Future!", has none of these connotations, except in absence. summarizes the disappearance of optimism. Since then, not withstanding paid enthusiasms for the virtues of the market or for the everlasting development of new technologies, we have existed in a kind of stasis. The truth is that the future, has for us, disappeared—at least as an affirmative possibility. Despite the almost magical hopes that some vest in Silicon Valley (or in endless economic growth if one is Asian) the future is, for most, that which conjures up an underlying fearfulness about what may be to come. Yet so distant are we from this, so wrapped in the short-term that not even fearfulness is allowed to reach the condition of impelling action.[1]

That we feel our future no longer assured is not surprising. The exponential increase in destructive capacity developed across the seventy or so years up until 1945 (and represented not only by the two world wars but the apparatuses of human desolation perfected in the concentration camps and the gulag) issued in the postwar nuclear stand-off: an intensification of destructive capacity that for almost 45 years threatened possible annihilation on a daily basis. The fall of the Berlin Wall in 1989 did not change things with respect to the future as much as might have been hoped. It did not quite usher in Francis Fukayama's end of history. If the "quick" (atomic) end to history seemed to recede a little with the end of the Cold War, it was replaced, soon after, not only by a succession of economic crises but also by increasing evidence of man-made climate change. The latter, acting at scales that threaten a severe break with patterns of climate, and thus of natural ecology and settlement that we have known as a species since the end of the last ice age, threatens permanent systemic crises. Today, no *serious* person denies climate change. Yet the very lack of action with respect to this threat means that, on the contrary, as the sub-headline of one of the despairing pair of articles already referenced had it, "We will watch the rise in greenhouse gases until it is too late to do anything about it."[2]

Not only the scale of what we are now engaged with warrant pessimism. The real problem lies elsewhere, in our collective compulsive inability *not* to continue to act disastrously with respect to destructiveness, and the equal, perhaps even more abject, inability to act collectively and decisively to deal with these threats.[3] On the one side therefore the drive, unchecked. On the other, "contemporary nihilism"—but, as already suggested, in its prosaic not in a romantic formulation: nihilism not as revolt against what-is but on the contrary as absolute resignation to what-is (so often, today, justified as a virtue) underpinned by "a purely negative, if not destructive, will."[4]

The inability to act collectively to avert system crises is the structural consequence of this fatal combination. But this cannot be achieved by a simple assertion—or by naïve hope. Neither dogmatic assertion of "will"[5] nor "greening" will suffice. No age (and our short industrial-economic epoch constitutes an age) allows itself to be superseded by will. If we are going to attempt to move from the nihilistic despair of self-interest we need a more structural look at the position we now inhabit. In an essay that has more to say about material change than we might imagine from its title, the historian Stephen Yeo reminds us that "to change social relations ... means *to realize them in one of the other forms they make materially possible at any one time*."[6] To grasp what is now possible for us means to begin to understand what is today *objectively* made possible by the emerging determining conditions of our time.

*

To understand fully what is in play here we need to grasp the development of the artificial-as-world in two ways—first as a distinct, and wholly new, development in human history; and second in terms of the characteristics and conditions of the artificial, especially, in this context, in terms of what these both demand of us (as that which we must rise to) and, crucially, what they offer to us as resources vis-à-vis crafting a future or, as we see below, in terms of contending (successfully) with destructiveness.[7]

We can begin initially with the second. The question we are asking overall here (re the future as history) is whether the onset of the artificial gives rise, as was noted above, to the possibility of an entirely different set of relations with nature and with others. To be sure, the onset of the artificial as world is not nirvana. The watershed that we have been passing through in the last seventy years is signified in its beginning in World War II by the development of the capacity to offer wholesale, and in effect species-wide, destruction (the A-bomb, followed *c*.1955 by the H-bomb).[8] As this transition reaches maturity it does so, via its designation as the Anthropocene Age, the epoch (to repeat) in which the scale of man-made actions now have consequential and probably irreversible impact on the largest natural systems.

Needless to say, in its first instance these impacts (at least from our own perspective)[9] are wholly destructive—at least in terms of the range of climatic variation that human beings have settled to since the end of the last ice age. In that sense Kristeva is right, deploying artifice at ever new levels of scale and impact, we have not only increased exponentially human destructive capacity but seemingly internalized destructiveness as our way of being in the world—and we should add, at the moment our *only* way of being in the world:

> We, as civilizations, we know not only that we are mortal ... we also know that we can inflict death upon ourselves. Auschwitz and Hiroshima have revealed that the "malady of death" as Marguerite Duras might say, informs our most concealed inner recesses ... a passion for death, the latter has been revealed to rule even the once noble kingdom of the spirit. A tremendous crisis has emerged ... never

has the power of destructive forces appeared as unquestionable and unavoidable as now, within and without society and the individual.[10]

The onset of the artificial as the effective horizon for human beings therefore *first of all* marks the transition to a global political and technological economy in which destructive capacity is externalized and internalized in acute form—at extreme as defuturing. Defuturing is the paradoxical condition in which even that which is most certain (that there *will* be a future) becomes placed in doubt. Defuturing (and with it the concomitant requirement that we begin, urgently, to *cultivate* the future into being) is an inescapable condition of our time.

Were this everything then the "danger" (as Heidegger would say) would be acute. Indeed it *is* acute, but it is, fortunately, not all. The artificial as the horizon and medium of existence is *also* the onset of conditions whose objective characteristics and potentials are quite other than those of the era of domination that we are now, albeit with extreme difficulty, leaving behind. The artificial, in other words, is not *only* the continuation and intensification of the technological. It is *also* the setting into being of qualitatively different modes of becoming. Thus while on the one hand we continue to reap the implications of our inability to deal with or contend adequately with the consequences of acute expropriation (and with the violence that inevitably accompanies and determines this) on the other we also find ourselves in a world where the objective dynamics that are now emerging potentially work in quite different ways. Part of our current task is to begin to perceive these dynamics, which are obscured for us, not least by our inherited modes of knowing, even those of the recent past, which work against comprehending the dynamics of the artificial. The requisite initial recognition is that the artificial sets into being

1 a different logic of becoming (emergence, the proposition)

2 a different understanding of what-is (from being to becoming; from what-is to the possible)

3 a different comprehension of truth (from correspondence to possibility).

It is on this basis that we can turn to grasping the artificial as a distinct and wholly new development in human history—and as a new form of dependency, since from our original dependency on nature we have arrived at a dependency no less ambiguous in regard to the artificial.

Hegel notes at one point that human beings repress acknowledgement of that on which they most depend. Part of our intellectual task is to accept and think this new dependence. Our success (or failure) in so doing will be the index of our maturity vis-à-vis our own making. "Contending adequately with what we have made" means the responsibility of dealing with the artificial in regard to all other living systems. Precisely because the artificial is ours, and precisely because the scale of human impact of the world-as-artificial is such, then "dependency" means here thinking consequentially concerning all that sustains. It is also therefore to step back from the egocentric into the web of that through which (and only through which) we are able to be. As we shall see later, that which arises out of our compulsion cannot be thought from within the terms of that compulsion.

But the converse is also true, precisely because what changes for us in all this are the fundamental conditions of our *becoming*—i.e., the conditions of our possibility (Bauman) then our *affirmative* task is to grasp the implications of these changes—and above all to learn how to translate what they offer as resource into viable action that can secure a humane future. "The simple fact of one's own existence as possibility,"[11] thought as the "essence" of the human, places the ethical demand upon us to think and act in terms of our potentiality. The specific ethical demand the artificial makes here is that this possibility is thought in relation to what the world-as-artificial opens to us as possibilities. Possibility here means the qualitatively possible. It is the negotiation with actuality and not the escalation of what-is. To be absolutely clear on this, possibility or potentiality is *not* the free space of what is free. Possibility or potentiality is possibility *within* the ambit of the possible, this means within the ambit and web of what makes possibility possible. Possibility is the exploration or discovery of what possibility can be in actuality, i.e., in negotiation with the material and other conditions of existence in relation to which we exist. Since all human possibility is today conducted through the mediation of artifice, be it actualized as an artifact, considered in relation to nature or in terms of symbolic thought, language or representation, then all possibility is negotiation with the possible through the artificial, just as it is also negotiation through the conditions of natural existence.

But if we can learn to think possibility in this way then it perhaps means that we can at last begin to think past the tendency escalation/disaster. To think possibility in this relational, manner is *perhaps* to be able to posit the means of an "overcoming" of the tendency towards destructiveness. This possibility installs a requirement on us to understand that the artificial as the horizon and medium of existence is *also* the onset of conditions whose objective characteristics and potentials are quite other than those of the era of domination that we are now, albeit with extreme difficulty, leaving behind. To repeat, the artificial is not *only* the continuation and intensification of the technological (in its most expanded sense). It is *also* the setting into being of qualitatively different modes of becoming. Thus, while on the one hand we continue to reap the implications of our inability to deal with or contend adequately with the consequences of acute expropriation (and with the violence that inevitably accompanies and determines this) on the other we also find ourselves in a world whose emerging objective dynamics potentially work in quite different ways and which perhaps offer us new resources for becoming otherwise.

We cannot yet think this, and this is a major source of our unhappiness. The abject capitulation to what-is is maintained by our inability to grasp what is emerging. On one side, because we cannot think the determining condition of our time we are unable to think what determines us. This means we mistake continually how we act and fail to act because we fail to see what is now determining action. On the other, because we cannot think the resources the artificial offers we cannot think *past* the present.[12] Not to be able to think what-is emerging therefore renders impossible any *real* affirmative apprehension of the future.

Part of our current task is to begin to perceive these dynamics. We can proceed in two ways. First, by considering the artificial as a structurally and qualitatively new historical condition; second by examining some aspects of what the artificial opens towards, especially vis-à-vis the destructiveness of what is.

The artificial as a qualitatively new historical condition

The easiest way to grasp what is involved in the artificial, not just as continuation of what is but as the emergence of a new historical condition, is to consider the three diagrams, Figures 1, 2, and 3. Crude to the point of absurdity, their value is not, for all that, negligible. Taken together they map the place and condition of the artificial in three human periods: in the long era defined essentially by hand-labor (from the beginnings of hominid development to around 1800); in what we can now see as the transitional moment of the industrial revolution 1800–2000; and in the era that we are now entering into, that of the artificial-as-world. This era opens a new epoch for humans, and one that is essentially unsurpassable.

For reasons of space I will say relatively little about the first two.

In the first, artifice (represented by the gray dot) is central but limited. It is central because there can be no human becoming without artifice; artifice is the realm of the revealing to humans of what they and the world might be. But under the conditions of (hand)labor artifice is always difficult, always limited. Labor is hard, things are scarce—Shakespeare's "second-best bed." The formula is: things are crucial, but except in certain

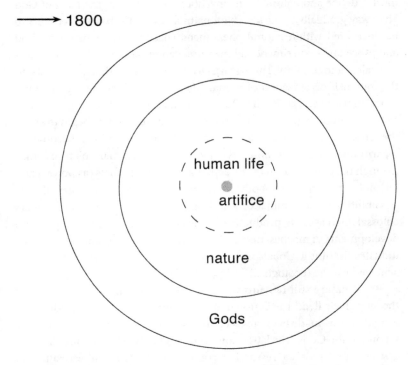

FIGURE 1 Artifice and the artificial across human history down to the industrial revolution.

instances, *comparatively* rare.[13] We forget too easily the degree of difficulty of handwork—of making a plane surface, say. We underestimate the effort involved. Hence while the artificial, or at least instances of it, may well be all the more valued (conceived as formative) it can itself easily seem as nothing against the immensity of nature and the universe, to say nothing of fate. (Except in defined locations the ability to have consequent, and other than local, effect on nature is limited—the horse-drawn plough cuts less than three inches.)[14]

Thus notwithstanding that our relation with artifice is how we become human—and not displacing that other moment of the artificial, language and all that accrues to it, in this era, attention was bound to be therefore not on artifacture but on the vagaries of chance. Here is the invention of the gods and the attempts to access fate by determining and obeying Law, first those of the Gods, (and their representatives on earth) later those of nature. To be within the Law is both the secret of happiness and the source of power, mortal, divine and natural.[15] The invention of the Law or the Laws of God gives way, gradually, to the search for natural law, for the basis of certainty to be uncovered within natural phenomena (Bacon) from whence method and procedure (experiment and measure) can make of these laws the basis of a calculable certainty. This in turns leads—or it is felt that it can lead—to the "rational" organization of human affairs, especially in production and (scientific) knowledge. By the 18th century all this is in place.[16]

The second diagram—which pictures what we can now begin to see as the short, transitional, era of industrialization—artifice becomes a logarithmic spiral of continuous expansion. The summary picture is this: through the combination of the exploitation of fossil fuels (as power) and technology-as-method—both set in motion by the perception of new possibilities for accumulation—industrialization ("machination") offers colossal increases in productive capacity. By 1917 Fordism opens up developments in machination and mass production that, after 1945, make industrialization a global phenomenon—albeit in the form of stability achieved via the (ecological) "using-up" of what-is.

But if nature still remains the ultimate horizon, in Nietzsche's terms the "gods have fled." The fiction that law springs from supra-worldly what is made is not-made becomes seen for what it is, first in relation to kings, second to the Gods. The latter now command only religion. But scientific law and its models ("research") command mentality. It was after all representation, procedure, method, organization and (embryonic) mechanization, developed in Europe from the 15th century onwards,[17]

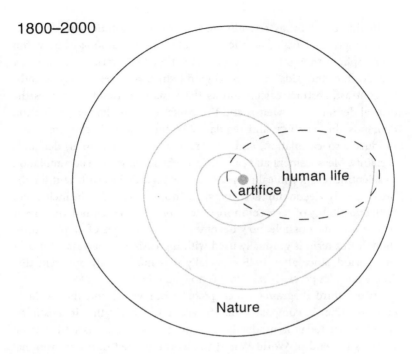

1800–2000

FIGURE 2 The expansion of artifice and the artificial in the short epoch of industrialization 1800–2000.

which set the stage for the organizational and methodological conditions of existence for European industrialization proper—which takes off when to these are added the energy gained from burning fossil fuels. It is the latter, first as steam power, then as electricity and the internal combustion engine, which permits, for the first time, a genuine ease of production, *ease* meaning here also that the domination of nature now becomes so complete that nature is scarcely any longer a resistant factor. The domination promised in the Bible is now realized (and superficially it appears as if it is so without anxiety, so completely does technology and the mechanization of agriculture appear to subdue it).[18] This domination extends to persons and territories. Through the focused violence that now becomes possible in the mid- to late-19th century, then by 1914 the world is in effect a European plantation. This gives rise to resistance, first as labor, then by the colonized, but not until after 1945 (with the exception of the USSR) do either truly enter into politics.

In this era, Law, as scientific law, becomes institutionalized and is increasingly the basis of practice, not only within technology but within every sphere thought capable of adaptation to "metrics." Thus, while the "death of the gods" reduces religion (which survives merely as faith) by contrast, abstract calculation as the basis of certainty becomes the central definition of what-is and the arbiter of truth. Just as production demands the passivity and regularity of the objects it consumes and produces, so calculation, and the organization based on it, demands certainty. Measurement and calculation, which spans from accumulation to scientific and technical projects, is now regarded as sufficient for the organization of economic activity, which in any case, under the incitement of the possibility of scales of more or less *continuous* accumulation never before thought possible, now becomes the entire basis of civilization—though this term is gradually used with increasing embarrassment over this period, since after 1945 especially it is increasingly apparent that "civilization" is precisely *not* what is now on offer.[19]

In the third diagram—which pictures our world and the world to come—artifice encompasses all. The accurate term is that it *constitutes* world. What today is gradually becoming apparent to us is that from towards the end of World War II the world entered into a transitional phase in which industrialization becomes global, and what we can call the "incomplete" artificial world of the early 20th century transmutes into the condition we are now beginning to experience; i.e., where the artificial, and no longer nature, constitutes the horizon, medium and determining condition of the world. This is the artificial as the *effective* totality.[20]

The historical markers at either end of the transition are destructive (the A-bomb; the acceptance of global warming, the definition of ours as the "anthropocene" age and the onset of permanent financial crisis) but the new conditions opened by the artificial-as-world are by no means only so.

In retrospect we can see the transition to the artificial as having two stages. The first half is in effect the "completion" of industrialization—i.e., industrialization as a social-democratic (in the US "mass") civilization, the only global period it should be noted where indeed there was the allowance of a democracy that was not simply to be identified with the market—and the only point in history where equality for all was seriously placed on the political agenda.

This thirty-year window comes to end around 1973–74. What follows is the social violence of neoliberalism coexisting with what artifice is

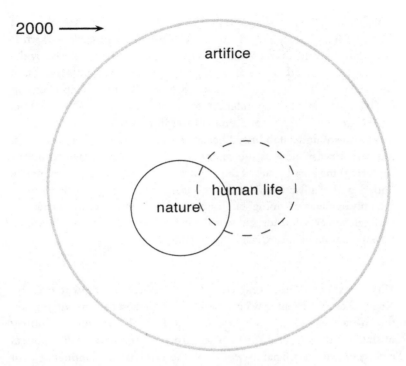

FIGURE 3 The artificial constituting "world" 2000.

setting in train. This violence is the transition out of industrialization, which emphatically does away with the older idea of "labour reaching metaphysical rank" (Heidegger).[21] Production is now farmed out to the cheapest bidder. This sets the stage for the dominant financial-service economy. The latter draws upon digital technology to organize itself on a global basis. But as technology integrates the previously *relatively* disparate zones of technological systems, symbol production and nature-become-artifice, so artifice totalizes, becomes world and intensifies its impact on natural systems—which now act the "return of the repressed."

Tensions over these natural reactions and their consequences defines the politics of what is to come, the only likely certainty of which is even further intensification of inequality.[22] But the world-as-artificial throws up other implications by no means so in line with "the economic appropriation of what is most blind in technics."[23] The artificial in dominance instantiates a different logic of becoming, and thus a different understanding of what-is: emergence, the proposition and the possible, replace being, the actual and what-is. The Real, for so long the object of desire both scientifically and culturally cedes to the possible—which is now *objectively* the deep condition of our time. Similarly, replaced by the speculative structure of the artificial, Law gives way to contingency and configuration. The absolute is bracketed, and a different comprehension of truth—from correspondence to possibility—begins to obtain. Artifacture, under these conditions, moves from instrumentality (means) to a means of understanding; it becomes an instrument of knowledge in a different sense, now as the central means of grasping (which means exploring) the possibilities of the artificial (which by definition cannot be understood in advance). Ethically, this is the exploration of artefacture as not only as an act of "doing" but the agency of attuning complex relations between subjects, artifice and world/earth.[24] It is also the work by which *perhaps* a humane future can be brought into being.

*

This transition is not complete—nor by definition could it ever be. Nonetheless, sufficient may have been said to suggest that the supposition that we are entering into a new historical epoch may not be entirely mistaken. In any case, distinct perhaps from the argument over historical emergence, the artificial-as-world, or the artificial in dominance as it were, sets in being other emphases or conditions or possibilities for acting. It is to the (over-brief) examination of these that we should now turn.

II

What the artificial opens towards/ overcoming destructiveness

The full elucidation of what the artificial opens towards requires more deliberation than can be compressed into a single essay. Here, just six sets of attributes or affordances will be briefly examined. Yet even at this level, the degree to which these developments or emphases offer challenges to how we have considered the world will become clear. Each offers, potentially, radically new spheres of operation. Of course the form that the artificial will take is by definition incomplete. Yet if the artificial cannot be known as such, its outlines, or at least some of its salient aspects, are already visible. take out this sentence. They are by no means definitive, tendencies more than literal fact, indications or implications rather than direct recipes for action. Nonetheless they are not irrelevant to noting necessary directions for thought and action across the next decades. There is nothing "utopic" proposed in these developments. If the artificial contains or offers opportunity it is as such, and it is not without ambiguity. In any case, destructiveness shadows the artificial as its *permanent* accompaniment.[25] This alone puts the demand that the issues opened here should also be read in relation to their potential (if any) for contending with destructiveness. Six issues will be cursorily examined, they concern Law (and its absence, but also its opposite, the configurative, and the question of propositions and possibility); mediation and negotiation; the "going beyond" of technology; the problem of will and its overcoming; the question of nihilism as the proscription of possibility; and finally the situation as the site, simultaneously, of ethics, design and politics.

Issue 1—No law, the propositional, the possible

Much was made, in talking about the "stages" of the artificial across human history, of the role of law. Given the manifest indifference of nature to our fate it was natural (or at least, so we say) that in early human epochs we would seek both to personify fate and to attempt to formulate laws that explained and accounted for fate. As this gradually transforms into seeking to grasp the nature of what-is, it becomes equally natural (or so we say) to seek not only for God's law but for the laws of nature, and thus that the realm of laws that effectively connect life to what is enduring should be valued over mere realms of appearance. Even as the more theological aspects of this projection lose force under the pressure of the rise of science, the latter, we saw, provides compensatory logic for the relevance of law—in that, as Francis Bacon intimated, it is precisely access to natural law that gives us the knowledge to create instruments of power beyond those gained by empirical experience alone. And Heidegger, too, has maintained that law is the very subject of experimental science; that one experiments (in the modern sense) in order to prove law, to prove that which is the case (and that which is not).[26] Law, then, is central to the modern project for on it depends the certainty of things in their condition of objective measurability.

But when we turn to the artificial we find a peculiarity. The prime condition of the artificial is not that things "are," but that they could be other. In the artificial there is no absolute "what-is." It follows then that in the artificial there is no Law as such in the absolute sense. Since this statement seems at first sight absurd, let me explain.

Previously, it seemed possible that law as scientific laws could determine, wholly, artifice—thus giving the artificial something of the authority of the given (making artifice an objective fact).[27] But in fact, as we pursue this we see that, in artifice, no law is ultimately possible. Obscured both ideologically and practically under the view of technology in the narrow sense, this fact becomes evident once the artificial becomes world. To be sure, as Simon pointed out, "those things we call artefacts are not apart from nature. They have no dispensation to ignore or violate natural law."[28] But this is to incompletely state the matter. That which cannot ignore or violate natural law nonetheless cannot, *in its configuration, be subject to law*. Consider, as an instance, half-a-dozen chairs of different configurations. While each may obey, in detail, the natural laws appertaining to the forming of timber or the bending of metal, *in their configuration* they obey no law. Plato's rhetoric in this instance is confounded. No ideal chair exists. In artifice there are only chair*s*.

The instance might be thought to be trivial. It is not. It reflects the general truth that the artificial does not know law but *only* instances and possibility. In the artificial, the real is wholly contingent. In a sense, there is *only* semblance, the "real" is not. There are no "things-in-themselves" (using this term now in its vulgar, literal, sense). What matters, in the artificial, is the configuration that things take—and hence their directional force, the manner in which they work.[29] In nature, configuration is the physical structuring of something such that it has directional effect. In is no different in artifacts. The form of things—be they real or virtual, in the world or in mind—gives the work they perform. Thus what matters, for humans, are for example, the *forms* through which material and sentient human needs are met.[30] The application of science to technology is the attempt (which ultimately fails) to give objectivity (law, certainty) to this process; it is the dream of discovering in law the certain recipe for form, which in fact can only be discovered by experience.[31]

The artificial as a whole is *beyond (or beneath)* law. The world-as-artificial consists of an array of configurations, but these do not constitute a regime of "fact" (law) but *only* (yet what is the status of this "only"?) more or less persistent propositions concerning what could-be. Because configuration deals simultaneously with form and its operation (since it is through form that a thing operates; a thing is designed with its operations in mind) and because its essence lies neither in the form itself nor the operation but in what is between both (the reciprocity and resonance of the thing) we have a great deal of trouble in thinking it. Both thought and action (design) shy away from it, in opposite directions. But the artificial requires to be thought configuratively.

Yet this is a problem. As François Jullien has pointed out with respect to some similar concepts in Chinese,[32] the term lies stranded between the overpowering distinction between things or objects (their condition, configuration, and structure, above all their facticity) and forces or effects (or is this case, the processes that give to things their form and therefore also their efficacy, their implications, their force). Like all such dichotomies, this one is abstract, and inadequate to understanding—as design indeed precisely exposes. Nonetheless for just this reason configurative (and hence design) remains largely unconceptualized, even though that we sense that is at stake here is everything that really matters, particularly in regard to the realm of the artificial, which is of course the realm within which design comes to be, and the realm within which it finds its meaning.

*

At the same time, the artificial as a whole, and artificial or artifactual configurations in their instances, require to be thought as *propositions*. Configuration in the realm of the artificial is always the negotiation of (complex) incommensurable requirements, requirements that meet, and are to some degree resolved (though never completely) in the artifact.[33] Since the artifact is always in the end the contingent and unpredictable outcome of an essentially unstable relation of forces, no final resolution of a configuration can ever be achieved. All artifice (from artifacts per se to the symbolic realm as a whole) has therefore the character of a proposition. It is *always* an exploration of the *possibility* of what an X might be.[34] In artifice, what replaces law (rule) and the certainty of method is the radical uncertainty of the proposition. In this condition the artifact—any artifact—inhabits a double condition, one that can scarcely be expressed verbally but can be expressed typographically in the form "This!?" This formula expresses the fact that the artifact is at once "This!"—i.e., that which is existent, possessed of reality, possessing these attributes and showing them forth, exemplifying them, the artifact as quasi-fact, as "like" nature in its quasi-objectivity; *and*, in the same moment, "This?"—i.e., a proposition, *constituted as a form*; that which implicitly, if not explicitly, offers a question to the world,[35] and that which is inherently fallible.[36]

That the artificial is therefore, in strict terms, beyond law and beyond certainty means that the propositional is *structurally inherent* to the artificial. This means in turn that the artificial is a world of the possible, *not* as extrapolation, or as subjective will ("I demand!") but as its deepest condition.[37] The artificial, we might say, brings possibility into objective being for us, or rather it reveals (according to the principle that the higher reveals the lower) that *possibility* is not only, now, the future and everlasting condition of the human—the human as *becoming* not being— but is perhaps the very condition of the universe, which we now understand and see revealed, less as determinate and law-like (in any absolute sense) and more as *radically* contingent.[38] In short we grasp a universe of possibility, of becoming, and not of Being. In that sense we break with what Adorno called the "pure self-presentation" of being. We understand rather that as the artificial constitutes the realm of our possibility, so possibility now becomes the very realm of our being. We now objectively occupy the realm of culture-as-possibility.

*

One might well argue that this *is*, in any case, the definition of the human; that the possible is what human culture has always stood for.

Yet this is not how we have historically seen it. As Zygmunt Bauman has argued, "all too often 'culture' (particularly in its classical anthropological uses) stood for a *soi-distant* service station of structure, an instrument of continuity, reproduction of sameness and resistance to change."[39]

By contrast, the onset of the artificial as *objectively* the realm of the possible sets the view of culture as possibility inescapably in motion. "Culture ... is about making things different from what they are; the future different from the present. It ... is that which accepts that, first, 'things are not necessarily what they seem to be', and second, that 'the world may be different from what it is.'[40] "The human world (the world moulded by the humans and the world which moulds the humans) is perpetually, unavoidably and unremediably *noch nicht geworden* (not-yet-accomplished), as Ernst Bloch beautifully put it."[41] Here, notions of the artificial and of culture-as-possibility resonate sharply. "Culture is a permanent revolution of sorts." It manifests "A concern with keeping the forever inexhausted and unfulfilled human potential open, fighting back all attempts to foreclose and preempt the further unravelling of human possibilities, prodding human society to go on questioning itself and preventing that questioning from ever stalling or being declared finished."[42]

We can add an earlier formulation of the same concepts:

> Culture pushes at human experience in that it brings into relief the discord between ideal and real ... it exposes the limitations and imperfections of reality ... it conjoins and blends knowledge and interests ... culture stands and falls on the assumption that accomplished reality is not the most authoritative much less is it the only object of interested knowledge. The unfinishedness, incompleteness, imperfectness of the real, its infirmity and frailty, undergirds the status of culture in the same way as the authority of the real buttresses science.[43]

The wager that the artificial gives us, the possibility that it objectively "places in our laps," is the challenge to think of culture not as the realm of the ideal but of the real—or since this last term still smacks too much of the search for certainty, as the realm of lived actuality, where possibility, objectively and subjectively, combines in uncertain configurations. The culture to come, by necessity, is the wrestling with this possibility, its difficulties and its opportunities.[44]

Issue 2—Mediation, negotiation, incommensurability

If the first set of transmutations that the artificial performs is on the double status of law and the possible, the second centers on mediation.

All artifice is essentially mediation. Seen through the lens of the artefact, this is Herbert Simon's basic proposition: "We can view the matter quite symmetrically. An artefact can be thought of as a meeting point—an "interface" in today's terms—between an "inner" environment, the substance and organization of the artefact itself, and an "outer" environment, the surroundings in which it operates. If the inner environment is appropriate to the outer environment, or vice versa, the artefact will serve its intended purpose."[45] "Meeting point," "interface," the more accurate term here is mediation, and the relations go (at least) two ways, not (as Simon suggests) merely one.[46] All artifice is made on behalf of human subjects.[47] Any artifact is therefore the meeting point of at least *two* external relations or "outer" environments; that of human subjects and their relations (to whom it is, irreducibly, addressed) and that of existing artifacts and the wider physical environments in relation to which, or in the context of which, it acts. The inner environment of the artifact itself—its *configuration*, referring here simultaneously to its mode of internal organization and its modes of operation—is therefore a mediation between the realm of the subject and the "objective" conditions of the (complex) contexts within which it operates.

If the artificial is a mediation between the "inner" environment of the artifact itself (its configuration) and the "outer" environments to which it refers and in relation to which (on behalf of which) it must act, then once we see these environments not in the singular, as matter of physical law (Simon/technology), but in their existential, social and ecological pluralities then it becomes clear that relations

1   between any artefact or system (physical or political) and human subjects in social relations;

2   between existing artefacts likewise in complex social, technical and economic relations (and operating within complex and irreducible systems of power)

3   and between both of these and natural laws and conditions;

are *necessarily* a matter of complex negotiation[48] between irreconcilable or incommensurable moments and demands. All artifice is constructed within this condition.

Put differently, if the artificial *is* mediation (if that is its essential *status*) then transformational acts within the frame of artifice-as-world (be they design or politics) are by definition acts of complex mediation which take place between irreducible demands and conditions which cannot be bracketed or wished way, nor can they be simply dominated. They must rather be taken up in their weight and *negotiated* with in terms of a propositional configuration.[49] In this situation—the situation of the artificial as world—the speculative, propositional and negotiative/ mediatory conditions of configuration become the prime—and *necessary* characteristics—of practice (praxis) as a whole. In fact, as we will see, and harking back to some points made in section I, we are no longer within praxis considered merely as will. We are instead in "pro-duction" in Agamben's wider and more useful sense of the term.

Much of technology (in the older sense of the term) has been devoted to the attempt to deny this last condition, first through the lessening of the status of the configuration of the artifact (in favor of the laws determining it) second as a disavowal of complex negotiation.[50] Technology dissolves, or seeks to dissolve, incommensurability—and therefore substantive negotiation—in two ways: first, by thinking technologies on the basis of their putative operation in a law-determined, and (ideally) in socially and environmentally null (abstracted) world; and second on the basis of "drastic simplification of the real-world situation in representing it for the purposes of the design process."[51] Just so can one create systems or moments of "bounded rationality"—i.e., moments and systems which are, in many ways, the prerequisite for successful action, but which are not natural, and are in fact, in every aspect, already acute abstractions concerning what is.[52] At extreme this approach allows for the technology to be determined, as far as possible, on the basis of single ideal representation—a mathematical equation that establishes performative certainty before it is configuratively codified. Thus for example, in technology that takes its cue from science relations are essentially twofold: self-directed *obedience* to understood rules (or idioms of knowledge/s) as the determination of the configuration (the quest for certainty); and *minimal* second-order adaptation of the technology to the demands of the environments—economic, technical, human, social, ecological— within which the artifact will operate. The obvious example here is nuclear technology. Nuclear power is possible only because of the separation made between the operation of the reactor (considered purely in terms of the efficiency of the fission reaction) and the dangers of this process. The latter are dealt with *externally* to the fission reaction itself. The ongoing crisis with the Japanese reactors at Fukushima perfectly illustrates both points.

The problem here—besides the associated disdain for even short-term, let alone longer-term, costs[53]—is that by breaking with substantive contexts, and by refusing the need to negotiate with the forces and factors involved in real relations, "technology" (in the 20th-century sense of the term) is without organic relation to its contexts. As early as 1935, Walter Benjamin already saw in this the seeds of disaster: "The destructiveness of war furnishes proof that society has not been mature enough to incorporate technology as its organ, that technology has not been sufficiently developed to cope with the elemental forces of society."[54,55]

By contrast when we move to accepting complex relations we are confronted with incommensurable moments and demands. These moments are incommensurable because in belonging to qualitatively different realms they can neither be subsumed within a null environment nor adequately represented a priori before their (always incomplete) "resolution" in a configuration. Once we think of the artifact in terms of these wider relations then we see that any artifact—and thus all artificiality, whether of symbol systems our adaptation of nature or our political arrangements—is *necessarily* the relational outcome of complex negotiation between incommensurable moments and demands.[56]

Put differently, if the artificial is mediation—if that is its essential, radically contingent, status—then transformational acts within the frame of artifice-as-world (be they design or politics) are by definition *always* acts of complex mediation which take place *between* irreducible demands and conditions which cannot be bracketed or wished away nor merely dominated but must be taken up in their weight and negotiated with in terms of a propositional configuration.[57] In this situation—the situation of the artificial as world—the speculative, propositional and negotiated conditions of configuration and mediation (critical affirmation) become the prime and *necessary* characteristics of acting in general.[58]

Issue 3—Surpassing technology

Forty-five years after Simon first drafted *The Sciences of the Artificial*, what he perceived as emergently in process is intensified, expanded massively in scale and impact and today constitutes an effective—though by no means seamless—totality. By the late 1930s Heidegger was already disinclined to see "technology" purely as such. Today we can go much further. The realms of technical systems, symbol systems and the artificial adaptation of nature that, in 1968, were still relatively distinct (at least in our minds, though less so even then in praxis) have today become almost coterminous—or at least it is now impossible, in practice, to make a clear distinction between the one and the other.[59] The most obvious linkage, and perhaps the one of ultimately the furthest reach, is that between technologies and language, where the old distinctions between "work" and "interaction" (on which an entire sociology was built) have given way to a much more uncanny condition.

The designer Jamer Hunt offers some acute observations on this condition. Beginning by noting that Donna Haraway, exploring the dissolution of this boundary in 1985, prophetically declared "Late twentieth-century machines have made thoroughly ambiguous the difference between natural and artificial, mind and body, self-developing and externally designed ... our machines are disturbingly lively, and we ourselves frighteningly inert." He continues: "The designed, artificial world that envelops us is coming alive with communicative possibilities ... we are drifting into a new alignment, in both mind and body, with technology that is far more immersive, encompassing, and confounding. We are entering an age of uncanny technologies."[60]

What is of significance here, both intellectually and practically, is that this merging of "symbolic" and "technological" capacities renders the idea of a pure technology redundant. "Technology" as a concept can now be seen to belong only to the short industrial era. Born out of a division of labor useful in utilitarian terms in order to differentiate that which could be objectified and treated as if it lacked relation to the subject, the objective movements within technology itself are pushing beyond the limits technology gives itself.[61] Technology arrives then, in dominance, for humans, just at the point where it reveals itself as in excess of itself as concept, and thus now finds itself as dissimulated in a world of the artificial that cannot be other than our world.[62]

That technology is "overcome" by being incorporated into the wider notion of the artificial, makes us more aware of the degree to which our mental capacities—including of course language but all symbol-making capabilities—are not simply "natural" but are themselves artifacts.[63] If, on one side, this calls forth the hubristic projects of artificial intelligence with their declared ambitions of creating an artificial brain, on the other this also causes us to be more aware that human mental sensibility was formed, came into being as such, through artifice; that the artificial is therefore both the condition of human becoming (that without which the human could not be)[64] and that through which we may become, in Vattimo's telling phrase "(finally) human."

The condition of the latter is seeing our own conceptions of what constitutes artifice transformed under the workings of the artificial itself. The end of technology, which is also the end of representation (we are living through the high wave of the latter, at the point where representation, so constitutive of the modern, begins to be eclipsed) is the beginning of the artificial proper, where what becomes central, as already suggested, is the resonance and attuning of artifice to subjects, world(s) and nature. Thinking the artificial in this sense is therefore that *transitive*[65] appropriation of what-is as that-which-we-have-made which overcomes the older splitting and brings us back to technology not as a pseudo-mastery (which actually masters us) but as a dialogical and dialectical relationship of mediation.[66] On that basis, it is conceivable that destructiveness can be accepted and incorporated without illusion and without mastery.

*

Against the view that would see this as a far too optimistic view of the situation—and one can of course easily see this argument—it has to be insisted that the essence of the technological is the artificial, or mediation. Hence "opening to technology" does not mean affirming technology (in the noncritical sense of affirming) nor is it its opposite, the reaction against technology. It means grasping the artificial as mediation. In so doing, in "finding our way back" to the artificial, and to mediation, we find our way forward—to "the full breadth of space . . . proper to our essence."[67] What is proper to our "essence," subjectively as well as objectively, is potentiality.[68]

Since all human possibility is now conducted through the mediation of artifice—be it actualized as an artifact, considered in relation to nature or in terms of symbolic thought, language or representation—then all potentiality is negotiation with the possible through the artificial.

Technology belongs, *intimately one must insist*, to this qualitative exploration of the possible.

In this coming-to-technology, technology reveals itself as mediation, as negotiation, as proposition; as *more than* technology, operating in a world that is not in any manner "other" to it. In *this* world the lack of identity between subjects who make and what is made, between a society "not ... mature enough" to incorporate the technology it has constituted as its own, and a technology "not ... sufficiently developed to cope with the elemental forces"[69] theoretically at least begins to collapse. Recognition forces understanding of the intimate and binding relation of dependence and mutuality between subject and object.

Three quotations by Elaine Scarry bring us back to a world from which we can think past the endemic brutality of unbridled technology, hard or soft.

1   "The shape of the chair is not the shape of the skeleton, the shape of body weight, nor even the shape of pain perceived it is the shape of perceived-pain-wished-gone. The chair is therefore the materialized structure of a perception. It is sentient awareness materialized into a freestanding design."[70]

2   "Anonymous mass-produced objects contain a collective and equally extraordinary message: Whoever you are, and whether or not I personally like or even know you, in at least this small way, be well."[71]

3   The "general distribution of material objects to a population means that a certain minimum level of objectified human compassion is built into the revised structure of the external [non-sentient] world."[72]

There is nothing sentimental in these observations.

They describe accurately the [obscured] structure of reciprocity that underpins all making of things (which has as its target the remaking of the person)—and they propel the *directly* political statement, which requires careful reflection, that "that achieving an understanding of political justice may require that we first arrive at an understanding of making and unmaking."[73]

The internalization of technology as *making* (and thus as designing in the sense intended in Scarry's sentence above) is a grasping of this relation of reciprocity—which means a grasping of the dependencies (and freeing from dependence) that this entails. Thinking the artificial in this way is then that transitive appropriation of what-is as that-which-we-have-made that overcomes the modern diremption or splitting of the technological. This brings us back to technology not as pseudo-mastery (that which actually masters us) but as a dialogical and dialectical relationship of mediation. Design, as the "reconciling of incommensurate requirements," is perhaps the first space in which this belonging can be explored and brought at least to proto-typical visibility—if, that is, what is presented as actuality *through* design can also be grasped and articulated in terms of what it achieves as a model of future praxis.

Issue 4—The question of the drive

(a) Destructiveness and its overcoming

No attempt to reckon with what is, particularly one keen to discern from amongst the potential wreckage that which could be built upon as a bridge to the future, can avoid dealing with destructiveness. That the lack of relation between "society" and "technology" (in both its narrow and in its widest and emerging definitions, i.e., as encompassing also economics) *theoretically* shatters under the impact of the artificial, does not *yet* serve to make the dangers of desolation and catastrophe any the less. Not only, considered without illusion, is the global take-up of the possibilities opened by the artificial as yet all but infinitesimal when measured against the potential force of destructive tendencies; and not only do economic considerations in favor of what-is[74] trump futural judgment, but the best index of our position remains that which Adorno depressingly laid out 50 years ago i.e., (to repeat) that our society will choose total destruction, its objective potential, rather than rise to reflections that will threaten its basic stratum.[75]

It is clear then that the task of considering, analytically, both the character of this destructiveness and the chances of "overcoming" it—which means incorporating and passing beyond that which *structurally* gives rise to it—is nonnegotiable. To think of "history" in this sense is therefore to think the question of how destructiveness can be overcome. "Overcome" does not mean here vanquished. As Heidegger said of metaphysics, it cannot be overcome by wishing it so ("it cannot be abolished like an opinion. One can by no means leave it behind as a doctrine no longer believed and represented").[76] Overcoming therefore means something closer to incorporation, but in the condition where the incorporation is the state of passing-out-from-the-domination-of, where what is incorporated remains, but now *without primary formative capacity*. This seems to me the key move that we must now conceive. Desolation (like defuturing) is a *structural* possibility of the artificial, and *thus of all of future human history, including futures that are, in theory, "sustainable."* The goal, therefore, is not to eradicate the possibility of destructiveness (for such is impossible) but rather to discover the means for the incorporation of it within a wider corpus of practices. The formula, "where what is incorporated remains, but now *without primary formative capacity*" therefore represents both the *minimally necessary* ambition for what we must attain (no humane future if this cannot be achieved) and the *maximum possible* that we *could* attain (there can be no possible erasure of the destructive per se). Yet, if we have no warrant to be cheerful in the face of disaster the requirement to act to the best of our ability to avert catastrophe *also* demands an orientation towards intervention that is affirmative in the sense of being capable of taking from the resources now made available, some tools to deal with the paradox that *we have made that which we cannot yet think*.[77] Thinking the artificial affirmatively is the attempt to discover some of those resources within what is now emerging. It is the attempt at an active (transitive) thinking that tries to think through this nonrelation and proposes means of overcoming this diremption. By "active thinking" is meant here practice. Thinking the paradox of the artificial through the manner in which we remake the world is the attempt to turning the prosaic and destructive nihilism of our age towards a resonant affirmation of what is possible for our history beyond accumulation and catastrophe.

(b) The problem of will

The openings provided by the conceptions of mediation and negotiation bear, we might immediately realize, on the question—which is to say the problem—of will. On the latter, two quotations capture the problem. "It is first the will which arranges itself everywhere in technology that devours the earth in the exhaustion and consumption and change of what is artificial." "The will has forced the impossible as a goal upon the possible ... The desolation of the earth begins as a process which is willed, but not known in its being, and also not knowable at the time when the being of truth defines itself as certainty in which human representational thinking and producing first become sure of themselves."[78]

Taken from what is arguably Heidegger's most serious essay reflecting on destructiveness, these lines can only with loss be extracted from their argumentative context. Nonetheless, they reveal a consistent point of view. It is the conjunction of the drive and lack of reflection in the will that permits technology (in the expanded Heideggerean sense) to push "the earth beyond the developed sphere of its possibility into such things which are no longer a possibility and are thus the impossible."[79] This process, set in motion as such, cannot be thought, even cannot be understood, from the perspective of that mode of (representational) thinking which set it in motion. Hence our danger is the structural incomprehension of that which we have made. What obscures comprehension is the will.

The word "will" is used here in the sense of that which we might also name (and better) as the *drive* (in the Freudian sense); as the push towards the *absolute* (religion, politics); as the *compulsion to domination*, as the *urge to accumulation*, or as what Heidegger named as "conscription" (*Gestellung*) the economic and technological process "that adopts and compels whatever it encounters into the order of the *standing reserve*."[80] The drive is therefore that willing that not only demands (subjective and objective) domination, but which prescribes that the world appears in terms of the *active disposability* of everything that is, including persons and the earth. Or, as Heidegger put it in a later and more succinct phrase (which captures precisely the essence of our future disaster) our danger is the dynamic of our modern capitalist anthropology which presses toward "a guarantee of stability as a constant form of using things up."[81]

The will that "arranges itself" in technology—meaning that it both appropriates the apparatus of technology for its own ends and reconfigures it in its own interests—makes of technology its basic form of (objectivated) appearance. Will is the intensification of an "opening" where the opening Its possibility is thought without regard for consequence. It finds expression in the immediacy of an act. This act can be immediate, i.e., without reflection, because it pushes to extreme what is already latent in the situation as power. In economics the drive for profit discounts, i.e. defers or externalizes, at every moment. In technology, the immediate logic of technical possibility as increased power overruns consideration of second- and third-order consequences. In politics, will is the pure drive, irrespective of implication. The Holocaust was precisely this.[82] The latter reminds us that, at base, the will (the urge to domination, the drive) is always subjective (no matter what degree of objective appearance—above all in the form of the "necessary" or necessity—it takes on). But conversely, in relation to domination, the will is equally necessary. Necessity of the will means here *felt* necessity: the felt necessity of the will as domination as the means—in practice the *only* means—of expropriating the infinite material beneficence of nature.

Particularly in the modern period, and above all in America, interactions with nature have existed under a model where nature is at once infinitely beneficent (bestowed by God) yet where what is beneficent to us must be taken by force from nature not sufficiently mindful to offer it just-so. It is thus by domination (will) that man is distinguished. But then domination is the first proscription God puts on man.[83] The "difficulty" here is that, even though it has the imprimatur of God, domination is less easily realized in practice than the declaration might suppose. Violence is inescapable: it is the exercise of will through violence that is the only means of maintaining the force of the subject against that which is designated as object.[84] But the demand for domination breeds acute anxiety. This is even more the case when expropriation moves from nature to the site of persons and requires endless vigilance and violence. Here, as every witness on slavery and colonization will attest, anxiety—and consequent violence—ratchet to new levels.[85]

A story illustrates perfectly the point. It comes from the diary of an officer on one of Stanley's *peaceful* expeditions in Africa around 1887:

> It was most interesting, lying in the bush watching the natives quietly at their daily work. Some women were making banana flour by pounding up dried bananas, men we could see building huts ... boys and girls running about, singing ... I opened the game by shooting one chap through the chest. He fell like a stone ... immediately a volley was poured into the village.[86]

Such violence must sooner or later turn against the deploying subject. In the 20th century this turn was manifest in a variety of pathological forms: the extreme drive for accumulation, "the unconditional rule of calculating reason"; the extreme violence of imperialism and ethnocide;[87] the nervous zeal for the absolute in radical politics of right and left (Fascism, Stalinism). It was perhaps most manifest in the European civil wars.[88] Today it is most evident in the parasitic abstracted drive of the financial economy, in the economics of crime, financial and extortive,[89] and of course as "return"—the violence inflected on nature returning as climate change.[90]

In the light of this the challenge to be faced is clear: to access what is affirmatively made possible by the onset of the artificial-as-world depends upon the surpassing of will. But "will" or the drive cannot simply be overcome by the action of thought—even if the latter is not negligible in terms of preparing relational understanding. From the standpoint of action, If the notion of "will" stands in for the structuring dynamic and destructive force of expropriation in the wide sense, then the argument has to be that it is the *practical* transcending or overcoming of will which is key. The target, again, is attainment of what is *objectively both emergent and affirmatively possible*, namely a realm of the artificial in which the necessity of will (and thus domination) is no longer paramount.[91]

'That dimension is for us mediation; or, to put it alternately, the underlying creative and affirmative figure of the emerging epoch is mediation.

Four points can illustrate what is involved here.

1   The first notes that the overcoming of will that is argued here is *not* itself a projection, a matter of will, not simply "overcoming," and not simply the positing of a desired condition, it is rather an outcome [or at least possibility] of the most salient shift in our times. The artificial puts into place the *objective* possibility of a different way of standing to things, persons and nature. It hence also puts into place the possibility of different forms of what we call design, as well as different forms of what we have called up until now politics.

2   The second is that the onset of the artificial marks the possibility of the dissolution of the abject *necessity* of will. Will is appropriate, if at all, only to a world that sees itself as uniquely vested with the necessity for domination. *Objectively*, this is no longer the case. Will occurs most ferociously (and dangerously, i.e., destructively) when object and subject are construed and separated, when the subject becomes assured that only through domination can the object be mastered and the subject retain its subjectivity and mastery. But in the artificial subject and object mediate. Adorno's injunction from *Negative Dialectics*—"Mediation of the object means that it must not be statically dogmatically hypostatized but can be known only as it

entwines with subjectivity; mediation of the subject means that without the moment of objectivity it would be literally nil"[92]—is today already being worked out in practice. All "interaction" is the practice of mediation in the deep sense—even if its ethical consequences are not yet fully realized.

3   Third, the new centrality of mediation as the objective characteristic of the artificial as totality allows us to grasp that in this new context questions of *politics* and questions of artifice and its shaping and forming in relation to the meeting of human needs and wants—in short, questions of *design*[93]—become, if not identical, then at least coterminous to a degree that even fifty years ago could not be grasped. *Then* the requisite formula would have been design *and* politics, the ampersand revealing the separation, the awkwardness of the (non)-relation. Today, we are in a quite different situation, first in relation to the artificial as a whole—which now constitutes the horizon and medium of our world—and second, as a consequence of the first, between the agencies of design and politics, which grow closer and perhaps even take on something of the other's identity.[94] This shift from a nonrelation, or relation of externality, of design and politics to a kind of internal relation is potentially a "saving" capacity. This relation has agency because it is grounded in the attributes of what now is.

4   Where this becomes politics and ethics, is that under these emergent conditions both are necessarily negotiation in the wide sense. This is negotiation not with the political per se (negotiation within politics—the politics Obama so disastrously wished to pursue) but negotiation as a mode of transformative praxis orientated towards bringing a humane future into being. We can postulate therefore that under the pressure of the artificial becoming the effective horizon and medium of our time, the shaping of the artificial, at every level from individual artifact to global system will become simultaneously both the field for (an expanded practice of) design and—because the scale of these questions of how we deal with the artificial and its consequences and implications cannot be divorced from the question of how we organize towards contending, politically, socially, economically, with their implications—an arena of political contention and work.

Issue 5—Overcoming the proscription of possibility

As a fifth level of the malady of destructiveness, the violence externalized as a consequence of the drive, finds its internal correspondence in the political inability or "incapacity ... to name and strive for a Good"—by which is meant the incapacity to strive for a public good, a good for all. The "nihilism" that results is the name Badiou gives to what then defines the worst aspects of our times, the "distinctive (*singuliere*) combination of resignation in the face of necessity together with a purely negative, if not destructive, will."[95]

"Nihilism" (a term as unsatisfactory as will) is here both the abject capitulation to what-is and the impotent resentment of this capitulation, whether the latter is expressed in active, self-destructive, nationalist fundamentalist politics and theologies (one of whose ends is terror: the symmetry of a Brevik or a McVee and Islamist violence) or in the "passive" modes of what has been called "Californian Buddhism," i.e., the escape into highly subjective modes of living that withdraw the self from the world and disdain intervention in its operation.

Yet this last characterization has elements of unfairness. Impotent resentment of capitulation or resignation in the face of necessity that issues in a negative, if not destructive, will is by no means confined to the most obvious or most visible extreme points of its manifestation. Nihilism is not the subjective poetic or the theological extreme, it is not romanticism of any variety but the norm: nihilism is the name that politics takes in an age of economic conformity. In this sense nihilism is no longer (if it ever was) confined to the fringes of theologies active or passive, rather—and this is its real danger—it enters into the body politic as a whole, "in such a way that subjectivity in general is inevitably dragged down into a kind of belligerent impotence."[96] That what-is benefits from this is indisputable. Not only does a "socius" of resentment all but ensure the collective absence of any real project or of any emancipatory politics, but resentment finds its other expression in the longing for the "false plenitude" of substitute collectivism where identity ("us") is bought at another's expense ("them"). Today, there is no European country where this politics is *not* an active part of the governing process. If most overt in Eastern Europe (Hungary, Poland) it is no less present in the officially sanctioned animosity shown to "immigrants" and those unemployed or on welfare in the theoretically more sophisticated democracies.[97]

*

But if all this works, at least in the short term, to reinforce that-which-is (to erase the possibility of an alternative) there is still, for politics, and ultimately for the economy, a problem. That nihilism is *structurally* that which blocks the way "towards the positive prescription of possibilities," means that it is also that which reduces thereby the scope of maneuver for social steering mechanisms. Once this reaches a certain point, the inability to respond to objective external problems opens the potential for disaster. We return yet again to the fear that Adorno so often mentioned that we will embrace the objective potential of catastrophe, rather than rise to reflections that will threaten the basic stratum of that which keeps what-is in place.

If Adorno's proposition speaks to the deepest implication of the reluctance to engage in the scale and originality of reflection that our situation demands. we might still register a surprise. For this thesis also marks a remarkable failure of enlightened self-interest—a failure to take oneself and one's future seriously enough to begin to "face and face and face down" all that is erosive of the conditions of humane life. But this cannot be *only a* subjective or individual failure. That it is not so indicates that the blindness that nihilism induces (as closure) extends to thinking in general and so too, to action. Adorno (and Horkheimer) again offer the essential insight: "If a malady so deeply embedded in civilization is not properly accounted for by knowledge, the individual too, though he may be as well intentioned as the victim himself, cannot mitigate it through understanding"—meaning that he or she cannot mitigate it merely through *individual* understanding, and cannot do so *even by appealing to reason*: "The plausibly rational, economic, and political explanations and counterarguments—however correct their individual observations— cannot appease it, since rationality itself, through its links to power, is submerged in the same malady."[98] Nihilism, in other words, enters into reason—all reason[99]—and does precisely at the point at which thought wishes to think and act vis-à-vis the future.

One aspect that this implies is that the critique of the failure of subjects to open themselves to being able to take on board the challenges that the future demands is mediated by the fact that, in the wider absence of a full and public accounting of our situation, even well-intentioned and well-executed practice is without the consequence that it is due. It *occurs*, but what it achieves is not understood. As Barthes once said in a quite different context but with much the same meaning, such projects can be "the motor of no development"— which means that emerging practice fails *not* because of the efficacy that it models but because these efficacies cannot be "seen," specifically, such practices cannot issue *in new thought* (new reason) and therefore they can challenge neither existing practices, nor, what is now revealed as more serious, the limitations of the reason that dismisses them and refuses to take on board what they imply.[100]

*

On what possible basis can we then go forward? On what foundations can we recoup historical possibility—which depends upon our being able to prototype new possibilities of existence and to translate what is achieved in these (modeled) possibilities into thought.

What has become clear, as we have worked through some of the issues surrounding destructives and the artificial, is that we have, at the heart of our praxis, a void that instrumental action cannot fill—except as the illusion of the plenitude of technology-as-entertainment and the objective illusion that stability bought at the cost of "using things up" can be maintained indefinitely without crisis.

In truth, perhaps no-one truly believes any more in either of these. But since these are both all-powerful and in any case effectively dismiss all but peripheral alternatives they remain in dominance. Nonetheless the void is real and is felt, to a variable degree, as disappointment.[101]

This void, or disappointment, is undeniably political[102] but it is centrally that which has been continuously referred to by implication in this book, that is the disappointment, or the void, the lack, of modes of ethical, political *and material* acting that can begin to reconstruct the inverted and displaced priorities of now.

Previously, we noted that one emergent logic of the artificial was that we would see the generalization of "negotiation as a mode of transformative praxis orientated towards bringing a humane future into being." Under the pressure of the artificial becoming the effective horizon and medium of our time, we said that "the shaping of the artificial ... will become simultaneously both the field for (an expanded practice of) design and ... an arena of political contention and work."

This changes, in important ways, the "meta-" framework of acting. It is to this that we can now turn, through looking principally at the concept of the situation and what it entails.

Issue 6—The situation as the site of ethics, design and politics

Three points are perhaps worth mentioning, each links, to some degree, what is emergent in the artificial with ethics or politics and with modes of acting that are congruent with design.

The first concerns the situation, in its structural essence.

The replacement of law by the possible, and the primacy given to mediation and negotiation, transforms the ethical situation that obtains between possibility or the proposition and mediation. We have seen that we can call the "outer" environments with which an artifact engages *the situation*. Simon captures this understanding in his famous definition of design as the "devising of courses of acting to move from existing to preferred *situations*."[103] The sentence reminds us that the artifact is not the end of poietic activity—that its end is in the situation and even more precisely and essentially in the humans who are the actors or subjects in that situation. Since situations are irredeemably bound to the human, activities that engage actively with them (as design and politics do as *essential moments of their acting*—the situation as the very nexus of their work) are necessarily ethical—and in two senses, first because the situation is the very locus of ethics:—"There is no need for an "ethics" but only for a clear vision of *the* situation ... to be faithful to the situation means to deal with the situation according to the rule of maximum possibility; to treat it right to the limit of the possible. Or, if you prefer, to draw from the situation, to the greatest possible extent, the affirmative humanity that it contains."[104]

Equally, because the situation necessarily has the human as its center it calls for a concomitant responsibility by the subject. If the subject is *always* immediately or ultimately the subject of artifice—that to whom it is *without exception* addressed—then subjects must acknowledge (vis-à-vis the world, vis-à-vis others, vis-à-vis generations to come) this radical anthropomorphism; must take on board the responsibility (the cost, consequences) for being the *necessary* center of all situated activity.

The first of these two ethical transformations gives content—demand—to Simon's "preferred situations" and thus to mediation in general. The second delineates the radical responsibilities that the inescapably anthropomorphic subject must take on board as the price paid for centrality—what Joyce in *Ulysses* famously telegraphed, in a different context, as the necessity to acknowledge "the immense debtorship for the thing done"[105]—a statement that can also stand for the even wider necessity that we begin to contend adequately with all that we have made and set in motion. In relation to the latter, the artificial-as-world is the condition where this responsibility can no longer be *so easily* sloughed off. A transitive politics (an ethics) adequate to the condition of the artificial as world begins here.

The second point concerns the subjectivity of ethics and the overcoming of its limitations.

A slogan that has recently been used as one way of attempting to reinvigorate both politics and ethics—and, more importantly, each simultaneously and with consequence for the other—is "If ethics without politics is empty, then politics without ethics is blind."[106] But the context in which this is uttered confines both ethics and politics to the subjective realm. Simon Critchley, for example, passes from defining our time "by a state of war," to this provoking "the question of justice," which provokes in turn the need "for an ethics" and thus in its turn the need for a theory of "ethical experience and subjectivity."[107] There is nothing wrong in this sequence, except that it misses out on the praxiological dimension of the manner in which we engage the world. What we also require—and with equal urgency—is an ethics, a politics and a mode of acting in and on the socio-material world, where the first two are conjoined to the latter, just as the latter is inextricably bound with the former. Such acting is subjective, but it does not stay in the subjective realm. It is capable of passing into the world.[108] On the other side, such understanding of ethics/politics/acting would deprive instrumental action (here including that design which tends to align itself with instrumental logic) of its alibi to be somehow distinct from these questions. This would be a mode of ethical acting then that brings poiesis actively into ethical and political relations and makes it possible to see our thinking/acting in these terms. In terms of the question of how we contend with nihilism, we could characterize this work as the attempt at overcoming the latter *through taking the risk of acting with universal aim* in world-transformation directions.

In *Mourning Before the Law*, one of the last volumes she published before her untimely death, the political and ethical philosopher Gillian Rose was concerned to develop (if implicitly) a model of ethico-political practice that she called "activity beyond activity," an ethical politics of *positing action*. Positing action is thought of by Rose as acting capable of working in the world as action; acting which is not afraid to engage with actuality (with law, with power) and which does not succumb to the poles of domination and suffering. In cursory summary, we can say that, for Rose, four elements of political-ethical action are crucial those of:

- *risk*, or action without guarantee:—"for politics does not happen when you act on behalf of your own damaged good but when you act, without guarantee, for the good of all—this is to take the risk of the universal interest";

- *learning, for learning "mediates the social and the political: it works* precisely by making mistakes, by taking the risk of action, and then by reflecting on its unintended consequences, and then taking the risk, yet again, of further action";

- *creative action as negotiation*, for acknowledgment of the "creative involvement of action in the configurations of power and law" and of "the risk of action, arising out of negotiation with the law" is a precondition to being able to act in relation to these configurations, as against merely evading the ambiguities and anxieties that they give rise to; and

- *positing*, which refers, in Rose's language, to the "temporarily constitutive positings" of actors which "form and reform both selves"; this "constant risk of positing and failing and positing again," Rose says, she will call "activity beyond activity" to both cover the ethical nature of the description and to distinguish it sharply from the Levinasian "passivity beyond passivity."[109]

To take the risk of the "universal interest" is to enter on acting from a point that includes but goes beyond one's subjective limit. One acts—takes the risk of acting—because one tells oneself the nature of the situation.[110] This acting necessarily takes the form of learning—for one is acting beyond the limits of how one has previously acted (one is acting outside of narrow interest) and this acting is itself between the social and the political. This acting is iterative—and, to connect with a notion noted above, and explored further below *necessarily* fallible. This is politics and ethics as creative action, as negotiation with configurations of power and law. This is the opposite of evasion: it is acting not through certainty but through positing: the "constitutive positings," Rose says, that both generate action and are capable of transforming both self and activity in the process. This is ethics in the active mode, an ethics capable of contending with law, and because of this capable of contending both with the realities of (material) practice and politics. What Rose acheived in her from points is the positing of an ethics that is capable of conjoining with "politically operated justice," i.e., an ethics capable of acting as an internal relation of politics, at the same time as the latter is understood as internally to it. Where this touches on design, or material configuration, is that the ethically transitive mode of acting that is implied here is not only congruent with acting in an artificial world, it is perhaps the only form of ethical acting that can be contiguous with what the latter necessitates.

*

If we now finally turn from ethics to politics we can augment Rose's points in ways that are at once congruent with her ethics, that show how these constitute the basis of an active extension of ethics in the world and at the same time are (unexpectedly) close to design thought in the wide sense.

A quick indicative way to do this is to turn to Badiou's short essay "Politics as a truth procedure."[111] This chapter of *Metapolitics* usefully delineates three fundamental conditions of the political qua politics: *the universal or the address to all; the possibilities of the situation*; and *the taking of a measure (of a situation)*. Read in context of this discussion however they can be made to reveal an *internal* correspondence to the issues we are exploring here. Together with Rose's four points, they provide a basic lexicon of ethico-political concepts which are consonant with design and which echo, in significant ways, a number of the issues explored above as the conditions of the artificial.

Re 1. *The universal or the address to all.* So often captured by particular interests, the political (which can be distinguished from politics in the everyday sense and this can be thought of a politics no longer confined by the given, situated, limits of "politics") is *universal* because (like design) it takes the risk of asserting a universal interest (a universal problem—or affirmatively, a universal possibility) and thus intrinsically addresses a universal subject; a subject capable of engaging with this need, of dealing with this problem, of rising to this possibility.[112] Qua Rose above, here acting takes the risk of asserting a universal interest and need and thus a universal subject. Design, on behalf of the subject (this is its gift) speaks to a universal subject or more accurately (the nuance is key) to that which is universal within each subject. The truths that design explores are the truths of a subject in search of what Simon called "good designs," i.e., in the language of the artificial, mediations. We can pay attention here to the sentences in which Simon notes that the "proper study of mankind has been said to be man. But I have argued that people—at least in their intellective component—may be relatively simple, that most of the complexity of their behavior maybe drawn from their environment, from their search for good designs."[113] In other words, the "search for good designs" is the basic socio-political work we undertake. It is what humans do.

Re 2. *The possibilities of the situation.* Politics presents as such the *infinite character of situations.* Politics summons or exhibits the infinity of the situation. Since politics includes in the situation the thought of all, it is engaged in rendering explicit the subjective infinity of situations. Badiou puts it: of course every situation is ontologically infinite [is] never closed … But only politics summons this infinity immediately, as subjective universality … only in politics is deliberation about the possible … constitutive of the process itself.[114]

Against Badiou's "only" it is easy to insist that design too is nothing other than an address to situations. Design summons the infinity (of a situation) immediately, as subjective universality, this time by summoning the universal capability to move from "existing to preferred situations" and the universal (in the artificial) possibility of possibility. Design is in fact the "science" of possibility, what I have elsewhere called the "science of uncertainty";[115] it is that which translates the given into uncertainty (possibility) and therefore opens as question its possibility. Not only is design nothing other than an address to situations, but politics and design are both faced not merely with the proposing of or the prefiguring of the possibilities of a situation, but with the realization of what is possible within the situation. We already noted Badiou's strong ethics of the situation. We can understand a structural variation of this where we see both design and politics as fungible agencies of capability, capable of engaging in what, from a Chinese perspective, we might call the play between the notion of a situation or configuration (xing) as it develops and takes shape before our eyes (as a relation of forces) and its development, through the grammar of iterative positing in terms of our understanding of the potential (shi), which is implied by that situation and can be made to play in one's favor.[116] Looked at from this perspective design/politics would be that where

1   we act towards/design for that which has potential: or better,

2   we act/design in such a way as be able to realize the potential latent in a situation, or even better,

3   (and closer to Badiou's ethics of the situation) we act/design so that what we create has the propensity to realize to the *maximum* all that the situation and the persons within that situation are capable of.

This last reminds us that what is emergent in design is precisely design for capabilities: that the engagement in situations is in terms of how one deploys the capabilities of design in service of developing capabilities. Such a project has recently been indicatively set in motion, in both theory and practice by the Swedish designer Otto van Busch. Working from the development theory of Amartya Sen the basic case Busch makes for such a strategy is simple, but is not for that reason to be gainsaid.[117]

Re 3. *the taking of a measure (of a situation)*. Finally, there is the question of the measure (of a situation). Errancy occurs when a situation (a power, e.g. that of the State) cannot be put at a distance, meaning that it cannot be measured, cannot be gauged. "Politics is the interruption of this errancy"[118] meaning that it gives measure to what is immeasurable; it gauges (in Heidegger's sense) and shows that that to which we are resigned—because its power consists in its immeasurability— can indeed be thought and thus acted in relation to. *If politics is the act that makes power reveal itself, design is the act that makes the power of the artificial reveal itself in modes accessible to appropriation from an ethical and then political standpoint.* Measure is challenge. One measures by making a challenge to what is. The affirmation ("This!") is an implicit, potentially explicit, challenge to the limits of what-is. It is through asserting—i.e., proposing—this that what-is comes into view as limit. Movement from "an existing to a preferred situation" is also this; it is the result of both a measure(ing) and is itself a new measure of the situation. It is the result of a private measure as it were (i.e., a measure originally internal to the designer) which then emerges as a public measure and thus as a challenge. Designing (like politics) is a perpetual challenging-forth, a testing of measure.[119]

We have seen that the artificial, understood is perhaps, as well as the source of the dangers that beset us, our possibility; that it offers, in potential, objective and subjective resources for action.[120] The question that we might ask is whether the possibility of acting to overcome (incorporate and pass beyond) destructiveness is in fact latent in what is now emerging, and capable of providing some means for engaging with that which is most dangerous to us. It is to this I will now turn, but as history. A moment from Berlin, in 1993, provides us with an instance with which to work.

3 ACTING IN REGARD TO HISTORY

I

The problem of how to act

Much has been made, earlier in this essay, of the notion of affirmation.

In its contemporary form, the one most useful to a theory of acting, the basic concept comes from Badiou. Affirmation is required, he insists, as one moves from critique to intervention. Why affirmation? Because

> if you intervene with respect to a paradoxical situation, or if you intervene with regard to a relation that is not a relation, you will have to propose a new framework of thought, and you will have to affirm that it is possible to think this paradoxical situation, on condition, of course, that a certain number of parameters be abandoned, and a certain number of novelties introduced.[1]

Badiou was speaking about philosophy. But we can see immediately that the concept applies no less—perhaps even more—to design and to making. In this strict sense design *is* affirmation. It is acting affirmatively because acting, in the sense meant here, is always intervention into a "paradoxical situation, into relations that are not *in* relation."[2] In any case, design is always also intervening, not only as "changing existing situations into preferred ones," but ethically too. It acts, or ethically it is demanded that it acts, such that we draw from the situation into which the intervention occurs, to "the greatest possible extent, the affirmative humanity that it contains."[3]

Such, we have said, is the essence of intervention, and thus the essence of the acting we wish and need to undertake. But we have also already indicated that the question of how we act is the very question of our time—because it is our acting (which includes also our failure or inability to act) that may well drive us towards disasters with potentially catastrophic outcomes. It is thus our acting which today most needs our intervention—that which most needs drawing from it the "affirmative humanity" that it contains. So we are asking not just about how we intervene into specific concrete situations, nor even only about how we can intervene into the present in terms of a situation and of our (futural) history—and thus into historical and political questions—but about how we intervene into acting in general in relation to these situations. We are asking then about how we design "acting" and how we do so such that acting can be an act of *actively thinking through* the contradiction and diremption of our peculiar historical position.

(i) Affirmation and intervention

So that we can perhaps begin to think more clearly about the nature of the "affirmative interventions" that we need to make it is perhaps worth reviewing briefly the structure of the thinking that led Badiou towards his notion of "affirmation."

Affirmation in this context is the name of how philosophy intervenes in such situations of incommensurability and absence. It names what is absent by thinking past the paradoxical relations involved in a situation, thinking past relations-that-are-not-relations. The text in which the construct arises in its simplest form is a lecture that Badiou gave in 2004. In it, he asks a simple question: "To what extent does philosophy intervene in the present, in historical and political questions? And in the end, what is the nature of this intervention? Why would the philosopher be called to intervene in questions regarding the present?"[4]

The answer is at once succinct and telling, not least from the perspective of design. The philosopher, Badiou says,

> constructs his own problems, he is an inventor of problems ... A genuine philosopher is someone who decides on his own account what the important problems are, someone who proposes new problems for everyone. Philosophy is first and foremost this: the invention of new problems. It follows that the philosopher intervenes

when in the situation ... there are things that appear to him as signs, signs that it is necessary to invent a new problem ... signs that point to the need for a new ... invention.[5]

So we have the invention of new problems—*for all*, we have the derivation of these problems "*from the present*," and we have the basis of these problems, the (philosophical) "*situation*" as Badiou calls it. The latter devolves from moments where what is understood as a sign requiring the formulation of a problem is so because it demonstrates the existence of a paradoxical situation, a disjunctive synthesis, a relation-that-is-not a relation. The formulation of the problem is the bringing of the paradoxical situation to light and thus to understanding—such that it can be named, as a problem, and then thought, affirmatively, as intervention.

Badiou's philosopher therefore:

1   reads his times (his present) on behalf of all;

2   does so by identifying those contradictions, paradoxical situations, incommensurabilities and the like that are productive and constitutive of the situation(s) in question; that describe its forces but also outline its potential;

3   grasps these incommensurabilities as signs that point to the need to formulate (identify, name) a new problem (and hence a new possibility);

4   intervenes into their times through thinking these "disjunctive syntheses" (the relations-that-are-not-a-relation (always multiple) affirmatively, i.e., with a view to thinking past their incommensurability, "on condition, of course, that a certain number of parameters be abandoned, and a certain number of novelties introduced."

There is no need even to translate this from one field to the other. Allowing for the substitution of "possibility" for "problem" (but even this is not totally necessary) the *structural* relation between the philosopher who intervenes in this way and the designer is sufficiently identical as makes no difference. What else, after all, is the process of design, other than the working through of these stages?

Let us simply say then that the designer—the *genuine designer* (i.e., the designer who refuses a priori limits on what they should concern themselves with, the *critical* designer)—inhabits, structurally, the same position as the "genuine philosopher." "Genuine design" is therefore a matter of the designer or designers deciding *on their own account* what the important problems are: "Problems" means here opportunities. These problems, or these possibilities,[6] do not arise arbitrarily; rather the designer, like the philosopher, intervenes when "in the present"—*which means in the historical situation*—there are issues, discrepancies, unused potentialities that appear as "signs" that a new (historical) possibility (problem) has emerged. In these circumstances it is necessary to invent a new configurative, which is also a new conceptual schema in order to model and demonstrate this opportunity—providing of course that one accepts that "a certain number of parameters be abandoned, and a certain number of novelties introduced."[7]

*

But in so doing the designer does not remain the same, does not remain in a subaltern position. In breaking with the blind tyranny of "problem-solving" economically defined—that is, service to another's problem, but service within the framework of an already given, already anticipated, solution and service to another's (private) interest—the designer breaks with repetition.

More strongly, since this more usual form of designing (problem-solving) enclosed as it is in the narrowest of parameters, is as inaccessible to the truth of design as "opinion mongering" is for philosophy, then to think design in this way is to begin to recover the truth of design, which is not given in the industrial division of labor, but only discovered through the free assertion of the abilities to perceive and intervene exercised in the light of the role of articulating new problems and possibilities for all—of taking the risk, to link back to Gillian Rose in §2, "of universal interest," i.e., the risk of thinking ethically concerning our situation. It is also to recover the acting of designing in history, that is, in relation to the present and the future.

We can put it like this because the situation we inhabit—our historical situation—is both the context of this intervention *and* today the subject matter of design. In other words, our task today is to design our history, both retrospectively *and* as forward-looking anticipatory practice. Of course our historical situation is in no wise unitary. It possesses no natural flow from past to present. It is, in many respects "broken"; structured by the "entanglements" of approaches and forces that do not constitute a "dialectical correlation" but a situation of antinomy bordering on incipient system-wide crisis. And if "crisis" is necessarily a shorthand, rhetorical, term here—and by no means the best[8]—it nonetheless suffices as such to describe both the prevalent underlying (and one must insist, *objective*) sense of danger that we face and the "lack-of-relation" between moments, which is our historical task to attempt to think through. Opportunity, after all, can only be thought without glibness by thinking of possibility *within* the context of "danger." In that sense, the demand that Adorno made of his own field, that in the face of "indefatigable self-destructiveness" philosophy must discard "even the last vestiges of innocence in regard to the habits and tendencies of the spirit of the age,"[9] applies today no less to design. "Innocence" is an alibi that can no longer be accepted.

All of this links to the task that now confronts us as we seek to create our future within a series of relations-that-are-not-relations, "disjunctive syntheses," paradoxical conditions. The notion of "affirmation" we can now see grows out of the sense—tangible today even to the social sciences—that it is no longer sufficient or satisfactory to merely critique these conditions. There must be an intervention and this must be so because in the case of paradoxical situations and the like these do not, and cannot, issue in any natural resolution. The systemic inability to manage the forces that relations in disjunction generate (cf. Benjamin's thesis on war) means that the outcome of entanglements between structurally incommensurate forces and capacities in an epoch of the artificial can only be destructive. Incommensurabilities of this character *cannot* be reconciled in pure thought. The objective reason for this is that within the artificial (i.e., within what is for us "world") incommensurate forces and demands become fully visible *only* in the act of seeking to bring them into relation. Considered in isolation, the incommensurablity of elements does not become fully apparent. The economy considered qua economy does not reveal desolation as a consequence until it is placed in a relation of with that which sustains it. Only them does the incommensurability of capital vis-à-vis the web of dependencies that sustains it become apparent. The violence of technology only becomes fully apparent when placed in relation to the vulnerabilities of the subject. Climate change is inconsequential for nature. It only becomes consequential when experienced in relation to patterns of sedimented human settlement.

Incommensurate conditions can only be "dealt with" in some form of practice—from which perhaps a new idiom of thought, i.e., a new "compound body" of knowledge that opens towards a new understanding, can be derived. "Dealt with" means here "reconciled." The immediate problem is that this sounds too passive, as if the reconciliation is of what is given, without the ability to truly transform either the situation or the moments to be reconciled. But reconciliation as affirmation is quite different. The active demand ("that a certain number of parameters be abandoned, and a certain number of novelties introduced") implies the transformation of what is given, both in thought and in actuality. Affirmation in this sense can only be fully realized through a *configuative* possibility or proposition in which the incommensurate elements are *themselves* subject to transformation.

To put this another way, mediation is not passive. Once the mediation of subject and object is set in motion neither pole in the equation remains intact. Purity dissolves under the pressure of thought dissolving the illusory valorization of each. This transformation does not stay at the level of thought. It enters the world. In fact, this reverses the order of thinking. It is not now that practice puts into play that which thought first thinks and legitimates. It is rather that, as in the subject-object dialectic, practice is "ahead of the game." The dialectic is already in play. The task of thought in this case is *to think that which is already in exploration*, already modeled, in embryo and in prototypical forms. The converse of this is that the exploration of practice, and the creation of new, prototypical, forms of negotiating incommensurability are *themselves thinking*—the creation, once grasped, of new idioms of thought (new compound bodies of knowledge).

(ii) Designing, intervening, thinking

We said earlier that Badiou's lines are at once "bracing" for thought and in themselves an effective description of what, at best, design does. Design *is* the capacity to intervene into a situation precisely by affirming that it is possible to "think" a paradoxical or a limiting situation. The invention of the London Underground diagram in 1931 can be instanced as a textbook example of precisely such. But what is also important is the strong equation this allows to be recovered between designing, intervening and thinking (without this, design is condemned to impotence).

The term "think" in design means to configure, i.e., it means thinking *through* configurations. Contrary to those views that wrap language and cognition so hermetically that the latter cannot exist outside the space of the former—as if, extraordinarily, language eclipsed all thought—configurations (material, visual, social) *think*. Cognition and understanding is endemic to *all* configurative work. The visual no less than the linguistic is orientated towards understanding; such configurations are no less propositional, in this respect, than their linguistic cousins.[10] Nelson Goodman captures the matter beautifully:

> the primary purpose [of symbolic activity] is cognition in and for itself: the practicality, pleasure, compulsion and communicative utility all depend on this. Symbolization, then, is to be judged fundamentally by how well it serves the cognitive purpose: by the delicacy of its discriminations and the aptness of its allusions; by the way it works in grasping, exploring and informing the world; by how it analyses, sorts and organizes; by how it participates in the making, manipulation, retention and transformation of knowledge. Considerations of simplicity and subtlety, power and precision, scope and selectivity, familiarity and freshness, are all relevant and often contend with one another; their weighting is relative to our interests, our information, our inquiry.[11]

The argument that configurative *thinks* is important because a significant part of the ideology that creates design as a subaltern field is the argument that "design does not think," that the configurative is not a contribution to understanding.[12] But vehicles of design discovery—i.e., designed configurations—are themselves vehicles of thought. It is not that somehow thought is in "addition to" practice; *practice thinks*. The question to be considered is how it does so. What we need to understand is how, through practice, practice thinks—and how, *in* practice, and *through* practice, practice can think affirmatively, that is establish a thinking that is capable of thinking past the paradoxical conditions of now and therefore capable of opening our history, which is to say our future, to reflection.

(iii) A gesture whose retroactivity reconstitutes the past

What we are looking for is a gesture whose retroactivity reconstitutes the past—not, obviously, the "actual" past but the past as we receive it, as we measure it, and as we allow it to determine how we act. Slavoj Žižek has called this "the most succinct definition of what an authentic act is." In our ordinary activity, Žižek notes, we effectively simply follow the given "coordinates" of our identities (individual, collective, as a culture). But an "act proper ... is the paradox of an actual move which (retroactively) changes the very virtual 'transcendental' coordinates of its agent's being";[13] it is an act which changes the actuality of our world by changing what determines our notion of actuality; by introducing into what has inevitably become a fixed or determined relation the possibility of thinking it otherwise. If the past is the transcendental condition for our acts, and the past brought forward into the present is one of the deepest conditioning mechanisms of how we think that we can act, then an act that looks hard at this history and which undoes its false grip on us (which *analytically* abandons certain unnecessary parameters therefore making space to introduce "novelties" of thought and action) creates an actual new reality by retroactively changing what determines and fixes us and by changing the existing parameters and norms of acting.

What Žižek is trying to tell us here is that we are "simultaneously less free and more free than we think: we are thoroughly passive, determined by and dependent on the past, but we have freedom to determine the scope of this determination."[14]

> I am determined by causes, but I (can) retroactively determine which causes will determine me: we, subjects, are passively affected by pathological objects and motivations; but, in a reflexive way, we ourselves have the minimal power to accept (or reject) being affected in this way, in other words we retroactively determine the causes allowed to determine us, or, at least, the *mode* of this linear determination. "Freedom" is thus inherently retroactive: at its most elementary, it is not a free act which out of nowhere starts a new casual link, but a retroactive act of endorsing which link/sequence of necessities will determine me.[15]

What we are interested in then is a (designed) gesture which explores this while also reflecting on itself as act, and twice over; first in regard to history—above all as the breaking of "fate" and as the true "Working through the past" which Adorno demanded,[16] and then once again in regard to acting—where it *enacts*, even symbolically, what can occur when we break the supposed limits on our acting and through that (re) discover something of what it can be to act.

There are two moments or tasks here. One is Adorno's—"the past will have been worked through only when the causes of what happened then have been eliminated . . . only because the causes continue to exist does the captivating spell of the past remain to this day unbroken"—the other is Žižek's, "the texture which predestines us belongs to the purely virtual eternal past which can, as such, be retroactively rewritten by our act.[17]. The first puts to us the task of thinking historical cause—which means in our terms rethinking it, understanding it over again, realizing where fateful steps were taken, recovering, in a word, the "real" of our determination. The second—and this is not at all in contradiction with the first—realizes that the history that determines us is not only "real" but is "virtual" and "eternal" in ways that can be rewritten by our acts. Acts change destiny, both by proffering comprehension, concerning what actually determines; and by the gesture that changes the nature of the fate that apparently grips us. What brings these two together is (to repeat) the act which changes the actuality of our world by changing what determines our notion of actuality; by introducing into what has inevitably become a fixed or determined relation *the possibility of thinking it otherwise*. This acting gets all the more weight when we remember that we too only "are" through the *eventful* manner in which we *interpret* our historical condition or situation and through that to repeat, past, present and the future. Today, design is in the position to explore such acts, at once in relation to history and to the future. That we can explore this possibility is given by a project established in Berlin in 1993.

II

A Berlin Moment

A project

Orte des Erinnerns/Places of Remembrance, a Memorial for Jews Living in Berlin 1933–42, was enacted in Berlin, in 1993, by the artist and art historian couple Renata Stih and Frieder Schnock.[18] The project is a designed commemoration—though this word is loaded and is, as we shall see, by no means exact—of the former presence of a considerable Jewish community who inhabited the Schöneberg district of Berlin up until World War II. (Both Einstein and Hannah Arendt lived there at various times before 1933; the neighborhood was something of an intellectual center for upper middle-class Jewish life in Berlin.)[19]

Focusing on the Bayerischer Platz, the historic hub of the district, Stith and Schnock's project does not take the form of a conventional memorial, rather, in a gesture that is both remarkably simple and astonishingly compelling, they created and erected in the adjacent streets eighty pictorial/textual signs.

Hung on lampposts, perhaps three meters off the ground, and of a size to be legible from a distance,[20] each consists of a single brightly printed illustration, done, it seems at first, in the slightly naïve style of a child's first reader.[21] A few are words or graphic emblems—"Haberland Straße," the sign "name plate," a sketch of the chalked outline of the child's game "Hopscotch," but the vast majority are depictions of simple domestic objects—a loaf of bread, a house, a cake, of pair of swimming trunks, a dog, a hat, a violin case, car keys, an electrical plug, a pacifier.

Despite, or perhaps because, of their literalness, they are at first sight oddly equivocal and enigmatic. What does it mean for example to encounter in the small park near the Bayerischer Platz subway stop, the image "envelope,"[22] or to suddenly turn a corner and come across an abstracted image of a beach?[23]

Their meaning only becomes clear when one examines the reverse of each sign. Affixed below the sign is a small plaque. On the reverse of each image is a text. Plaque and text together begin to offer a clue as to what these illustrations are about. The plaque gives the title, and very importantly the subtitle, of the project as a whole—"Memorial: Places of Remembrance: Bayerisches Viertel: Isolation and deprivation of rights, expulsion, deportation and murder of Berlin Jews in the years 1933 to 1945." The texts are edited extracts from one of the decrees that were applied to Jews in Berlin between 1933 and 1942.

Thus, for example, the text for the sign noted earlier, "House," reads "Jews may inherit only when national socialist morals are upheld, July 31, 1938." The reverse of the sign "Bread" carries the edict that "Jews in Berlin are allowed to shop for food only between 4 and 5 o'clock in the afternoon, July 4th 1940," that of the game "Hopscotch," "Aryan and Jewish children may not play together," 1938. The texts therefore record, as each sign illustrates—sometimes literally, sometimes allusively, almost always with a degree of pathos—the net of persecutory and humiliating prohibitions that, between 1933 and 1942, eroded Jewish life and increasingly set the community apart from their non-Jewish neighbors. See for example, the sign "Chalk board" whose reverse records the expulsion of Jewish children from public schools, or the sign denoting the curfews enforced on Jews ("Jews are not permitted to leave their Apartments after 8pm (9pm in Summer) September 1st, 1939").

The relationships between text and image are at once direct and elusive. The pearl necklace on the sign "Jewellery" almost literally marks the edict "Jewellery, items made of gold, silver, or platinum, and pearls belonging to Jews are to be turned to the State. February 21, 1939," but the sign "Herzlich Willkommen" ("Good Welcome") which records the order sent out during the Berlin Olympics of 1936, "To avoid giving foreign visitors a negative impression, signs with strong language will be removed ... Signs such as 'Jews are unwanted here' will suffice, January 29, 1936," is deliberately ironic.

Signs and texts between them make emblematic—and not at all insignificantly represent the objective evidence of—the often seemingly petty legal and juridical processes by which the Jewish population was gradually deprived of all rights. It is indicative in this respect that the series opens, chronologically, not with a dramatic gesture but with one of the first regulations passed by the Nazi city authorities ("Costs of treatment by a Jewish doctor after April 1 1933 will not be reimbursed by the City of Berlin's public health insurance company. March 31, 1933").

The apparent minutiae of the issue tells one immediately that the emphasis is not on the events of the Holocaust per se as we now think of them (only a few of the signs refer to the removal of the Jews from Berlin and their subsequent murder) but rather on the daily humiliations and cruelties that prepared the way for the Jews as victims-to-be (and which later enabled their fate to be seen as both logical and necessary).[24] Thus, for example, the sign "Chess Board" records the early edict (July 9, 1933) that "Jewish members of the Greater German Chess Association are expelled"; that of "Armband" that "Jews may not be members of the German Red Cross, January 1st 1938." Taken one by one these and like decrees may scarcely seem to matter. But of course they are never taken— nor are they intended—in singularity. What is of consequence for the Jewish targets of such regulations is the range and the cascading accumulation of the edicts imposed.

As to range, while some can be expected, others surprise, either because one had scarcely thought of this or that activity subject to regulation ("Book: Jews may not purchase books, October 9th 1942") or because one is still reluctant to attest to the premediated degree of cruelty imagined in the even in the smallest moments ("Cat: Jews are no longer allowed to have household pets, 15th March 1942.")[25] Even while the escalation towards their murder was developing, decrees of astonishing banality were still being issued: "*Extrablatt*: Jews are forbidden from buying newspapers and magazines, February 17, 1942"; "Ashtray: Cigarettes and cigars are no longer sold to Jews, June 19, 1942." The bathetic final regulation applied to the Jewish population before their almost total deportation to the camps[26] is "Jews may no longer purchase meat, meat products and other rationed goods, September 18th 1942."

As to their cascading accumulation, the point, of course, is that it is precisely the fact that these never-ending, logical-yet-arbitrary edicts reach into even the most petty areas of life and thus bear with particular or peculiar force on the character of everyday life as a whole, that they succeed in taking the Jewish population of Berlin (as of course across Germany as a whole) out of civil society and thus make them capable of being murdered with impunity.

One can watch the entwined escalation of this process through the dates on the few signs that bear directly on the processes that led gradually to murder. The sign "Factory" denotes the edict from March 1941 that all adult Jews must do hard labor; The sign "Shirt," that "All Jews over the age of 6 must wear a yellow star with the word 'Jew', September 1941." A black rectangle is the visual marker for the decree which came only a month later that "The emigration of Jews is forbidden" (October 23, 1941), while the sign that simply bears the acronym "DR" (i.e., Deutsche Reichsbahn) stands for the double legend, "First mass deportations of Berlin Jews, October 18, 1941" and "First deportations directly to the death camp at Auschwitz, July 11, 1942."[27]

Nonetheless, precisely because these moments are "known," these are by no means the significant signs. To the contrary, the overall lesson borne in on the spectator is that it is impossible not to perceive the deep intertwining between petty cruelty and humiliations and what was to come.[28]

Experiencing the event

(i) Locale

As one encounters it today on the streets of Schöneberg, the project is remarkable in its ability to achieve precisely what its authors describe:

> together the words and images force passers-by to remember the almost-forgotten history of this neighborhood. The decrees set by the National Socialists systematically forced the Jews out of daily life and gradually robbed them of their basic right. Isolation and discrimination paved the way for deportations and mass murder ... By walking through the streets, the observer can relate to the way in which these regulations eroded basic human rights. Instinctively, questions about the past and about present events evolve.[29]

The affect the work produces is deeply connected to its locale, and to the parallel experience of walking at once through the memorial and through the neighborhood. Devastated through fire bombing in the war, today the area around the Bayerischer Platz is a comfortable, even desirable neighborhood. Traversing it, one gets a strong sense of community: tree-lined streets, a church, shops, a children's playground. Both memorial and visitor feel as something of an intrusion into this world.

But this is perhaps a point. For the awkwardness that is the *necessary* accompaniment to experiencing this piece is wholly different to the sense that one experiences (or feels one should experience) in relation to the standard war-memorial. The latter, almost by necessity, carves out for itself a quasi-sacred or at least an honorific space. This is most obvious, even in a secular sense, in the war graves of eastern France. But it is present, as aura, around every monument to the dead. Not for nothing are memorials traditionally rendered in that which will endure. As Victor Hugo points out in *Notre-Dame de Paris* (in the remarkable chapter on stone and print "This will kill that") humanity stores its unbearable and essential memories in forms visible but above all durable. For millennia, the geological endurance of stone made it the natural material for enacting enduring memory. Even the effort of working it inscribes the monument with the weight of human investment. In such memorials one pays tribute as much to the act of inscription as to what was inscribed. Even contemporary monuments continue this tradition, hence the fall-back to neoclassicism in the worst and most trite of recent memorials—the United States monument to World War II; the more recent British monument to the crews of war-time Bomber Command—broken only by the occasional reinvention of the tradition, Maya Lin's sunken granite walls of the Vietnam Memorial, or Peter Eisenman's sea of concrete blocks in Berlin.[30]

The Schöneberg memorial is quite different. Though it is called—and was ostensibly created as—a "memorial" in fact it is neither experienced as, nor does it function as a monument in any traditional sense.[31] It is in fact—and this is the first of a number of deflations that the project manages—an *anti-monument*, both in the extreme modesty of its means—as compared not only to the massive investment in some of the World War I monuments (think of Edwin Lutyens' immense memorial to the dead of the Somme for example) but also vis-à-vis what seems, from this perspective, as the rhetorical excesses of Daniel Libeskind's Jewish Museum (1998) or Peter Eisenmann's more recent monument in central Berlin to the destruction of European Jewry. Instead of creating itself as a space other-to-life, the project weaves itself into the fabric of the quarter and therefore, by necessity, intimately into the conditions of daily life.

Put another way, we can say that counter to the logic of almost every other memorial of death, Stih and Schnock's project insists on the continuity between what is memorialized or recollected and the present, not as memory or the attempt to hold in mind what-was, but as the realization of what is still present.

Here again locale is key. Instead of (to repeat) as with a traditional memorial, withdrawing or subtracting the memorial to a discrete place where lamentation is permitted to take place in an quasi-sacred setting *outside* of the everyday and outside of this history—our history, the history of now and the history to come for us—"Places of Remembrance," on the contrary, deliberately, even *profanely*, inverts this notion. No matter the extent to which the populace discounts the signs, distributing them across the twenty or so streets across the area weaves the project inextricably into the daily moments of the neighborhood.[32] This placement within the everyday threatens its purity as a monument as such (which is perhaps one reason why, amongst others, it has not become a site of Holocaust tourism or pilgrimage) but it changes immediately the works relation to time. It enables it to operate, or better *to cut across*, time.[33] It neither cuts out a sacred time or tries to turn what was of its time into an eternal moment (which is what every reading or every monument or memorial to the Holocaust almost cannot help but want to achieve). The sense gathered as one walks the streets of "Places of Remembrance" is quite different: a considered fusing of past and present, of a project operating with something of Adorno's sharp awareness that "the past that one would like to evade is still very much alive."[34] The time of *this* monument is in other words *now*.[35]

(ii) Choreographing the visual

But an indissoluble part of what creates something of the awkwardness and the force of the Schöneberg memorial is the visual form it takes, or, to put it better, the manner in which it visually and experientially organizes how we encounter it.

In the Schöneberg piece the items are simply printed metal images, 80 of them, distributed around the streets of the neighborhood. Are they paintings? Hardly, in any direct sense (even if derived, it would seem, from acrylic originals). As noted, they have something of the quality of a child's book illustration but at this scale they are broken somewhat from the sense that they are merely illustrative. They evoke some sense of a poster or at least of the image as an announcement, so in that sense they might be seen as simply the herald to the true content of the work.

In some respects this is accurate. It might well be argued that the texts, the extracts from the decrees, are the real "message" of the memorial, but the effect of the work as we encounter it via these images is by no means the same as simply reading the list of regulations and orders. It is one thing to read or even to hear these regulations, shocking as some of them are (above all in their still disconcerting banality and petty cruelty) quite another to discover them reproduced on the reverse of an image hung on a lamppost in a pleasant Berlin quarter.

And one does indeed *discover* them. There is a cursory center to the memorial (the small park at the Bayerischer Platz U-Bahn) but with only two or three images to a street (they are usually 100 to 200 meters apart) one walks the surrounding streets will almost no sense of when or if you will find the signs.[36] Even on repeated visits one never sees all of them. At times it can seem as if the signs go on in almost endless procession, so that it becomes easy to imagine them distributed across the entire city, if not across Germany as a whole, a side effect of their distribution that the artists doubtless welcome.

The effect of this encounter (and one can only call it that) is the stranger because of how, even on the most immediate and visceral level, the signs are presented. One is at a loss, at first, to account for them. Lying between the literal and the enigmatic, but always staying this side of emotional expression, they have something of a deadpan quality. Their nonengagement with any overt emotion produces puzzlement. Even if one knows that this is indeed, somehow (but how?), a "Holocaust memorial" what could these images possibly reference? If the work of someone like Käthe Kollwitz is the epitome of the emotional anguish of murder translated into a visual image these are at the opposite extreme. There is nothing "bandaged" or "expressive" in what they depict. Later, one realizes that they are in this sense the equivalent, from the other side (though not-identically so) of the prosaic matter-of-factness of the regulations themselves. They are both a concretization of the regulations, yet not simply literal illustrations of them. They are ostensive—in that they point to segments of life (the necklace that indicates jewelry; the five rings of the Olympic movement that points us to 1936) but there is an emblematic quality to them, a slightly elliptical stance vis-à-vis the regulation they refer to, that gives them a certain independence, even vitality, against the deceptive neutrality of the language of the edicts and orders.

But if they are not expressive of "life" they are emblematic of it. As I put it in a recent lecture:

> What is the role of the visual in this project? It is not easy, I think, to precisely explain it. First, there is an involvement as question or puzzle—what are these images doing here? What are they of? Second, there is a human involvement, heightened, I think, by the (clearly deliberate) lack of finesse in the images. They are somehow too crude or too naïve to be "art" in the accepted sense.[37] Third, the fact there is not quite a literal transposition between regulation and illustration means that there is a kind of wavering, a zone of uncertainty that is only resolved by reading and pondering the regulation printed on the reverse side, but which then take on the smack of raw data or pure fact—law in all its inevitability and consequence.

This quality between literalness and enigma is significant. In one of the last lectures he gave before his untimely death (on the occasion of the opening of a "House of Literature" in Stuttgart in 2001) the writer W. G. Sebald argued that only in literature "can there be an attempt at restitution over and above the mere recital of facts, and over and above scholarship."[38]

In its literalness *Memorial in Berlin-Schöneberg* would seem, at first sight, to refute Sebald, but in fact its brilliance lies in staying as close as possible to the "recitation of facts" and yet, through their emblematization, and though their enactment as a strange kind of poetic project (if a sort of poetry at degree zero) it creates a space in which an *understanding* can emerge, *not* as restitution (this would be quite the wrong word) but as that which both makes suffering concrete in specific instance—in itself a significant act[39]—and seeks the end of the abstraction of the event.[40]

(iii) Objects (1)

This last point is important. It is emphasized by how "Places of Remembrance" bridges the scale of the event it deals with by fragmenting it into objects and actions that balance the difference between the immensity of the scale of what happened[41] and the intimate moments that constituted the "building blocks" of that event. Take for example the sign "Powder Box" from 1942 where the text reads "my powder box is a personal reminder for you. Use it often and think of me. With deep sorrow, yours, Else Stern. Before being deported, January 16 1942."

This sign is one of the very few that contains a personal narrative. While ensuing that just sufficient is told to remind us of the *then* human consequences, there is good reason for this limitation. "We said we don't work with names ... We didn't want to show it from the point of view of victims but from perpetrators." "We took the anti-Jewish laws and regulations,"[42] and presented them. Reading these statements we can understand Stih and Schnock's insistence that the project's emphasis not be on individual stories but on the "impersonal" (but in fact, in their consequence not so impersonal) means whereby (legally) these stories were produced, indicated to them that a memorial adequate to dealing with the perpetration of the event demanded a less subjective, less narratological approach than that today found in the Holocaust Industry. Whereas the latter prefers the story,[43] the strength of the memorial is that Stih and Schnock create and utilize one "apparatus"[44] to contest another and much larger (the legal preparation for the killing of the Jews).

The second reason to limit these stories is to force us to imagine *for ourselves* the consequences of these regulations and edicts. This is in line with Adorno's contention that the only way to cross the bridge to the subject who suffers is to see ourselves as *also* the potential victims of history, but it is, at the same time, also to seek to deliberately take attention away from the category and concept of the "victim" while placing it back, with emphasis, on the *living subject*.

It is not only however that, in such moments as that revealed by Else Stern's powder box that we are reminded of what we often wish to forget—i.e., that suffering at mass scale is always the product of an entire series of previous steps and decisions made, the interruption of any one of which might have had considerable impact on whether the project was realized—it is also that it is through working around and *through* such objects, that the project *connects*, at once dissolving all ideas of it as a contained event and placing it back within the webs of implication of daily life from which it began. After all, little, if anything remains in absolution from the Holocaust. At its widest it crossed Europe, both geographically and in the sense of touching every moment of European life; neither politics, nor thought, nor religion, nor (as this memorial makes most evident) law escape implication. Yet the brilliance of the memorial is precisely how it restores, critically, and I will say at the end paradoxically *affirmatively*, the implication of the Holocaust in the every day and does so though its unique use of the everyday object as the central mediation through which we are able to grasp the Holocaust.

Psychologically, we know that the object world is capable of putting the self through complex psychosomatic experience.[45] Like the small interjections used in expressive utterance, these objects live close to us. And there is clearly something about the way in which the wholly familiar, that which we are so used to handling, physically and mentally, that we feel at home with it, is particularly resonant for the psyche. A line in Calvino is pertinent here: "I would say that the moment that an object appears in a narrative that it is charged with a special force and becomes like a pole of a magnetic field, a knot in the network of invisible relationships."[46] It is perhaps for just that reason, when rendered emblematic as signs, that they can be particularly and peculiarly powerful, all the more that they are not only "close" but now address us, if with an enigmatic command.

But their affect is not confined to our own sensibilities. As was said in a note to me recently,

> if you are able to use small words and objects, you are much closer to how it is to experience first hand. The small thing often expresses the most direct and primary understanding of the other person's situation. If you understand the objects most closely connected to the person going through something, it means you able to put yourself in the

other person's shoes. If you think about words and objects as things we place between each other, it makes sense perhaps, that the smaller the object/word, the smaller the distance between us.[47]

Given the Nazi project of splitting, the politics of this identification hardly need to be spelt out. The objects, mediating the regulations—and thus behind them the terror—bridge experience. The divide breaks. "Victim" is no longer simply so—or, what comes to the same thing, is us.

But there is also another level on to which the objects work. That Stih and Schnock wanted to show it not "from the point of view of victims but from perpetrators" and "took the anti-Jewish laws and regulations and presented them" is of course the single most powerful—and original— aspect of the memorial. But the regulations, while they are in retrospect the "missing element" which links politics and terror—which make the former concrete by endowing will with actual effects, while, in a culture of obedience, legitimating the latter—are nonetheless, in themselves, as cold as the cynicism (and rationality) which drove them.[48] They require therefore that which can make them alive, which can cause their consequences and implications to be grasped viscerally and emotively as well as intellectually. Here we come back to the resolute "object-ness" or at least the implied materiality, the matter-of-factness, of the signs. Pictures of things, or if not of items or moments equivalently modest and close, they allow precisely what the preceding paragraphs spelt out, i.e., the establishment of a resolute connection between our experience of now and the experience of then.[49] In this sense it is their use of objects that is the agency of their thought and in the end the basis of the politics of the memorial.

(iv) An economy of presence and the question of history

Finally, in terms of how we experience the work, there is the question of the astonishing economy of what we are presented with. This is undoubtedly related to the works' all-but-utilitarian, almost anonymous, manner of presence. But it is not only this. There is a configurative economy at work here. The work touches lightly on the streets it inhabits. This is played out in the physical condition of the memorial, which is at once infinitely smaller (in architectonic or structural volume, or in expense) and infinitely greater (in terms of the geographic area of Berlin covered) than Libeskind's or Eisenman's memorials. Indeed the contrast between the excess yet held-in (economically restrained) conditions of the latter two versus the open, if not potentially all-but-infinite, condition of the Schöneberg memorial is marked. Against it the (formal) gestures of Libeskind and the monumentality of Eisenman look overwrought, inert, full of the opacity of the world as-is, but strangely empty in content, as if they had in fact nothing to say concerning the *historical* truth of the Holocaust.[50]

And this is perhaps the case. For they propose nothing concerning it, other than that we should recall it in their presence. Both proffer themselves as "experience." But we might ask: experience in relation to what? And the answer comes back: in relation to the Holocaust as we receive it through the lens of the "Holocaust industry," which today, as in the working of any other apparatus, perpetuates what maintains it. Even more to the point, history—meaning the *problem* of history—is an afterthought in the one (Libeskind's museum was clearly never conceived to show anything but itself) and is buried underground in the other[51] (for why should history disturb immaculate gesture—even that of the tomb?). By contrast, in "Places of Remembrance," while its resonance is to what is outside of itself, its reference to *history*, meaning both to the history of the Holocaust as it came to be (rather than to what is already digested as tragedy, and thus as myth) and to our history as a whole, is internal. It is *history* that is here recorded, made emblematic and presented for thought. And it is this that makes this work emblematic for the wider problems that we are dealing with in our culture as a whole.

Writing history: What an event does

Essentially it is a matter of the way in which the past is made present whether one remains at the level of reproach or whether one withstands the horror by having the strength to comprehend even the incomprehensible.

THEODOR ADORNO[52]

(i) Problems of memory

We saw earlier that it was Nelson Goodman's brave contention (brave because he goes here against the grain of our times) that the "primary purpose" of all complex symbolic activity—which includes all complex ensembles of the character of the Schöneberg memorial—"is cognition in and for itself."[53] On these grounds we could reasonably be disappointed in the majority of Holocaust memorials, few of which rise to the challenge of enabling us to comprehend the only real question which matters, which is the question that Stih and Schnock asked themselves, namely, "How could this ever have happened?"[54]

But then of course it is not intended they do so. "Memory" plays fast and loose here. Its invocation as necessity comes with the ready idea that without it "the murdered are to be cheated out of the one single remaining thing that powerlessness can offer them: remembrance."[55]

The problem arises however when one realizes also that memory (as memorial, as monument) is as easily invoked in the cause of *not* having to think. The monument memorializes, but around the dead thought stops. The atrophy of historical continuity is thus not necessarily resisted by it. On the contrary, the suspicion remains is that it is perhaps accelerated. Virtue replaces the more difficult task of understanding. The comforting ideology grows that one should *not* understand, lest what is transcendent (a person, a people) is thereby soiled.[56] Unfortunately, this merely resurrects again gross stupidity. What is put out to memory in this way—as one puts out a horse to grass—returns as the compulsion to repeat, even in the name of that memory. Adorno was right, the adage that "The past will have been worked through only when the causes of what happened then have been eliminated"[57] remains the necessary political watchword. But there is no relation between cause and elimination that does not pass through understanding—and this means an understanding capable of overcoming cause through its affirmative incorporation. In that sense memory does not belong to the present but to the future. Adorno's requirement, noted above, therefore needs to be slightly redrafted: "The murdered are not to be cheated out of the one single remaining thing that powerlessness can offer them: *the capacity to affect the future*."

In this respect Stih and Schnock are correct. Not even the extraordinary project of naming all the dead, magnificent though it is—and itself that which stands as a silent rebuke against judgments which can only count and thus against those for whom only number matter—suffices to begin understanding of this event, let alone of the trajectory of (modern) history of which it was *not* the culmination.[58] There is no less useful way of seeing the Holocaust than this. It is not the culmination because, uneliminated, cause—all that enabled the Holocaust—continues to "captivate."[59] There is thus nothing teleological in the Holocaust. Thought in abstraction, as "idea," such thinking participates in the same structure of thought and will. The notion of a "tragedy," unthought, turns into myth. That which was contradiction is mediated to the point where it is assimilated as an "unknowable excess," and this excessiveness and unknowability is then turned into a virtue, as if this talisman will alone ward off future evil while keeping memory alive. This slippage—ultimately a slippage of responsibility and of understanding of causation—is at the very opposite end of Stih and Schnock's ambitions for their project. Their aim is precisely to *reverse* the direction taken, wittingly or no, by many of the major Holocaust memorials.[60]

*

The project arose, after all, from historical research into the former Jewish population of Schöneberg. Stih and Schnock's project directly took up some of this material. In so doing, in transposing literal historical fact into demonstrative practice, they were working in accordance with the idea that if one *thinks* history, in a political or a philosophical sense (in terms of thinking of the meaning of history, i.e., its consequences and implications for subjects, across time) then this merges with "the writing of history," and thus with entry into "the subject matter of history itself." And this moves naturally, as it were, to the necessity to "write" history oneself in order to explicate it, and hence to the need to address and engage with "the specific configurations of historical processes."[61]

Now it will be objected immediately that artists or designers do not "write" history.

But this is to fail to observe the term "configurations" in the last sentence, and to fail to reflect in what ways that designers and artists may, in and through *their* configurations, make parallels (literal or no) between the configurations, events and sequences of history, and the events and sequences which they can establish through their own configurations. The achievement of Stih and Schnock is to have deployed a number of traditional artistic, poetic and design tropes (selection, discrimination, invention amongst them) in such a way that they have discovered (created) a configuration—a *designed* configuration one must insist— through which it is possible not simply to *use* history (in an extractive sense) but to "write" it, in the language of a configurative and poetic event. But the only way the project can do this—can make its seemingly insignificant gestures leverage such huge questions—is if the *apparatus* that actors devise both "does" and "sees," i.e., if the work functions (as a memorial) but also acts as lens through which history (past, present, future; at extreme, the nature of own evil can be enacted) can be seen and understood differently.[62]

(ii) Making an apparatus that thinks

Why speak of the memorial as an *apparatus and why connect this apparatus and "writing"*? First, because it is literally so: the memorial is a choreographed ensemble of physical signs, images and words interwoven into the complex space of more than a dozen streets centered on the Bayerischer Platz U-Bahn. More significantly, it is clear that the memorial does not separate its moments: i.e., it does not separate the contents with which it deals: the overwhelming fact of the Holocaust; the (legal) history on which it focuses; the suffering which implies and references, and the even more fundamental question that it seeks to address: "How did this happen?," and the technical moments through which it thinks, exemplifies and demonstrates these issues. Its thinking circulates *between* these elements and makes no absolute distinction between them; that is the memorial thinks *through* its apparatus,[63] and this "circulation is the movement of a unique thinking"[64]—a movement productive of a singular understanding.

That the memorial-as-apparatus thinks in this way means that is perhaps—this is its wager—at once (i) an apparatus working on behalf of subjectivity (in favor of what Agamben might call "profanity");[65] (ii) an event that is "transformative of the conditions of experience and knowing"; and (iii) something close to what Tony Fry in his essay in this volume called the creation of "something else, something new" with respect to the revitalization of writing history.

But how precisely does the "apparatus" of the memorial *think*?

To begin by repeating what is already apparent: "Places of Remembrance" is *not* a monument, or even a memorial, in the usual sense of the term. We can see it in many ways as the difference between responding to the project as a memorial to "the Jews" (the Other) and *thinking* Else Stern's experience. The first participates in an event that is "known" and *represents* that representation. The second *presents* a discovery concerning how this event occurred. The first ostensibly places the victims as central, but in fact puts the event first, an event whose historical and political definition is already prestructured by existing suppositions (those concerning evil, the Holocaust, the Jews, the war and so on) and is in any case subordinated to whatever is the prevailing consensual judgment of opinion concerning this event.[66] The second, by contrast, actually places the victims as central, but *not* as "victims." The difference can be put down to this. The first, "leave the identity of the [viewer as] voyeur intact, at a remove from the grievous events which she observes."[67] The second *deliberately* normalizes, or at least relativizes, the evil that it *explains*. At the same time, it refuses any overarching condition that could determine the point at which our participation would be *outside* of this order of relations. The first, then, leaves Fascism intact—because it leaves all "explanation" intact (refuses explanation indeed) and *in any case operates as ontologically as did the cause of what it memorializes*;[68] the second shakes Fascism, or more precisely "shakes" our conception of what Fascism might have been and of what it today consists (and shakes too our assumption of our lack of complicity in the act). The first operates through the category "Auschwitz,"—which is today the misunderstood shorthand for the Hell one is seeking to address. The second grasps that Auschwitz "comes too late," that to erect monuments in its name is already to cede too much.

Auschwitz is too late. It was even so, for the Germans. Planned, as is now beginning to be more generally understood, as the center of what was thought of as a vast network of slave-labor camps, Auschwitz was thought as an economic hub in the conquest of the East, in which camps would be established to work to death—at not inconsiderable profit to the SS and the companies involved[69]—the "subhuman" populations of Poland, the Ukraine and Russia.[70] Its role as a "death camp," in the way that its name now conjures, came late.

But even as this essential history is obscured by what, as a name, it now stands for, so the axiomatic connection "Auschwitz"/"murder" also obscures the only question that truly matters which is "How did this—i.e. the totality of the project of the destruction of European Jews—occur?" To answer that question one must come back before the transports; one must (re)discover to what enabled the transports to be; to what in retrospect announces not that the transports *would* be (inevitability) but that they *could* be (the requisite *political* decision having been made). One goes back then to what enables a subject to be murdered with ease (and this is perhaps what always grips about the Holocaust, the *ease* with which death happened, this was killing, in effect, "without a hair out of place"). What facilitates ease are mechanisms. Not just the pistol, the machine gun, the chambers and the ovens, but the ideological and organizational mechanisms that prepared both the subjects to be transported, and other subjects to participate, at every level, in this vast process of transporting subjects for labor and death.

(iii) Thinking the Holocaust from the perspective of the living

The question of law

But it is precisely because it is *not* the end, *not* death, and *not* Auschwitz that is the focus of the project that it *configures*—or better reconfigures—its subject matter so differently. The focus is on the necessary *primary* question "How was Auschwitz possible?" meaning here how was it possible that between 1933 and 1942 certain individuals, living in one of the most sophisticated societies on earth, were in the minds of the German population, including German Jews, reconstructed (we might almost say, reconfigured) such that they could be removed and killed with impunity, without these crimes being in any way attested as murder? [71]

To address this the memorial reverses the norm. Compared with the ostensible subject matter of the traditional monument, the Berlin memorial acts as if it followed the maxim attributed to Spinoza that "there is nothing to be thought concerning death." The subtitle—"A Memorial for Jews *Living* in Berlin 1933–45"—gives us its orientation. What matters, to this project, are the processes of living. It is a memorial—if we can call it that, it might be better to say that it is primarily a commentary—on the processes whereby the *material means that enable socialized living to take place* were gradually *legally* denied to one segment of the Berlin population. What *Places of Remembrance* speaks to is not the tragic myth of the Holocaust, where the focus comes down to the tiny interval between the trains and the gas chambers and the event is crystallized in death, but the real horror of the legal processes whereby lives are readied for death. The evil that is spoken to is therefore not the brutality of death (for which so few were ever convicted) but that of *denial* (for which it is quite certain no-one was ever convicted). The former happened "outside" the ostensible norms of German society. The latter happened in plain sight within and through German society, at every level.

If this is a "memorial" to anything it is to the regulations that were the other side of the terror, the legal apparatus in all its authority and dispassionate professional instrumentality. What Stih and Schnock discovered (and there is a way this term can be justified)[72] was the "missing mechanism" of the Holocaust—*the mechanism that every conventional monument had to miss*. To at once show—demonstrate—this mechanism of legal terror and at the same time to make its human consequences central to the experience of encountering it, the memorial has to do three things.

- First, to make immediate suffering visible and speakable—but through the voice *not*, except for a couple of rare exceptions, of the victim but that of the perpetrators. And yet this suffering has to be transferable, through the simplest means, to the spectator.

- Second, it must re-present these regulations in the context of the configuration of power and its legal legitimation (backed by terror) which constituted the ever-narrowing limits of the "world" of the Berlin Jew.

- Third, Stih and Schnock had to do this by creating a configuration—a simulation if you like—that could both capture the relation between the political project of the Nazis from 1933–1942 (in which the name of the Jew figures as the appalling and contaminated other to the inclusive homogeneity of the German), law (as the visible face of administration) and force or terror (that which secures law, makes it absolute for those to whom it is addressed) *and* offer the sharpest possible *inexplicit* critique of that nexus.

Everything that has been said so far indicates that they achieved this. In this way—by the fact that their entire subject matter concerns the *legal* means by which denial was enforced on the Jewish population of Berlin—they contribute to history, meaning to understanding. Looked at retrospectively, we can see that even the Nazi regime had to summon its courage for death. The ultimate denial (life) was practiced first in the denial of the attributes and conditions of living. The one almost seamlessly prepared the way for the other. If law gives the *character* of history to a moment (its manner, its modality) if law engenders, then law in this form—or these laws—are not neutral but the very agency of evil. The nazi political project used the idea of the Jew as the means of rallying a Germany population to the Nazi cause. It follows that their erasure, rationally, is the mark of the achieved plenitude of Germany. Law was an agency, perhaps the agency by which the second was made possible.

What "Places of Remembrance" achieves is the presentation and *thinking* of *this* fact, i.e., the rational logic of the Nazi political project.[73] It presents law in its falling away from mutuality,[74] and it thinks the consequences of this falling. This is a presentation of law at an extreme moment of its betrayal as that which should serve the universal interest. Through it, an ascribed class of persons lose their relations to "desire, work and otherness"[75] and with it their subjectivity in the eyes of others. What social propaganda propagates, law *enacts*. It *positions*, and it readies (in their roles) the participants in the Holocaust. With law in play, terror can take a back seat (as indeed, between 1935 and 1938, *relatively*, it did so).[76] It need reappear only in the seizure of these persons for transportation and death. The modern diremption of law and ethics is here complete.

It is in showing this—in presenting it—that the memorial begins to rework it. Invoking the force of terror, law claims its innocence vis-à-vis evil. But the absolution it wishes only perpetuates the underlying diremption. The Schöneberg memorial confirms this and shatters the "innocence" of the law.

(iv) Reconstructing suffering, and the victim

This does not mean (as of course we have seen) that the project fails to recollect suffering. If the focus is on the juridical deprivation of rights, the regulations that Stih and Schnock present are not simply an index of the processes of eroding, in varying ways, the civil standing of the Jewish population, they are also *in themselves* suffering. All of the signs, without exception, refer to decrees, laws, regulations that are regulations of denial. All are direct or indirect referents of suffering—and all the more effectively sadistic in their mock impersonality and what we can only call the sentimentality of their legality. The relationship between suffering and denial is in each case more or less one-to-one. Suffering and humiliation is therefore not just the *ultimate* outcome of these processes but its immediate intended consequence. Historically suffering did not begin in the transports, or with the execution squads. It was built into legalized anti-Semitism from the beginning; it is what these processes were *designed* to do.[77] The project records this and speaks to it directly (as we have seen) occasionally in the texts. But as we have also seen, the project radically limits these stories, in part "to force us to imagine for ourselves the consequences of these regulations and edicts" but also to deliberately take attention *away* from the category and concept of the "victim" while placing it firmly back on the living subject and their slow, deliberate deconstruction as a subject, their transformation into a "specimen" for use and disposal.

This is important. The narrative and ideology of the victim are both deeply entrenched in the traditional representation of the Holocaust. However, the recovery of the victim once they have been consigned to that role—once the *shame* (Primo Levi's word) of allowing oneself to become *placed* as the victim has been internalized—is very difficult. It is not least of the evils of the Holocaust that after it the concept of the victim has become "impossible", above all perhaps because of associations of passivity (the victim is the at the opposite end to will and the philosophy of action that we still lean towards) but also because we cannot take the victim as anything *except* an all-but nonsubject. The reduction and deprivation of potentiality that defines "becoming a victim" (or being made into a victim) passes into the character and identity of the subject marked for death. What is necessary to the suffering they receive—that they are regarded as fit only for disposal—marks their identity, even in advance of the event itself. "Suffering does not awaken transformation"[78] (Heidegger) because suffering happens to the victim—who the will marks anyway for contempt (and fear of contamination).[79]

To "acquiesce" in becoming a victim (to be forced into acquiescence) is to invite suffering. Just as the exercise of deprivation created the proto-victim, so the legal identification of Berlin's Jewish population as proto-victims "invited" the exercise of imposition. This is deeper than the view that the victim has, in some manner, a part to play in their own damnation—that they "furnished some kind of instigation."[80] It is rather a sense that the ideology of the victim is fundamentally corrosive—obviously to those who are assigned this role; equally perhaps to those who are not victims yet who fear, deeply, to be assigned or to "fall into to" the status of the victim; and (not least) to those caught up, willingly or not, in this apparatus, and who, again willingly or no, adopt the roles—*and the legal sanctity*—of those charged with enforcing the denials that will knowingly produce suffering (and who, in the end, organize and effect death).

But one might want also want to pull back from the very concept of the victim because the notion transforms substantive suffering from the concrete consequence of decisions made to something very close to fate— or what is as bad, to "that-which-happens." There is a too close affinity between notions of destiny, tragedy and the victim. In genocide this association has baleful consequences. For this way of viewing "what happened" too easily gives alibi to those whose decisions were responsible for what transpired—just as it de-fangs the political and criminal actuality of what transpired. Even today we have difficulty in assessing genocide or mass political murder as criminal activity. Deaths incurred in the Holocaust have never been charged under the criminal statues dealing with homicide. And we know that today, lacking the will to engage with the "difficulties" involved, it has proved all but impossible to bring to trial most of those accused of more recent genocides and human rights violations.

That is why there are almost no victims in this memorial. Rather, the address is to all. On one side the negation of mutual recognition through law is revealed as the agency of denial—ultimately of life. On the other this denial is not worked as abstraction, but in terms of what the laws themselves address that is the very specific material and social conditions through which lives are lived.

If law is the first move of this memorial, and the refusal of the status of "victim" the second, the third and final moment I will identify here concerning how the memorial "thinks" the Holocaust is in terms of the weight it gives to small material things and the everyday.

(iv) Affirmation, or the object (2)

I can begin this point by trying to redeem a curious comment I made earlier that there is an affirmative moment in the memorial. To propose that there is something affirmable in the Holocaust would seem to be— is—obscene. But I am not referring to the event, but to what the *memorial* discovers.

All monuments are also affirmations. The nation affirms itself, in its myth, through the sacrifice of others for its cause. The monument is the mark of this.[81] Likewise, the family affirms itself through the grave plot it annually visits. In the case of Holocaust monuments of the usual class the affirmation is largely to those who erected them.[82] But what then is the affirmation of the Schöneberg memorial? It lies, to repeat, in what it essentially discovers. What it discovers is that it is in relation to the moments of material existence that both evil and the good are revealed in their emphatic nature—we can even say, in their truth. How does it do this? It shows us irrefutably that evil has its roots in denial—and thus that (sovereignty) of the Good is located equally emphatically in the provision of objectified compassion.[83]

One of the last signs in the sequence in the memorial (#78) is "Canary Cage." It bears this legend:

> We had a canary. When we received the notice that Jews are forbidden from keeping pets, my husband found it impossible to part from the animal. Every sunny day he put the bird-cage out on the windowsill. Perhaps someone reported him because one day he was summoned to the Gestapo. (. . .) After living in fear from many weeks, the police sent a postcard saying that I must pay a fee of 3 Reich-marks to pick up my husbands ashes. Report 1943.[84]

What is as significant as the terror is *what* was denied. What is denied is access to the small material things and occasions of life. This is not only denial of that without which the "higher things" of life cannot be (though it is obviously this too—cf. the signs denying Jews access to the theatre, opera, cinemas—and eventually books) it is more directly the denial of access to what enables life to be. It is the denial of the truth elucidated so articulately by Elaine Scarry when, apropos of the work that things do, she notes, "the general distribution of material objects to a population means that a certain minimum level of objectified human compassion is built into the revised structure of the world, and does not depend on the day-to-day generosity of other inhabitants which cannot itself be legislated." She continues: "This is why . . . the first act of tyrants and other egoists is often to replace a materially bountiful world (with its implicit if anonymous, human wish for the individual's basic comfort) with a starkly empty one in which each nuance of comfort depends on the vagaries of the egoist's own disposition."[85]

Nothing could be closer to what Stih and Schnock enact for us in Schöneberg. Thought in terms of their entwinement with the everyday, the "materialist motifs" (Adorno) of the project—and what better characterization of the signs than this?—now reveal their double work, as the emblems, simultaneously, of denial as the agency of sadism and the betrayal of the universal truth of objectified human compassion) and, on the affirmative side, of the translation and building of objectified human compassion into "the revised structure of the world", as the very essence of the Good.

The latter is not insignificant, neither for ethics, nor even for what can be, for us, "metaphysics". Adorno, in 1965, had already argued that, it is not in "pure thought that morality lives on, but in 'materialist motifs'."[86] "Once the totality, the 'great whole' has been actively discredited as the primary object of philosophy, and once 'as good as nothing remains of its metaphysical truth content' the experience of small things of unimportant and unobtrusive things, acquires a completely new dignity . . . 'metaphysics migrates into the micrological.'"[87] As origin reveals its insignificance, the proximate begins to occupy the place of deepest reflection. Agamben, in the appendix to *The Coming Community*, explores something similar, "Revelation does not mean revelation of the sacredness of the world but only … of its irredeemably profane character … The possibility of salvation begins only at this point; it is the salvation of profanity of the world, its being thus."[88] The Berlin memorial can thus be read as a memorial to the micrological, to profanity, where the latter are not abstract concepts but as the material things on which a life depends, the very medium through which life flows, or is denied—and hence, in ways we might not have previously realized, the moments of good and evil. The paradoxical affirmation that Stih and Schnock make then arises here. Richard Ellmann, deducing that Joyce's *Ulysses* was, amongst other things, but not least, a statement concerning the overcoming of denial, ends his lectures on the book with the line, "Having completed his plan, Joyce might well feel that he has succeeded in disengaging what was affirmable in existence, and had affirmed that."[89] If we adapt this to the Berlin memorial we might say: "Having enacted their work Stih and Schnock might well feel that they have succeeded, against the forces at work in both the destruction of the Jews and in later representations of this event, in *disengaging* what was affirmable, and had affirmed that."[90]

*

The Schöneberg memorial is in the end an ethical, a historical and a political project. It is the reinvention of the conjunction of these, not as abstractions but as ways of grasping the histories that determine us such that it is possible to move from stasis and evasion, from *fear*. The fear that they address is not the fear that Auschwitz will "occur again." It already has, and was little noticed—because it did not look like Auschwitz, because it did not have the same actors. The fear of Auschwitz is the fear of the same. It is the impossibility of accepting responsibility. "Ineffability," the prohibition of thought, the desire to preserve a "mystical" moment, almost a sublime sensation of horror vis-à-vis what happened, is the desire, as Gillian Rose has pointed out, "to mystify something we dare not understand because we fear it may be all too understandable, all too continuous with what we are."[91] Above all, it is the fear of accepting the nature of evil as the Holocaust as a whole—or better the Nazi project— reveals it. For this evil is substantive, and is founded on denial. It is neither banal nor trivial (neither term is appropriate for what they show)[92] but neither is it "radical." It is, on the contrary, ordinary—but then so too is the good.[93] *They are located in the same place.*

If we finally try to bring all this together we can say that through their memorial (their configuration) Stih and Schnock manage a fourfold resituating or repositioning of the Holocaust

1   a situating of its singularity (by making their own situation and creating their own singularity that is capable of reflecting, acutely, both on the originating event and how that event is received today);

2   a repositioning of the categories of participants (perpetrator, "victim") and their relation within the political—social, legal, cultural—sequence of the Holocaust, then and now;

3   this repositioning includes a repositioning of the place of "Auschwitz" in the understanding of the Holocaust ("Auschwitz comes too late") and a reemphasis on how the Jews were created such that they could be destroyed;

4   at the widest, a radical repositing regarding the substantive categories of evil and the good, and the relocation of these firmly in the most material of things and relations.

Here is a work *of history* that retroactively reconstitutes the past (as we receive it, as we measure it, and as we allow it to determine how we act) in the light of the present-becoming-future. In these terms Stih and Schnock achieve what Žižek called an "act proper," the paradox of an "actual move which (retroactively) changes the virtual coordinates of our possibility," and which hence opens the possibility of changing the actuality of our world by changing (through offering understanding) what determines our notions of how things are. It is an act, in other words, that allows the possibility of thinking our determining history otherwise.[94] It thus also points to a different future, a future which, *as understanding*, is contained within its own configuration.

In lieu of a conclusion

(i) Without mitigation

In the end, despite the presuppositions that surround his thought, the comment "History promises no salvation and offers the possibility of hope only to the concept whose movement follows history's path to the very extreme"[95] need not be thought only pessimistically. What the fifty years since Adorno made this proposition have shown us is the essential truth of a second proposition few have ever taken sufficiently seriously. The force of the argument that "after having missed its opportunity, philosophy must come to know, without any mitigation, why the world— which could be paradise here and now—can become hell itself tomorrow"[96] can now be seen to lie not only in what it urges for philosophy (essential though this still is) but as much—if not more—in the substantive declaration. "Paradise here and now" and "hell" are not abstract referents. The condition where *both* are eminently realizable (even if one, clearly, at the moment predominates) is immanent not theoretical. On one side then a matter of choice, the question of how one lines up with respect to these possibilities; on the other a matter of grasping what is implied in the sentence that precedes Adorno's first injunction: "The undiminished persistence of suffering, fear, and menace necessitates that the thought that cannot be realized should not be discarded."[97]

The former places us in a state of decision as to our standing to the world. "Between Man as the possible basis for the uncertainty of truths, or Man as the being-for-death (or being-for-happiness, it is the same thing)."[98] The strangeness of this choice for our times is that it boils down to a choice between the easy certainty of a likely hell, or the immense transitive difficulties of realizing "paradise" in a form other than economics and technology in the modes we understand them today.

The latter propels choosing the second decision by requiring that we work to protect the real possibility of finite paradise. To do otherwise would be to diminish the reality and force of finite "suffering, fear, and menace." To lose the dimension of possibility would be to make these the norm, and thus lose all hope of forcing their historical overcoming. It would make the world as a whole too close to what, across the last two centuries, it has too often been—that is a rehearsal for hell. This is to echo J.M. Bernstein's fear, quoted above, that without the dimension of historical possibility "the present would be reduced to sheer actuality without potentially ... a blind fate" and the possibility of the qualitatively other truncated. Heaven, in other words, disappears as immanent possibility and the work of philosophy—which means any thought, any dimension of significant action aimed at understanding, *including material practice*—would be (as Bernstein says) reduced to forever hinting at what eludes it.[99] We need to remember here that hell is not only the substantive suffering borne by others (who tomorrow may become ourselves) it is also the condition given in Heidegger's terrible indictment of our times, that: "even the immense suffering that surrounds the world is unable to awaken transformation".[100] Hell, in other words, is the inability to act well. It is the inability to measure where and how we are; to tell it "like it is" and to act on that telling; to take the logical consequence of this telling as the basis on which one acts. The escape from Hell is therefore the process of beginning to see again historically. We could say that it is to begin to grasp again one's historicality; to see one's being—one's potentiality—worked *through* the active grasping of historical circumstance.

But just this also tells us that we have reached the limits of pure thought. Today, we cannot read Adorno's observation that "the past will have been worked through only when the causes of what happened then have been eliminated ... Only because the causes continue to exist does the captivating spell of the past remain to this day unbroken,"[101] as a merely intellectual advisement. "Only because the causes continue to exist" means that the causes of suffering—and for us the potential of destructiveness manifesting itself as catastrophe—must be overcome (i.e., incorporated and thus rendered no longer formative) *in reality*. Paradise and Hell are no longer only matters of subjective will. As we have seen, they are better thought as immanent to what is emerging. For this reason neither can be dealt with by thought alone. Just as no-one could conceive of merely thinking these theologically, so they cannot only be thought philosophically. But this same injunction words in reverse. If thought is insufficient to "think" our historical position immanently, then action cannot be equally blind. On acting now descends the same obligation as Adorno gave philosophy: to know, without any mitigation, why the world—which could be paradise here and now—can become hell itself tomorrow. But there is this change: "Working through the past"—which is also, as we have seen, working in relation to the future—means to realize the past in some other form objectively made possible by the emerging circumstances. Understanding is laced with realization, or in a word, with modelling. To know our historical position is to discover ways of modelling that understanding in practice.

(ii) Thought now finds itself in an entirely different situation

"Philosophy, as at once both rigorous and free thought, now finds itself in an entirely different situation."[102] To which the only response is, yes, but one that thought did not expect. "The real movement of history" has taken a surprising twist. The onset of the artificial as horizon and medium of the world changes the conditions for acting and knowing to at least the same degree as did industrialization. Philosophy (thought) is no longer adequate as disinterested contemplation, but neither is it sufficient as critical thought. Kant's Copernican turn at the end of the 18th century, the ending of the "great metaphysical dream of the soul moving frictionless towards knowledge of itself, things-in-themselves and God"[103] and its replacement by his "lesson in limitation," is itself now put under pressure by what always charges intellectual and practical work, that is a new "consciousness of needs"—which means a new consciousness concerning what is substantively required, by persons, collectively and individually, of both thought and action. This consciousness today twists thoughts' role tighter to the finite. The sharp necessity placed on thought is, we have said, to become capable of contending with what we have made. But to become capable of contending with what we have made means to go beyond knowledge divorced from intervention; from knowledge wholly separate from the understanding realized in action. This changes the nature of knowledge. Because thought must now be orientated to acting (is not thinking now the thought of *how* to act?) it demands that it be "permeated with the potential of what could be different."[104] That this brings thought closer to what we think of as design should not be a surprise given all that has been said above. But it is emphasized if we consider that to be capable of truly contending with what we have made means to develop the generalized capacity (and the specific but multifarious sets of capabilities) that can allow "us," at once collectively as a species and individually as subjects, to engage with and *re-configure* what-is. It is *only* in actively seeking to reconfigure the world, in pushing beyond the existing and the given, that we enter into what Badiou names as one of the key counter-conditions to nihilism—the "hazardous, precarious advent of possibility."[105] Against what nihilism represents, the mixture of the "distinctive combination of resignation ... together with a purely negative if not destructive will"[106] of "conservative propaganda with an obscure desire for catastrophe"[107] "we can set only that which is not yet in being, but which our thought declares itself able to conceive."[108] To think and act *against* nihilism is therefore to insist on the right to begin to take up, a to take more seriously than we have to date, "hitherto unexplored possibilities for our situation, and ultimately for ourselves."[109]

(iii) Human beings and things, each in their rightful place

All of this, to repeat, has today objective and not merely subjective weight. If the artificial mediates all: if it constitutes the apparatus of our lives without which we cannot live, then "thought" concerning all this must also be practice, must be manifest in alternate moments of the artificial. It is in this sense I believe that we can understand Herbert Simon's remarkable and early insight (1981) that one of the key future roles of design is as understanding: "One can envisage a future, however, in which our main interest in both science and design will lie in what they teach us about the world and not what they allow us to do to the world. Design, like science, is a tool for understanding as well as acting."[110] By "world" here I take Simon to be indicating both natural and artificial worlds. Designed configurations ("designs") are thus to be thought of as means of knowing in general: they reveal to us possibilities vis-à-vis our interaction with both nature and artifice. The dark underside of affirmative possibility too simply considered ("false plenitude") is negation. The ovens were as well designed (by "Topf and Sons") as the best Utopia. The challenge therefore is that there can be nothing innocent about this process. To repeat, the demand on thought, to "know without mitigation," now descends also on design. In that sense not only "philosophy must prove itself the most advanced consciousness." Design, no less than the former, must be at once "permeated with the potential of what could be different—but also a match for the power of regression, which it can transcend only after having incorporated and comprehended it."[111]

We can grasp here the possibilities of an exchange. That which, classically as it were, even temperamentally, is already prefigurative in its operation (design) exchanges with that which claims that it is a "match for the power of regression" (philosophy). We might posit that it is this potential binding that may save both design and philosophy from the danger of falling behind what is required of them. Traditional philosophy's exhaustion at the succession of its variations[112] and design's confusion and belittling at the hands of commodification might suggest that neither can still be "the order of the day," that both are no longer capable of engaging with the "state of the world rushing to catastrophe."[113] But while the potential for catastrophe is in part a product the belittling and exhaustion of both thought and practice, what is not too late, what is still capable of meaningful action, is that degree of reflective action capable of modeling both danger and a "saving power." In other words, there still lies the potential for a praxis that, as Adorno puts it, "could break the magic spell" of history.

This is all the more significant if we consider the two urgent tasks we would wish to give to such thought-praxis. The first, in Adorno's phrasing, derives from "Hegel's astounding proposition that philosophy is its own time comprehended in thought."[114] Philosophy, in the expanded sense meant here, comprehends and models the realization of the possibilities of our time understood as the possibilities for our future history. And we can give a twist to Adorno's Hegel. If it is not only to be a slogan, philosophy as its own time comprehended in thought, needs to consciously and actively grasp circumstance—needs, in a word, to think "its own time" *transitively* and not merely as image, not, as Barthes warned us above, as myth. How can that be done? One way is to grasp circumstance as the circumstance for action. There is a paragraph in the writings of the art historian Michael Baxandall that is oddly relevant here. In an essay on Picasso's portrait of Kanwheiler and in answer to the rhetorical question "Who set Picasso's charge?" He answered:

A preliminary half-answer would be that Picasso formulated his own. The painter registers his individuality ... by his particular perception of the circumstances he must address. Indeed, if one is to think of a painter expressing himself, it is most of all here, in the analysis of his environment which schematically speaking precedes the process of painting itself, that one can most securely locate an individuality ... But the painter's formulation of a Brief is a very personal affair indeed ... The elements of Picasso's problem were ... freely selected by Picasso out of an array, and arranged by Picasso into a problem constituting the immediate Brief. However, if Picasso is to be thought of as formulating his own Brief, he did so as a social being in cultural circumstances.[115]

Baxandall's comment has its own charge within the history of art. But the point here has more general applicability. Circumstances become so, a time becomes thought—above all in its possibility—in relation to acting. Baxandall's formulation brings in a language that is close and conducive to design ("the particular perception of the circumstances that must be addressed ... arranged ... into a problem constituting the immediate Brief"). It brings in too a general notion of active formation and it echoes Badiou's point that the philosopher—but no less the designer—intervenes "when he finds, *in the present*, the signs that point to the need for a new problem, a new invention."[116] This means—it cannot in truth be otherwise—that the designer is potentially *affirmatively* reactive to the character of history; or if this sounds too abstract, that the designer is reactive to historical circumstance, that they are pointing, ostentively, to circumstance and addressing them in a particular way, seeing in them both a problem and a possibility.

The second task, which is also the last statement of this essay, comes again from a sentence by Adorno. In its final phrase it gives the most concentrated injunction (axiom) for practice it is possible to conceive: "Only a thinking that has no mental sanctuary, no illusion of an inner realm, and that acknowledges its lack of function and power can perhaps catch a glimpse of an order of the possible and the non-existent, *where human beings and things each would be in their rightful place*."[117] No ethic—no axiom—captures better the aspiration of design. Put another way, design *is* the working towards this in thought and practice. It has no other project. This is, needless to say, a historical project.[118]

NOTES

1. Our history, our unhappiness

1 It will be seen as we progress that the question of acting or more precisely of how we should act and what form that acting should take is the very issue for this century. For design the question becomes in what manner do the capacities and capabilities of design provide resources towards such acting—meaning by this of course acting capable of engaging the tendency towards "defuturing" and disaster endemic in what is present and in what is emerging.

2 Disaster, that is, induced through climate change. Except that this formulation is incorrect. Climate change itself is not the disaster. The disaster is our inability to collectively organize action to deal preventatively with its worst consequences. Considered systemically, global steering mechanisms are radically inadequate to the task at hand. The true disaster will be their slow multiplicity gradually engulfing structures incapable of dealing with the multiple scale and instances of what will unfold. This "incapability" is not existential or ontological but structural. Even more it is a "side effect" of the limits of capitalism vis-à-vis its problem-solving capacities. On the latter see the somewhat neglected essay by Jurgen Habermas, *Legitimation Crisis* (London: Heinemann, 1976).

3 Slavoj Žižek, *In Defence of Lost Causes* (London: Verso, 2008) p. 314. See §3 below for further discussion of these points.

4 Hence there is no "the" to the past. No singular "past."

5 "Without committing the cardinal sin of insinuating meaning where none exists." Theodor Adorno, "Progress or regression" in *History and Freedom* (Cambridge: Polity, 2006), p. 9.

6 Structurally, this must be the case. If unsustainment is historically produced, then the possibility of "overcoming" unsustainment must also be latent within this same history. One task of history is therefore to recover— uncover, discover—within our history, resources towards sustainment.

7 Vilém Flusser, *The Philosophy of Photography* (London: Reaktion, 2001) p. 1.

8 A point should be made here to note what should, but may not, be self-evident: that one speaks of catastrophe in order to avoid it. There is a useful formulation in a lecture by Zygmunt Bauman which captures this well: "prophesying the advent of that catastrophe as passionately and vociferously as we can manage is the sole chance of making the unavoidable avoidable— and perhaps even the inevitable impossible to happen." Quoting Jean-Pierre Dupuy, Bauman continues: "We are condemned to perpetual vigilance he warns. A lapse of vigilance may prove a sufficient . . . condition of catastrophe's inevitability: . . . proclaiming that inevitability and so 'thinking of the continuation' of the human presence on Earth 'as the negation of autodestruction' is, on the other hand, a necessary (a hopefully the sufficient) condition of the 'unavoidable future not happening.'" The paragraph comes from Bauman's Miliband Memorial lecture at the London School of Economics in 2005, published as "Thought against fear" in *Liquid Fear* (Cambridge: Polity, 2006) pp. 160–77, this quotation p. 176. Bauman is quoting from Dupuy, *Pour un Catastrophisme éclairé. Quand impossible et certain* (Paris: Seuil, 2002) p. 167. Some of Dupuy's work has recently been translated into English. See *The Mark of the Sacred* (Stanford: Stanford University Press, 2013) especially chapter 1.

9 See for example Bill Joy, "Why the future doesn't need us," *Wired*, 8.04, April 2000.

10 Martin Heidegger, "Building dwelling thinking," in *Poetry, Language, Thought* (New York: Harper, 1971) pp. 143–61, see especially pp. 160–61. It is worth remarking that the three terms in the latter are also the very last words in the essay "Overcoming metaphysics," in Martin Heidegger, *The End of Philosophy*, Ed. Joan Stambaugh (Chicago: University of Chicago Press, 1973) pp. 84–110: "Appropriation ... brings mortals to the path of thinking, poetizing building." I have explored some of these issues in "Heidegger's essay, 'Building dwelling thinking,'" *Harvard Architectural Review*, 8, 1992, pp. 160–87.

11 We design and create things that "are" only in the moment of their commodity immediacy. There is no resilience to, or working with, time. Is this, in the end, one of the worst indictments that can be made about our comprehension of what the made is and should be?

12 Roland Barthes in the essay "From work to text," in *Image/Music/Text*, translated Stephen Heath (Glasgow: Collins, 1971) p. 163.

13 One should add, both as civilization and as barbarism.

14 "Adequately" means here to think responsibly concerning consequence. See section II.

15 J. M. Bernstein, *The Fate of Art* (University Park: Penn State Press, 1992) p. 189.

16 Not only as economics. Heidegger's point that for a subject to be able to make finite being comprehensible neither the present nor history alone is sufficient, that there has to be thought into historicity and thus into or through a philosophical inquiry of how our historicity occurs, for only this gives access to thinking about becoming, is equally to the point.

17 Alan Badiou captures what is at stake here. "We are living through the revenge of what is most blind and objective in the economic appropriation of technics over what is most subjective and voluntary in politics. And even, in a certain sense, the revenge of the scientific problem over the political project. Science—therein lies its grandeur—possesses problems; it does not have a project. "To change what is deepest in man" was a revolutionary project, doubtless a bad one; it has now become a scientific problem, or perhaps merely a technical problem, in any case a problem that allows for solutions. We know how or at least we will know. Of course we could ask: What is to be done about the fact that . . . science knows how to make a new man? . . . Since there is no project, or as long as there is no project, everyone knows there is only one answer: profit will tell us what to do." A. Badiou, *The Century* (Cambridge: Polity, 2007) p. 9.

18 Except as an eternal present of the "liberal" free market economy. See Francis Fukuyama's *The End of History and the Last Man* (New York: Free Press, 1992).

19 The victory of the market presents itself as a metaphysic in Heidegger's strict sense of the term—as that which defines the "essence of truth" through a "specific interpretation what is and a specific comprehension of truth." It thus gains (or seeks to gain) precisely what all metaphysics wish—the ability to give to an "age the basis on which it is essentially formed." Martin Heidegger, "The age of the world picture" in *The Question Concerning Technology and Other Essays* (New York: Harper, 1977), p. 115.

20 The phrase alludes, somewhat ironically, to C. M. Reinhardt and Kenneth Rogoff's study *This Time is Different: Eight Centuries of Financial Folly* (Princeton: Princeton University Press, 2009).

21 Jean-Paul Sartre, *Search for a Method* (New York: Knopf, 1963) p. 3.

22 Theodor Adorno and Max Horkheimer, *Dialectic of Enlightenment* (London: NLB, 1979) p. xv.

23 One way of seeing our times is that they are ruled by inversions in which narrow instrumentalities (the drive, technology, the economy as site of financial accumulation) invert, parasitically and to the point of pathology and potential disaster, the larger context of practices of which, socially, they are part. Thus the financially directed market economy is an inversion at once of money, markets and labor, none of which can be reduced to the private interest of accumulation. The latter, as drive, makes use of the former and in the process inverts the wider social and biological frameworks on which, in truth, it is dependent. The project of sustainment is the "setting to right" of such inversions. A useful note that bears on this can be found on pp. 62–3 of Michel Aglietta, "Into a new growth regime," *New Left Review*, 54, Nov/Dec 2008, pp. 61–74.

24 I use the term "affirmative" in this essay in a particular sense that is the opposite in many ways of how Marcuse used it in in his 1937 essay "Culture as affirmation." Marcuse was concerned to critique the self-interested affirmation of bourgeois culture. After a long period in which "affirmation" in Marcuse's sense has been transmuted into varieties of prosaic nihilisms, it becomes possible to use the concept again in a critical manner. This is the mode in which it is used in this essay, i.e., as counter to nihilism and in something of the sense that Adorno and Horkheimer intended when they wrote in the preface to *Dialectic of Enlightenment*, "today critical thought (which does abandon its commitment even in the face of progress) demands support for the residues of freedom, and for tendencies towards true humanism, even if these seem powerless in regard to the main course of history" (London: NLB, 1979) pp. ix–x. As will be seen later, the term is also used in the more active sense that Badiou deploys it in his lecture published as *Philosophy in the Present* (London: Verso, 2009), i.e., as the *necessary* corollary of moving from critique to intervention.

25 This notion of "bridging" is key. The entirety of thinking the "possible future" concerns thinking the creation of the durable bridges (scenarios sustained by prototypes at scale) by which we can span from "here" to "there."

26 Notice that as against science which "possesses problems" design is supposed merely to be "the solving of problems"—which, by definition, conventionally speaking are given by others. This ideology at once reduces and instrumentalizes design. It makes it incapable of grasping its role in grasping and prototyping ontological possibility in the realm of the artificial—which is today everything.

27 See the important paper by Anne-Marie Willis; "Ontological design—laying the ground," *Design Philosophy Papers Three*, pp. 80–98, 2007.

28 Elaine Scarry, *The Body in Pain* (Oxford: Oxford University Press, 1985), p. 279.

29 In the famous line, "the devising of courses of action aimed at changing existing situations into preferred ones." Herbert Simon, *The Sciences of the Artificial* (Cambridge: MIT Press, 1996), p. 111.

30 On private interests and their consequences see two essays by Jan van Toorn: "Thinking the visual; essayistic fragments on communicative action," in Ole Bouman, ed., *"And Justice For All . . ."* (Maastricht: Jan van Eyck Akadamie, 1994), pp.140–152; and "Communication design: a social practice" in Jan van Toorn, ed., *Design Beyond Design* (Maastricht: Jan van Eyck Akadamie, 1997), pp.153–166.

31 Artifice is our necessity, we are wedded to it symbiotically, however much we resent the dependency—thus, as a glance at any dictionary will show, the opprobrium in which the artificial is traditionally held. Herbert Simon points to this same point in *The Sciences of the Artificial*, p. 4.

32 Simon, *Science*, p. 138.

33 The sharpest and least forgiving analysis of this is Giorgio Agamben's essay "What is an apparatus?" in *What is an Apparatus and Other Essays* (Stanford: Stanford University Press, 2009), pp. 1–24.

34 I have explored this tension in C. Dilnot, "Design, knowledge and human interests" a working paper given at originally at the 2006 conference of the *Design Research Society* in Lisbon, Portugal.

35 Heidegger, "Overcoming metaphysics", pp. 110, 103.

36 The term is Vattimo's. It comes from the final line of the first chapter of *The Transparent Society* (Baltimore: Johns Hopkins University Press, 1992) p. 11.

37 The reference is to the concept developed by Horst Rittel and Melvin Webber in "Dilemmas in a general theory of planning," *Policy Sciences*, 4 (1973), pp. 155–69.

38 Giorgio Agamben, *Man Without Content* (Stanford: Stanford University Press, 2001) p. 68.

39 Agamben, *Man Without Content*, p. 76.

40 Agamben, *Man Without Content*, p. 69.

41 Heidegger, "Overcoming metaphysics," p. 99.

42 Heidegger, "Overcoming metaphysics," p. 101.

43 Heidegger, "Overcoming metaphysics," p. 101.

44 Heidegger, "Overcoming metaphysics," p. 101.

45 Heidegger, "Overcoming metaphysics," p. 101.

46 Heidegger, "Overcoming metaphysics," p. 102.

47 Bruce Sterling, *Shaping Things* (Cambridge: MIT Press, 2005) p. 44.

48 "At the level of concrete pathology, the compulsion to repeat is an ungovernable process originating in the unconscious. As a result of its action, the subject deliberately places himself in distressing situations, thereby repeating the old experience, but he does not recall this prototype; on the contrary, he has the strong impression that the situation is fully determined by the circumstances of the moment." J. Laplanche and J.-B. Pontalis, the entry for "Repetition compulsion," *The Language of Psycho-Analysis* (New York: Norton, 1973) p. 78.

49 This last point suggests that today we need to rewrite one of Walter Benjamin's most famous lines. The injunction that "Only that historian will have the gift of fanning the spark of hope in the past who is firmly convinced that even the dead will not be safe from the enemy if he wins" might now be re-drafted as "only that historian will have the gift of fanning the spark of hope in the past who is firmly convinced that *even the unborn* will not be safe from the enemy if he wins."

50 See Martin Wolf, "Why the world faces climate chaos," *Financial Times*, May 14, 2013 and Martin Wolf, "Global inaction shows that climate change sceptics have already won," *Financial Times*, May 21, 2013.

51 The intensity of reaction against this thesis suggests that Fukayama had touched a nerve that many did not want to deal with.

52 In the same way we appear to believe that our ability to deal with the future, i.e., with those emerging crises which we in any case disavow, will somehow be secured by simultaneously disembowelling government, curtailing future-focused investment in social and human capital and in decaying physical infrastructure, and by selling-off, or otherwise depleting, the wider public domain. See Mark Blyth, *Austerity: The History of a Dangerous Idea* (Oxford: Oxford University Press, 2013).

53 Alain Badiou, *Ethics* (London: Verso, 2005) p. 31.

54 Theodor W. Adorno, *Negative Dialectics*, trans. E. B. Ashton (London: Continuum, 1973), p. 398.

55 While it is said that Jones's book is about design methods, in fact its "methods" were grounded in a heuristic threefold model of staged historical development in design, encompassing the "unself-conscious" or craft epoch of designing-through- and in-making; the epoch of industrialization or design-by-drawing (the "self-conscious process") and finally, in our own time, not yet clearly distinguished, a third, "post industrial" epoch, which would demand a massively expanded field of the means of designing—the putative subject matter of Jones' book, even if to large degree, the methods that Jones offered were in fact transitional vis-à-vis the modes of technical practice that they engaged with: J. C. Jones, *Design Methods* (New York: Wiley, 2nd edn., 1992)

56 Manfredo Tafuri, *Architecture and Utopia: Design and Capitalist Development* (Cambridge: MIT Press, 1976).

57 Jean Baudrillard, *For a Critique of the Political Economy of the Sign* (St. Louis: Telos Press, 1972).

58 Adrian Forty, *Objects of Desire* (London: Thames and Hudson, 1986).

59 I have explored some of these issues in relation to the history of design: see C. Dilnot, "The state of design history: part one: mapping the field: part two; problems and possibilities," *Design Issues*, 1(1), Spring 1984, pp. 3–23; 1(2), Fall 1984, pp. 3–20. Reprinted in *Design Discourse: History: Theory: Criticism*, ed. V. Margolin (University of Chicago Press, Chicago, 1989) pp. 213–50; C. Dilnot, "Some futures for design history?," *The Journal of Design History*, 22 (4), 2009, pp. 377–94; "The question of agency in the understanding of design," *Journal of Design History*, 26(3), 2013, pp. 331–7.

60 The book series is *Design Thinking, Design Theory*, edited by Ken Friedman and Erik Stolterman (Cambridge: MIT Press).

61 Cyril Stanley Smith, "On art, invention and technology," in *Essays on Science and Art* (Cambridge: MIT Press, 1976) esp. pp. 325–6.

62 On the complexity of the decorative see the passages on the decorative in Hans-Georg Gadamer, *Truth and Method* (London: Sheen and Ward, 1960). The inflation of "tool-making" at the expense of all other aspects of human making is in the end little more than a sample of what Heidegger called "technological" thinking, the inability to reflect on the made world outside the categories and limits imposed by technological practices in the wide sense.

63 Gianni Vattimo, *The End of Modernity* (Baltimore: Johns Hopkins University Press, 1988) p. 3.

64 The real break is the early 1970s, "coincident," which is not a coincidence, with the oil-price shock to the Western industrial economics and the effective ending of the social-democratic project. It is just this point that there chime in the calls to renounce the "ideology" of progress (meaning politics) and from there we pass smoothly to the opening of China from 1978 and the onset of the neoliberal economy the year after. At that point the future shrinks to becoming identical with the permanent present of the economy as the horizon of human possibility. Design, ever attentive to the source of its market, follows suit.

65 "Just as all other mythic-traditional systems celebrate rituals and festivals to interrupt the homogeneity of profane time and, reactualizing the original mythic time, to allow man to become again the contemporary of the gods and to reattain the primordial dimension of creation, so in the work of art the *continuum* of linear time is broken, and man recovers, between past and future, his present space." Agamben, Ibid. pp. 101–102.

66 Agamben, *The Man Without Content*, p. 102.

67 Agamben, *The Man Without Content*, p. 102.

68 Agamben, *The Man Without Content*, p. 102.

69 Italo Calvino, *Six Memos for the Next Millennium* (New York, Vintage: 1996).

70 Milan Kundera, *The Unbearable Lightness of Being* (New York: Harper). The two quotations are taken respectively from his novels *The Joke* and *The Book of Laughter and Forgetting*. On page 137 of his *The Art of the Novel* (New York, Harper: 1986) Kundera quotes himself from *The Farewell Party* (New York: Harper): "Raskolnikov experienced his act of murder as a tragedy and staggered under the weight of the deed. Jacob was amazed to find that his deed was light, easy to bear, light as air. And he wondered whether there was not more horror in this lightness than in all the hysterical emotions of the Russian hero."

71 From the other side: in relation to a project's ascribed symbolic value. As this value reduces, so the need for formal expression of symbolism recedes. This was the case with the replacement for the towers of the World Trade Center. In 2001 it seemed important to mark these symbolically as well in restoring their presence. As each year has passed so it has became easier to slough off symbolism (poetics) and return to business. Today, we are almost back to where we began.

72 The Shard simply confirms Heidegger's prediction that our culture would go increasingly towards the "nullity" of gigantic but emptied gestures. See the final paragraphs of the essay Heidegger, "Age of the world picture," pp. 115–54. "Emptied gestures" is also literal—at the time of drafting this essay the building was substantially under let. On the other hand, this was also the early fate of the Empire State Building.

73 Architecture today is very largely an art of mass entertainment: its formal devices are as calculated for acceptable effects as anything in the media. It is difficult to think of a recent building that, configuratively speaking, is shocking in a manner genuinely challenging to intellect or sensibility.

74 The pretence that algorithmic or formal invention acting alone can generate material relations that possess and embody more than formal significance cannot survive minimal scrutiny.

75 Form makes a virtue of whim, but when gestures become merely aleatory then the ultimate arbiter is always force—or in architecture *interest*, which means private interest, the weight of money. For a powerful critique of the latter in design see the essays of Jan van Toorn noted above.

76 Agamben, *The Man Without Content*, p. 56.

77 Agamben, *The Man Without Content*, pp. 56, 57.

78 Anyone who has tried to teach, in a seminar with architects, Heidegger's essay "Building dwelling thinking" will know the relief that comes over students when they reach final pages with its brief paean to [Heidegger's own] "Black Forest hut" and thereby feel that they can dismiss all that has gone before as mere anti-modernism. It is a case not helped by those who take up Heidegger and blindly reproduce, quasi-theologically what Adorno rightly called "the Jargon of Authenticity."

79 "Dwelling" should never be read as what has been. It is not a temporal concept, not a state to which we aspire, but rather an axiomatic. Just as equality is not a state to be desired but a precept of immediate of political and economic and social action (and only *from this* can it then be realized, or worked toward politically and economically) so "dwelling" is the necessary axiom of thinking building. But what dwelling "is," or rather the forms or the modes or the manner that it can take, cannot be predicted, it must be discovered, ever anew.

80 See the discussion of "will" later in this essay.

81 As for example the camps were an extreme possibility developed out of existing modes of domination and the ideological, organizational and technological possibilities of modern Europe. On this see Zygmunt Bauman, *Modernity and the Holocaust* (Cambridge: Polity, 1989).

82 Reconfiguration is always *qualitative* transformation because reconfiguration implies the restructuring of the negotiation of incommensurabilities involved in the situation and therefore the remediation of relations.

83 This is thinking possibility not technologically or economically—as power—but as ethics: the possible being what it is that human beings are. Agamben again has some useful thoughts on this. See his early text *The Coming Community* (Minneapolis: University of Minnesota Press, 1993).

84 See Gui Bonsiepe, "The virtues of design" in Gui Bonsiepe, *Interface – An Approach to Design*, ed. Dawn Barrett (Maastricht: Jan Van Eyck Akademie, 1999) pp. 152–60.

85 See the web site of the Wolfsonian Institute, Miami, Florida under "Current Exhibits" (January 2013).

86 The phrase comes from the philosopher and novelist Iris Murdoch. See *The Sovereignty of the Good* (London: Routledge, 1970/2002).

87 Via design, that is, in terms of as the generic capability or set of capabilities drawn upon.

88 Kundera, *The Art of the Novel*, pp. 5–6.

89 *The Art of the Novel*, p. 42.

90 Agamben, *The Man Without Content*, p. 69.

91 Agamben, *The Man Without Content*, p. 101.

92 Agamben, *The Man Without Content*, p. 101.

93 And what capabilities we have vis-à-vis these situations and contexts.

94 Agamben, *The Man Without Content*, pp. 102–103.

2. The artificial and what it opens towards

1 Heidegger's savage post-war comment, that "even the immense suffering that surrounds the earth is unable to awaken transformation" today applies twice over, first as the indicator of our inability, despite claims to the contrary, to be moved to action with respect to suffering; second, to the future suffering of ourselves. Not even this motivates our beginning to act otherwise. On fear see Zygmunt Bauman's contemporary inventory, *Liquid Fear* (Cambridge: Polity, 2006).

2 Wolf, "Why the world faces climate chaos."

3 It is entirely typical in this respect that the only concentrated international action in the last decade was the brief moments of dealing with the banking crisis in 2008.

4 Badiou, *Ethics*, p. 30.

5 Cf. Bruce Mau, *Massive Change* (New York: Phaidon, 2004).

6 Stephen Yeo, "State and anti-state: reflections on social forms and struggles from 1850," in Philip Corrigan (ed.), *Capitalism, State Formation and Marxist Theory* (London: Quartet, 1980) p. 115.

7 Meaning by this of course, a humane future for all of those (human and non-human) living beings whose lives and conditions of their lives are bound up with the artificial—as ours (and theirs) are and will be, now in perpetuity.

8 The species-destructive as against "merely" local-destructive capacity of nuclear war is given by the nuclear winter that would follow a full exchange of nuclear weapons. See, in a complex literature, P. Crutzen and J. Birks "The atmosphere after a nuclear war: twilight at noon," *Ambio* 11(2): (1982), pp. 114–25.

9 It should always be remembered that climate change is not "destructive" to the earth per se, the latter, as a complex organism, is capable of stabilizing in a range of conditions. When we speak of climate change we are therefore speaking *entirely* anthropomorphically.

10 Julia Kristeva, *Black Sun* (New York: Columbia University Press, 2001), p. 221.

11 Giorgio Agamben, *The Communing Community* (Minneapolis: Minnesota University Press, 1993), p. 43.

12 Which means also that we cannot think past that which historically determines how we act. A culture that prides itself on dissembling history is in fact in thrall to it.

13 On the most obvious indicator. There are local potlatch economies at various moments but famine is present as threat in Western Europe until the early 19th century, Eastern Europe to the late 19th century, much of Asia and Africa well into the last century.

14 This is not to say that there are not instances of local ecological crises (deforestation) or, on the other side, remarkable instances of sustained care (the European peasant and soil conservation).

15 To put this another way, against endemic uncertainty (fear) certainty (or a degree of salvation from anxiety) is sought in the invention of secular law and the projection of theocratic law—which come together in the notion of the divine status of those who rule (a projection that therefore must always be denied; a projection that gives rise to the paradoxical condition of the *fear of acknowledging making*).

16 This last sounds like a "history written from the perspective of the victors." This is deliberate. Counterfactually one can envision a series of quite other historical outcomes, particularly vis-à-vis the history of Europe. But the structure of the epoch of hand-labor *in practice* falls into a relatively small series of tropes, each an attempt to deal with the tension between the desire for survival/expenditure and the difficulties of making.

17 A useful discussion of China's brush with both proto-industrialization and capitalism as early as the 12th century is in Etienne Balazs, *Chinese Civilization and Bureaucracy* (New Haven: Yale University Press, 1964) see especially Chapter 4, "The birth of capitalism in China."

18 This is the real transforming character of this epoch. Throughout previous human history nature is resistance. It is recalcitrant. From it, things are won only with colossal difficulty. Industrialization "breaks the back" of "static" natural resistance.

19 Who would today dare to issue a book with the simple title *Civilization*? Kenneth Clark's book of this title, published in 1969, is perhaps the last encomium to a vanishing idea.

20 Again as is noted below, in practice today the artificial and nature are entwined, but then they have been since the onset of human cultivation. By "horizon" and "totality" is meant here that how nature is and will be *for us* (and how we are and *can be*) is now as a *consequence* of the artificial. It is the nature, or better the character or manner—the *forms*—of artificiality that today determine how we can be. Put another way, it is the artificial—in the expanded sense detailed below—which is the context within which we now are. It is in that sense that the artificial—and not nature-is now the medium and horizon for becoming.

21 In "Overcoming metaphysics," p. 85.

22 This was the only all but unanimous conclusion of a recent poll of economists on likely scenarios over the next few decades. Reported in the *Financial Times*, January 25–26 2014.

23 Badiou, *The Century*, p. 11.

24 Cf. Herbert Simon on design and science as *both* "modes of knowing," *Sciences*, p. 164. Simon does not say what design is a mode of knowing of but reflection shows that it cannot other than the artificial, the subject dependent upon the artificial and the web of sustaining relations between these and world/earth. The difference is that science begins to know these relations as problem; design as an active project of intervention. In this epoch they are reciprocal.

25 Although I speak below of "overcoming" destructives this is a project both forever incomplete and ever tenuous. Given the artificial, destructiveness is endemic. The real question is how one deals with it.

26 See Heidegger, "The age of the world picture."

27 This is the point that Herbert Simon makes when he says at one point in *The Sciences of the Artificial*, "I have shown that a science of artificial phenomena is always in imminent danger of dissolving and vanishing. The peculiar properties of the artefact lie on the thin interface between the natural laws within it and the natural laws without. What can we say about it? What is there to study besides the boundary sciences—those that govern the means and the task environment?" p. 131.

28 Simon, *Sciences*, p. 3.

29 On the relevance of this last term see the section "Maneries" in Giorgio Agamben, *The Coming Community* (Minneapolis: Minnesota University Press, 1993), pp. 27–29.

30 See Yeo, "State and anti-state".

31 The perfect example is the domestic iron; a form that could not be discovered by law but which experience has endowed with an all but objective configuration—but "objective" means here, in relation to the (human) uses to which it is put.

32 See the opening remarks to François Julien *The Propensity of Things: Toward a History of Efficacy in China*, translated by J. Lloyd (New York: Zone Books, 1995).

33 See Philip Sargent, "Design science or non-science? A non-scientific theory of design," *Design Studies*, 15(4) (1994), pp. 389–402.

34 As will be made clear below, reconfiguration is *always* qualitative transformation because reconfiguration implies the restructuring of the negotiation of incommensurabilities involved in the situation and therefore the remediation of relations.

35 As Barthes says of Racine: see the introduction to Roland Barthes, *On Racine* (New York: Hill & Wang, 1964).

36 Adorno's comments on the fallible should be noted here. In the final lecture of the series on metaphysics he notes: "all metaphysical experiences—I should like to state this as a proposition here—are fallible. I would say, in general, that all experience that have to be lived, are not mere copies ... contain the possibility of error, the possibility that they may completely miss the mark. And in much the same way as I indicated earlier with regard to the concept of tradition, it may be that [among] the deceptions which the scientific-idealist tradition has enmeshed us, is that [according to the criterion of the certain] ... everything that really matters would be excluded as unworthy of being known, whereas in truth ... only what can be refuted, what can be disappointed, what can be wrong ... [only that] is not already subsumed under the identity of the concept. Fallibility, I would say is the condition of possibility of metaphysical experience. And it seems to attach most strongly to the weakest and most fragile experiences." From Theodor Adorno, "Selections from metaphysics," in Rolf Tiedemann (ed.), *Can One Live after Auschwitz?*, p. 465. This point has implication for the case study considered in section 3.

37 Cf. the points made earlier in section I.

38 In the sense that the configuration of the universe itself (and its laws) are not immune to the notion that underpins the configuration of all things—that they are not simply law-determined but are the outcome of the *contingent* negotiation of forces. I am interested here in the argument deployed by Quentin Meillassoux in *After Finitude: An Essay on the Necessity of Contingency* (London: Continuum, 2008) especially pages 82–3.

39 Zygmunt Bauman in Z. Bauman and Keith Tester, *Conversations with Zygmunt Bauman*, (Cambridge: Polity, 2001) pp. 31–2.

40 Bauman, *Conversations with Zygmunt Bauman*, pp. 31–2.

41 Zygmunt Bauman and Keith Tester, *Conversations with Zygmunt Bauman* (Cambridge: Polity Press, 2001) p. 32.

42 Bauman, *Conversations with Zygmunt Bauman*, pp. 31–2.

43 Zygmunt Bauman, *Culture as Praxis* (London: Routledge, 1973) p. 173.

44 This should be linked philosophically to the arguments that Gillian Rose makes in the final chapter of her book, *Hegel Contra Sociology* (London: Athlone, 1981, reprinted Verso books). See pages 204–20.

45 Simon, *Sciences*, p. 6.

46 If the artificial is a mediation between the "inner" environment of the artifact itself (its configuration) and the "outer" environments to which it refers and in relation to which (on behalf of which) it must act then, once we see these environments not in the singular and as matter of physical law (Simon) but in their existential, social and ecological pluralities then it is obvious that the relations between any artifact or system (physical or political) and (i) human subjects in social relations; (ii) existing artifacts likewise in complex social, technical and economic relations (and operating within complex and irreducible systems of power; and (iii) natural laws and conditions, is *necessarily* a matter of complex negotiation between irreconcilable or incommensurable moments and demands

47 This is Elaine Scarry's central argument in *The Body in Pain* (Oxford: Oxford University Press, 1985).

48 Negotiation happens because the moments in a conflict, or the requirements of a design problem, are incommensurable in a deep sense, that is they cannot be reduced to a single plane of representation out of which a calculation can be made to produce an optimum solution (as can be done in technology). If incommensurable elements and/or requirements cannot be so reduced then negotiation must occur.

49 If a single worldview is adequate to a design problem then the goals must have a common representation and thus a common measure of utility. A single utility measure can be calculated and the problem can be solved purely by optimization techniques. Conversely, a design problem exists *whenever* a single worldview is inadequate to encompass the multiple dimensions of the issue—the situation, problem and/or opportunity—at stake.

50 Technology happens, in the modern sense, when it is possible to reduce the effective contexts to which a thing is referred in its constitutive moments only to the realm of physical laws. In particular, in so far as technology can eliminate the subject as a context for which there needs to be significant accounting, it will. Such elimination after all allows technology maximum autonomy with respect to the creation of devices. To the degree that technology can eliminate incommensurability it can then proceed to an optimization of performance on the basis of a calculation in a single mode of representation—the mathematical.

51 Simon, *Sciences*, p. 141.

52 Simon, *Sciences*, p. 140.

53 A version of the displacement we looked at in section I.

54 Walter Benjamin, "The work of art in the age of mechanical reproduction" in *Illuminations*, p. 244.

55 We might note here as an aside that "the destructiveness of modern warfare," results not only from the objective development of the means of destructiveness, but from our inability to recognize and deal with destructive capacity as "ours." The lack of identity between subjects who make and what is made, between a society "not ... mature enough" to incorporate the technology it has constituted as its own, and a technology "not ... sufficiently developed to cope with the elemental forces" is sufficient to induce into this (non-)relation a destructiveness that plays out, ultimately not just in our inability to grasp how we act, technologically speaking, but to grasp ourselves as those who make, have made and will make further. The lack of determination of technology as "ours" plays into the doctrine of the subject as one who deploys the products of technology, but who does not conceive technology, in its essence, as "ours" and thus does not—in a certain sense *cannot*—take responsibility for its capacities or consequences.

56 This bears heavily on the issue of design as a model of future praxis. Cf. Philip Sargent: "Reconciling incommensurate requirements is an essential aspect of design, . . . the design process requires it and designed artefacts must always resolve it." Sargent, "Design science or non-science?," pp. 389–402.

57 Three ways in which design is negotiation of incommensurability: (1) mentally, in accepting the incommensurable demands of the situation; the irreducible complexity of the situation—its multiple levels and multiple demands; (2) literally, in the sense of establishing dialogue with those persons and factors involved in the situation—what Donald Schön calls the "conversation with the situation"; (3) configuratively, in the sense that what, in the end, design creates is a propositional configuration in which incommensurables are reconciled neither passively or definitively but as a proposition—*this* resolution, in *this* way, responding to *these* circumstances.

58 By contrast, design happens when it is not possible to so reduce the constitution of a thing and when the address to context cannot be devolved to a single plane of representation and we are in a condition of incommensurability. But it is not therefore that design simply "copes" with incommensurability. It would be more accurate to say (at least ideally) that design welcomes incommensurability; that it identifies and creates, within the design process, the elements of incommensurability with which it will work, recognizes them and gives them significance, i.e., endows them with the capacity to be incommensurable (and therefore demanding of recognition and negotiation-with). In other words, it is a signal capacity of design to bring the unrecognized to the table, to give recognition to these conditions or to those persons who must be negotiated with as a part of the design process. Whereas technology erases incommensurability, design celebrates it and uses it as the starting point for creative work.

59 The last place where such distinctions are still institutionalized are the universities whose litany of major subjects taught has barely altered over the last century.

60 Jamer Hunt, "Nervous systems and anxious infrastructures," in Paola Antonelli (ed.), *Talk to Me* (New York: MOMA, 2011) p. 48.

61 A small case in point is Kevin Kelly's book, *What Technology Wants* (New York, Penguin, 2010). At one point Kelly lists 13 aspects or virtues that his technology "seeks" to realize. It strikes anyone reading this list (that technology seeks increasing "efficiency, opportunity, emergence, complexity, diversity, specialization, ubiquity, freedom, mutualism, beauty, sentience, structure, evolvability" (p. 270) that comparatively few of these terms apply or are consonant with "technology" as we know it. Most go beyond. A few are all but incompatible thought within traditional limits. We might therefore say, technology *wishes* to exceed itself—to become no longer technology but to return to the wider condition of artifice.

62 Hence the colossal danger posed by those who continue to espouse, anachronistically, the autonomy of the technological. This is to try to create perverse technology. "Perverse" here has no emancipatory meaning.

63 The continuing, even increasing, relevance of Simon's *The Sciences of the Artificial* is that his interests in programming and psychology led him early to this understanding, hence his emphasis on the artificiality of (for example) economic rationality, the logic of thought processes, procedures of memory and learning.

64 A quotation from Philip Rawson may suffice. "To their makers and users pots have always been a kind of two-way revelation, first of man to himself as a creative and independently working agent, and second of the world to man as a medium, imbued with 'reality', which he is able to transform," Philip Rawson, *Ceramics* (Oxford: Oxford University Press, 1971), p. 8. In other words, artifice is the realm of revealing to humans the character of themselves as acting agents and of the world as that which is capable of transformation and adaptation.

65 The concept of the transitive is one that we need to recover for any activity involving making. Why this is so can be seen in this passage taken from Roland Barthes essay, "Myth today": "If Myth is depoliticized speech, there is at least one type of speech which is the opposite of myth, that which remains *political* . . . If I am a woodcutter and I am led to name the tree I am felling, whatever the force of my sentence 'I speak the tree.' I do not speak about it. This means my language is operational, transitively linked to its object, between the tree and myself there is nothing but my labor, that is to say, an action. This is a political language: it represents nature for me only in so far as I am going to transform it, it is language thanks to which 'I act the subject'; the tree is not an image for me, it is simply the meaning of my action. But if I am not a woodcutter I can no longer 'speak the tree,' I can only speak about it, *on* it . . . I no longer have anything more than an intransitive relationship with the tree; the tree is no longer the meaning of reality as a human action it is an image at one's disposal." Roland Barthes, *Mythologies*, trans. Annette Lavers (London: Jonathan Cape, 1972) pp. 145–6.

66 This is the absolute opposite of Heidegger's insight that "Technology, as the highest form of rational consciousness, technologically interpreted, and the lack of reflection as the arranged powerlessness, opaque to itself, to attain a relation to what is worthy of question, belong together, they are the same thing." Heidegger, "Overcoming metaphysics," p. 99.

67 Heidegger, "Overcoming metaphysics," p. 99.

68 Agamben has the neatest formulation on this. It is worth reproducing in full: "The fact that must constitute the point of departure for any discourse on ethics is that there is no essence, no historical or spiritual vocation, no logical destiny that humans must enact or realize. This is the only reason why something like an ethics can exist, because . . . if humans were or had to be this or that substance, this or that destiny, no ethical experience would be possible—there would only be tasks to be done. This does not mean however that humans are not, and do not have to be something. There is in effect something humans are and have to be, but that something is not an essence or properly a thing. It is the simple fact of one's own existence as possibility or potentiality." Agamben, *The Communing Community*, p. 43.

69 Walter Benjamin, the epilogue to "The work of art in the age of mechanical reproduction," English translation in *Illuminations*, translated by Harry Zohn (London: Fontana, 1970), see page 244.

70 Scarry, *The Body in Pain*, p. 290.

71 Scarry, *The Body in Pain*, p. 292.

72 Scarry, *The Body in Pain*, p. 291.

73 Scarry, *The Body in Pain*, p. 279.

74 And thus of what has been.

75 Adorno, *Negative Dialectics*, p. 398.

76 Heidegger, "Overcoming metaphysics," p. 85. Cf. also the lines "No age lets itself be done away with by a negating decree. Negating only throws the negator off the path"; "Age of the world picture," p. 138.

77 I am thinking here of the injunction that Badiou puts on thought at the end of his essay published under the English title "Philosophy and the 'War against Terrorism.'" "From this moment on, the task of philosophy is welcome everything into thought that maintains itself outside the synthesis [of the two nihilisms]. Everything which affirmatively seizes a point of the real and raises it to the symbol will be taken by philosophy as a condition of its own becoming." A. Badiou, *Infinite Thought* (London: Continuum, 2005) p. 122.

78 Heidegger, "Overcoming metaphysics," pp. 109, 110.

79 Heidegger, "Overcoming metaphysics," p.109.

80 Andrew J Mitchell, "Translator's introduction," in Martin Heidegger, *Bremen and Freiburg Lectures* (Bloomington: Indiana University Press, 2012) p. ix.

81 See Heidegger "Overcoming metaphysics," p. 104.

82 Rational as a Nazi political project (thought from within their own terms); irrational when pursued, at vast expense, in the midst of a War.

83 In the King James version, the Bible is remarkably clear on this point: Genesis, chapter I, 26: "And God said, let us make man in our image, after our likeness: and let them have dominion over the fish of the sea, and over the fowl of the air, and over the cattle, and over all the earth, and over every creeping thing that creepeth upon the earth. 27: So God created man in his own image, in the image of God created he him; male and female created he them. 28. . . . And God blessed them, and God said unto them. Be fruitful, and multiply, and replenish the earth, and subdue it: and have dominion over the fish of the sea, and over the fowl of the air, and over every living thing that moveth upon the earth."

84 Domination sequences the object in obedience to the subject. Representation in turn secures things as objects and reduces, on demand, other subjects to the status of objects—or most notoriously, and today increasingly, places them as essentially disposable. On the latter, as applied to persons see the essay by Zygmunt Bauman, *Wasted Lives* (Cambridge: Polity, 2003).

85 An excellent short text that grasps this with respect to Africa at the end of the 19th century is Sven Lindquist, *"Exterminate All the Brutes!"* (New York: New Press, 1997). For the logic of violence and colonization see the classic texts by Fritz Fanon, *Black Skin, White Masks* and *The Wretched of the Earth*; for the violence of economic expropriation in its extreme forms see also Adam Hochschild, *King Leopold's Ghost* (New York: Mariner, 1999). The recent histories of Rwanda and the Eastern Congo are also germane.

86 Quoted in Sven Lindquist, *"Exterminate All the Brutes"*.

87 The contemporary version of which will be the abandonment to immiseration and deaths of climate refugees.

88 In European history, the exported violence of the 19th century becomes, in the 20th, the age of European catastrophe in which violence comes home to roost in the orgy of internal bloodletting claimed over 100 million lives. An early and too little consulted attempt to measure this is Gil Eliot, *Twentieth Century Book of the Dead* (London: Allen Lane, 1972). The appellation "World Wars" to what has always seemed to me an attempt by Europe to involve by implication the rest of the world in what were, in truth European civil wars. Even World War II is two distinct wars: one European, one Asian.

89 See Clive Dilnot, "The triumph—and costs—of greed (Part I)" *Real-World Economics Review*, 49(March) (2009), p. 42–61.

90 The prediction for this century has to lie in the violence that will accompany the global failures, across the century, to contend with (i.e., manage) adequately the social consequences of climate change. Regretfully, the scale of violence deployed here will in all probability exceed even those levels we have come to accept as "normal" for the previous century.

91 For just this reason this essay is written *against* every proposal for the future that takes willing as its agency, be it the fantasies of economic or technological opportunism or those in design who ape this rhetoric.

92 Adorno, *Negative Dialectics*, p. 187.

93 I am using design here in the widest possible sense to indicate the intentional shaping of systems, not in the form restricted to the milieu of art-and-design. I am using it closer to Simon's sense when he speaks generically of "man's search for good designs" as the basis of his existence. Simon, *Sciences*, p. 138.

94 This logic is already anticipated in the title of Tony Fry's recent *Design as Politics* (Oxford: Berg, 2009).

95 Badiou, *Ethics*, p. 30.

96 Badiou, *Ethics*, p. 31.

97 One only need think of Sarkozy's demonization of Roma in France as responsible for France's social ills—all 20,000 of them that is, in a population of 65.8 million. Sarkozy had learned Hitler's Law in these matters: go after a minority, but make sure it is a very small one.

98 Adorno and Horkheimer, *Dialectic of Enlightenment*, pp. 139–40.

99 Nihilism enters because it deprives all reason of its praxiological or better its poietic and transitive capacities. It makes reason merely such, as impotent bewailing. Meanwhile action marches on, sans reflection.

100 Reason "submerged in the malady of the unsustainable" is both that which actively helps block the comprehension of what is (deficient as a tool of understanding) and that which undermines comprehension of what is achieved, even as model, in moments of new practices. All that in their configuration and their disposition—their potential efficacy—point beyond the limits of the unsustainable are held and limited. To put it another way, what practice struggles to bring to demonstrative light, reason, cast in the light of nihilism or caught in what-is, occludes and obscures.

101 See Critchley, *Infinitely Demanding* (London: Verso, 2007) especially page 3.

102 The apperception of increasingly obscene inequality—itself a historical move we should note, since it aims regressively at taking us backwards towards patterns of economic distribution of a century or more ago.

103 Simon, *Sciences*, p. 111.

104 Alain Badiou, *Ethics* (London: Verso, 2001) p. 15. Adapted quotation.

105 James Joyce, *Ulysses* (New York: Random House, 1934), p. 197. The full quotation from Joyce, who borrows it in turn from a line in George Meredith's *The Ordeal of Richard Feveral*, is "The sentimentalist is he who would enjoy without incurring the immense debtorship for the thing done." Placed in the context of this argument the suggestion would be that ours is essentially a sentimental economy. This may partially account for its violence, for it is well known that the two go together.

106 Critchley, *Infinitely Demanding*, p. 13. See also here the earlier work of Gillian Rose, especially *Hegel Contra Sociology* (London: Athlone Press, 1981) and *The Broken Middle* (Oxford: Blackwell, 1992).

107 Critchley, *Infinitely Demanding*, p. 3.

108 I have tried to make the case for the radical impurity of design in the extended essay "Ethics? Design?" (Chicago: *The Archeworks Papers*, I(2), 2005). See especially pp. 110–29.

109 Rose, *Mourning* (Cambridge: Cambridge University Press, 1996). See respectively pages 62; 38; 12–13, 76; 12–13.

110 On this see the important prologue to Badiou, *Metapolitics*, pp. 1–9.

111 In Badiou, *Metapolitics* (London: Verso, 2005).

112 "An event is political if its material is collective . . . the use of the term 'collective' is an acknowledgment that if . . . thought is political it belongs to all . . . in the case of politics the universality is intrinsic, and not simply a function of the address." Badiou, *Metapolitics*, p. 141.

113 Simon, *Sciences*, p. 138.

114 Simon, *Sciences*, p. 143.

115 Clive Dilnot, "The Science of Uncertainty or the Potential Contribution of Design to Knowledge," in *Doctoral Education in Design: Proceedings of the Ohio Conference, October 8–11 1998*, ed. R Buchanan et al, Carnegie Mellon University, Pittsburgh, 1999, pp. 65–97.

116 See Francois Jullien, *A Treatise on Efficacy* (Hawai'i: University of Hawai'i Press, 2004), p. 17.

117 See Otto van Busch, "Designing capabilities," in Jan Brand and Jose Teunissen (eds), *A Fashion Odyssey: Progress in Fashion and Sustainability* (Arnhem: Art EZ Press, 2013) pp. 226–9.

118 Badiou, *Metapolitics*, p. 145.

119 This finds take up in contemporary design. See the successive works of Anthony Dunne, *Hertzian Tales* (Cambridge: MIT Press, 2007); and Anthony Dunne and Fiona Raby, *Speculative Everything* (Cambridge: MIT Press, 2013). See also Carl DiSalvo, *Adversarial Design* (Cambridge: MIT Press, 2010).

120 Implied here, if not yet laid out, is a new doctrine of the subject. One consonant with what the artificial offers, both in its dangers and its possibilities.

3. Acting in regard to history

1 Alain Badiou, *Philosophy in the Present* (London: Verso, 2009) p. 81.

2 Or in design language, into situations that are a nexus of incommensurable requirements and forces. On this see Sargent, "Design science or non-science?", pp. 389–402.

3 Alain Badiou, *Ethics* (London: Verso, 2001) p. 15. Adapted quotation.

4 Badiou, *Philosophy in the Present*, p. 1.

5 Badiou, *Philosophy in the Present*, p. 1.

6 Designers tend to think problems immediately as possibility, indeed they define the problem from the stance of the possibility of they perceive. The necessary objective reason for this is wrapped with the structure of "wicked problems," i.e., those problems that do not allow for precise objective formulation, but which rather *only* become fully visible or evident through the "solution" that is proffered. See Rittel and Webber "Dilemmas in a general theory of planning," pp. 155–69.

7 Alain Badiou and Slavoj Žižek, *Philosophy in the Present* (London: Verso, 2005) p. 81.

8 On this see Janet Roitman, *Anti-Crisis* (Durham: Duke University Press, 2013). On the other hand, thinking "crisis" in terms of a crisis of "steering ability" through systemic limitation on problem-solving and steering capacities does seem to be a necessary component of understanding the danger of this situation. See Habermas, *Legitimation Crisis*.

9 Adorno and Horkheimer, *Dialectic of Enlightenment* (London: NLB, 1979) p. xi.

10 Analysis shows that that once we pay attention to the manner in which visual configurations work the notion that *only* the linguistic can establish propositional arguments can be refuted. I have made this argument in "Notes on the politics of configuration: Part one: 'Being prescient concerning Obama,'" *The Poster: A Critical Journal of Design*, 1(1), (2010), pp. 7–29.

11 Nelson Goodman, *Languages of Art* (Indianapolis: Bobbs-Merrill, 1968), p. 258.

12 The argument is ideological, from the side of language, which wishes to preserve anciently granted rights. "While the poetic 'image' may be acknowledged as a symbol or vehicle of truth, the implication always is that this truth is never due to any organic or effective presence in it of intellect or rational discourse or ideas." Galvano Della Volpe, *Critique of Taste* (London: NLB, 1978), p. 15.

13 Slavoj Žižek, *In Defence of Lost Causes* (London: Verso, 2008), p. 315.

14 Žižek, *In Defence of Lost Causes*, p. 314.

15 Žižek, *In Defence of Lost Causes*, p. 314.

16 Theodor Adorno, "The meaning of working through the past" in *Critical Models* (New York, Columbia University Press, 1998), p. 89–104.

17 Žižek, *In Defence of Lost Causes*, p. 314.

18 Renata Stih and Frieder Schnock, *Orte des Errinnerns/Places of Remembrance* (Berlin: Haude and Spenersche, 2002). I have drawn on some of the factual material in the essay included in this document by Caroline Wiedmer, "Remembrance in Schöneberg," at http://www.stih-schnock.de/Wiedmer_BV.pdf

19 The area encompassed around 16,000 of Berlin's roughly 200,000 Jews. It should always be remembered that the Jewish population of Germany in the early 1930s, *c.*550,000, was less than 1 percent of the then German population of *c.*67 million. More than 80 percent were German citizens. The vast majority of the rest were permanent resident Polish Jews.

20 70 cm high by 50 cm wide.

21 Because this book is primarily a theoretical text, and because art- or design-historical work as such was not its remit, I have decided not to illustrate the project here—it does in any case demand a multitude of illustrations, this is not a work that can be grasped in a single image. However, the artist's website provides a number of photographs of the project *in situ* (including some of the signs discussed below). See: http://www.stih-schnock.de/remembrance.html

22 The sign is one of the very few to tell a personal story: "'The time has come. Tomorrow I must leave and naturally, it is a heavy burden . . . I will write to you . . .:' Before being deported, January 16 1942."

23 Which in fact denotes the edict that Jews may not use the public beach at the Wanasee, August 22, 1933.

24 Similarly, the artists deliberately avoided any of the conventional signs of Jewishness: "We didn't want people to be able to say, 'Oh yes, that was that.' On the other hand the word 'Jew' is in the text in almost every sign." See "Jews aren't allowed to use phones: Berlin's most unsettling memorial," an interview with Renata Stih and Frieder Schnock by Ian Johnson, *New York Review of Books*, blog, June 15 2013.

25 This confirms another aspect of the memorial, that it references one's own ignorance and naivety, the limits of one's imagination in respect of the almost infinite cruelty that the National Socialists were capable of. The point is made more emphatic by reading Renata Stih's account of this sign. "The first sign we attached to a lamppost was a cat . . . [the reason for the regulation] is that the animals had to go then the owners could be removed. Because if the animals would stay in the apartment, they wouldn't get food, they'd make a noise, this would cause a commotion. Maybe the Aryan neighbors wouldn't care about the Jewish neighbor being deported but they would truly care about a little cat meowing. People think this sign is cute, adorable." Johnson, "Jews aren't allowed to use phones".

26 Perhaps 7,000 Berlin Jews survived the war, 4,700 as spouses of Aryans, 1,400 in hiding and 900 returnees from the camps. The Nazi's declared the city "Jew free" in June 1943, although the last transports ran in February and March 1945. Figures from *Berlin: the City and the Holocaust*, http://www.holocaustresearchproject.org/nazioccupation/berlin.html

27 As the transportations began the district was used as a kind of staging ground for deportation. "They turned a lot of the building into 'Jew Houses'—*Judenhauser*—so you had more than 6,000 Jews who were here for deportation. They were put together in five-room apartments, five families in such an apartment, making life really miserable." Frieder Schnock in Johnson, "Jews aren't allowed to use phones."

28 It is possible that these levels of tiny cruelty strike us all the harder today, in that both the continuing barbarism of our times and the Holocaust industry has inured us somewhat to the events in the camps. What now touches us, we realize, are those moments at which the political process comes down to earth. It is not the metaphysical tragedy that matters—since there was no tragedy in this sense, only *politics*; the use of one group of persons for the political benefit of another. Rather what matters are the intimate mechanisms through which persons are denied as such.

29 Statement by the artists on their website, *c.*2005.

30 Traditional monuments—and this includes the vast majority of avant-garde monuments, refer only to the fact of tragedy and not to cause. They refuse Brecht's argument that "criticism, to do more than whining, must make a diagnosis." In them, history is fixed and it comes down to us as the inevitability and unchangeability of what has now arrived.

31 One question this project raises is how we how we think such work, through which categories, and how we understand the work they achieve. The work can be placed within the tradition of memorials—to which it then becomes a critical counterpart. The problem with this categorization is that it is passive; it adds this example to the genre "monument" (albeit as counter-example) but it then closes thinking down by saying it is "only" a monument. The piece is less, in my view, a memorial than it is a tool for looking at history.

32 The placement of some of the signs at least is deliberate in order to heighten this connection. "In front of the delicatessen 'Butter Linder' we put the sign that Jews and Poles are not allowed to buy sweets. We placed it there on purpose, so people would see it coming in and out of the store. If you look across the street, there's the Bayerischer Platz U-Bahn station with the subway sign . . . next to it is one of our signs with the same symbol. But on the back it says that Jews aren't allowed to use the subway." Renate Stih, in Johnson, "Jews aren't allowed to use phones."

33 Renata Stih: "So in re-writing the [regulations] we used the present tense. But to put back time we used the date that it was passed at the end of the text," Johnson, "Jews aren't allowed to use phones." The deeper relation of "then" and "now" is that while on one side the memorial restores specificity, on the other it disallows any absolute barrier between then and now. What is impermeable in the monument (as myth) is here permeable (as experience).

34 Adorno's maxim concerning the impossibility of simply "breaking free" of the past: "One wants to break free of the past: rightly, because nothing at all can be in its shadow, and because there will be no end to the terror as long as guilt and violence are repaid with guilt and violence; wrongly, because the past that one would like to evade is still very much alive." Adorno, "The meaning of working through the past," p. 89.

35 We can add that it in so doing it comes close to rendering Benjamin's contention from the "Theses in the Philosophy of History" that "every image of the past that is not recognized by the present as one of its own concerns threatens to disappear irretrievably."

36 There is a map, in German, at three points in the area, but otherwise no information as to the location of the signs.

37 This is part I think of what enables the memorial not to be seen as simply a "work of art." The memorial emphatically takes its distance on "art" in the sense discussed in section I. It therefore moves closer to what Agamben called the "original space" (time) of art. An indication of what art can be "post-art."

38 In W. G. Sebald, *Campo Santo* (London, Hamish Hamilton, 2005) p. 215.

39 It is to the record of "Places of Remembrance" that of all the memorials to the Holocaust, this is one of the few that take up the weight of privation suffered by the Jewish population of Berlin *before* their extermination.

40 Sticking close to the facts is also sticking close to the materiality of things and the materiality of relations. It is the absolute opposite of the sublime in every way.

41 See for example Vilem Flusser, who assigns precisely this role to the Holocaust. V. Flusser, "The ground we tread" in V. Flusser, *Post-History* (Minneapolis, Univocal, 2013), pp. 3–10.

42 Flusser, "The ground we tread," pp. 3–10.

43 The charge against the Holocaust industry, especially in film but also in fiction, is that it trades upon individual stories as the substitute for understanding. The problem is not only the limitations of biography— powerful though those may be. The problem is rather the lack of self-referential skepticism about means and forms of representation. It is almost obscene to quote Heidegger here but his point made in the Appendix to the essay "Age of the world picture" that our times require an "originality and range of reflection" applies perhaps most of all to this question. On the question of fascism and its representation see the essay by Rose, "Beginnings of the day: fascism and representation", *Mourning*, pp. 41–62.

44 The work is best understood as a choreographed and configured apparatus for understanding. In that sense it is perhaps unclassifiable.

45 See the useful essay by Christopher Bollas, "The evocative object world" in *The Evocative Object World* (New York: Routledge, 2009) pp. 79–94.

46 Italo Calvino, *Six Memos for the Next Millennium* (New York, Vintage: 1996) p. 33.

47 Personal communication from the designer Helena Kjellgren.

48 One might think here of an insightful paragraph: "Why did Nietzsche's metaphysics lead to a scorn of thinking under the banner of 'life'? Because no-one realized how, according to Nietzsche's doctrine, the representational-calculative (empowering) guarantee of stability is just as essential for 'life' as 'increase' and escalation. Escalation itself has been only taken in the aspect of the intoxicating (psychologically) but not in the same time giving to the guarantee of stability the true and ever new impulse and justification for escalation. Hence it is the unconditional rule of calculating reason which belongs to the will to power, and not the fog and confusion of an opaque chaos of life." Heidegger, "Overcoming metaphysics", p. 94.

49 Note Luc Boltanski's formulation that the way to mitigate human suffering leads through "joining together," established in the connection between "a description of the person suffering and the concern of someone informed of the suffering." See L. Boltanski, *Distant Suffering: Morality, Media, Politics* (Cambridge: Cambridge University Press, 1993). Quoted in Bauman, *Conversations*, p. 158. In quoting these lines, Bauman's argument is that it this "joining" that is what "change of social understanding" amounts to; i.e., that it is connective understanding that leads to the commitment to change deficient social reality.

50 Re Eisenmann's monument: "From the perspective of victims, an experience of silent violence undertaken by German law and supported by the majority of 'citizens', is turned into another silent, passive experience, which is big only in scale but not in affection." Mahmoud Keshavarz, "*Tracing Un-: design, undocumentedness and possibilities of politics*," unpublished notes, 2013.

51 The museum or "place of information" was added to the project at a late stage in summer 1999 by order of the Bundestag. The museum was not designed by Eisenman.

52 Adorno, "The meaning of working through the past," English translation in Rolf Tiedemann (ed.), *Can One Live After Auschwitz? A Philosophical Reader* (Stanford: Stanford University Press) p. 15.

53 Goodman, *Languages of Art*, p. 258.

54 It would be worth looking critically at the range of Holocaust memorials in terms of the criteria that Goodman lays out so well and with such economy. See note 10.

55 Adorno, "The meaning of working through the past", p. 91.

56 The attitude of Claude Lanzmann (*Shoah*): "There is an absolute obscenity in the project of understanding. *Not* understanding was my iron law during all the years of preparing and directing *Shoah*: I held onto this refusal as the only ethical and workable attitude possible. He adds: "*Hier ist kein Warum*": this, Primo Levi tells us, was the law at Auschwitz that an SS guard taught him on arriving at the camp: "Here there is no why." But one might have thought that this statement, which is identical to that given everywhere by force, calls for precisely the opposite response. In truth, the camps are overdetermined with "why."

57 Theodor Adorno, "The Meaning of Working through the Past," English translation in Rolf Tiedemann (ed.), *Can One Live After Auschwitz? A Philosophical Reader* (Stanford: Stanford University Press) p. 18.

58 Part of the comfort of the Holocaust is the idea "this was the worst." But it was not the worst. The worst is yet to come. It was not even the worst *then*. Worse was the war itself in which in total some 60 million or so died. Worse again was the serious contemplation of initiating nuclear war (the "first strike" doctrines of the late 1970s and early 1980s). Worse again will be what occurs in this century.

59 Adorno's word here precisely capturing the enthralling of the will and the reduction of social reflection which permitted the holocaust to happen and will, in all likelihood, produce, in this century, monstrosities of equal scope and criminality.

60 Understanding does *not* mean reconciliation. It does mean incorporation.

61 Theodor Adorno, *History and Freedom*, ed. Rolf Tiedemann (Cambridge: Polity, 2006) pp. 39–40.

62 In the end this is also a contestation concerning decisions about "what is" (in this case about what was and what is now and what may be in the future) and about truth (the truth of an occurrence—the Holocaust—and the truth of history).

63 Just as discourses are deemed more than linguistic (Foucault) it follows that is perfectly capable that signs, artifacts, objects—real or virtual—engage in discourse, wage propositional war we might say, in discursive or propositional as well as enactive ways.

64 Alain Badiou in the essay "Philosophy and psychoanalysis," in *Infinite Thought* (New York: Continuum, 2005), p. 60.

65 There is not space here to discuss both Foucault's and Agamben's more recent explorations of the work of "apparatus" in constructing (Foucault) or deconstructing (Agamben) subjectivity. All one can point to is that a good argument can be made that the memorial works precisely how Agamben wishes for "profanity" to work, that is as "the restitution to common use of what has been captured and separated," theologically so to speak, by that which seizes and divides. See Agamben, "What is an apparatus?," pp. 1–24.

66 On this see the very important discussion of the concept of the Holocaust in Badiou, *Ethics*, pp. 62–6.

67 Rose, *Mourning Becomes the Law*, p. 54.

68 It takes categories as real and enshrines them with a quasi-metaphysical identity, "for all time."

69 One notices, always, a kind of embarrassment about the fact that the Holocaust was conceived in part as economic activity; that the Jews—and others let us not forget, particularly the intended populations of East—were seen as those who could be worked to death in the service of the Reich and the SS. By 1945 there was scarcely a German company that did *not* participate in the use of slave labor. Dachau alone had 123 such satellite camps by the end of the war. Auschwitz will not repeat. The slave economy will.

70 See Deborah Dwork and Robin Jan Van Pelt, *Auschwitz* (New York: Harper, 1992).

71 It is clear from this that Stih and Schnock are working emphatically against what we could call "Holocaust piety" and the idea that there is something about the Holocaust which is ineffable. Both notions they refuse and the memorial reflects this. There is no dimension of it that is either pious or mystificatory. In this both they and the memorial follow the logic that treating the Holocaust leads to mystification and thus to the undermining of both analysis ("How?") and political action. In their view—and this is implied in the entire structure of the memorial—acting "happens," i.e., is impelled, not when we secure apparent difference ("this happened, then") but when we recognize and accept the impossibility of our *not* being implicated in what occurred. They thus reverse the fear of "relativizing" the Holocaust, and against the valorization of the other as a deified category (the Jew as absolute victim, the victim of all victims) insist on treating the actual *German* inhabitants of Schöneberg, Jewish and non-Jewish. The identification is not categorical, through a named ontology of the "Jew," but with persons.

72 Cf. Kundera's notion of the ethics of discovery of hitherto unnoticed possibilities of experience discussed in §1.

73 This is what is wrong, we realize, with most memorials. In memorializing the Holocaust only the effects of a prior decision are commemorated. From the perspective of those deaths this is "beyond reason." But the Holocaust as political project—and in the end this is *all* that it is, it has no other "existential" weight beyond this contingent fact—is thereby made all but invisible. The real truth is that it is the *casualness* of the political gesture, the ease with which it was made, the tacit agreement to it by most of "respectable" Europe and the USA, at least up to 1938–1940, that is the real evil. The Holocaust is really nothing more than expediency. That is its tragedy. It is literally "wasted lives"—though not so from the Nazi perspective. But then Europe has been good, historically, at using the lives of others. It was inevitable, sooner or later, that this capability would be turned on its own populations.

74 Rose, *Mourning Becomes the Law*, p. 75.

75 *Mourning Becomes the Law*, p. 73.

76 The population of the concentration camps, does not, as if often supposed, rise inexorably across 1933–1944. After the brief burst in 1933–34 when the first groups of camps are established the camp populations decline in the late 1930s only to begin to rise again at the beginning of the War.

77 And humiliation. Suffering can be borne—just. It does not necessarily erode a sense of self. Humiliation is suffering-in-public, it always erodes the sense of self of those who are humiliated, just as, in parallel, it fortifies the self-worth, however illusory, of those who humiliate.

78 A paraphrase of the sentence: "Even the immense suffering that surrounds the earth is unable to waken transformation, because it is only experienced, as passive, and thus the opposite state of action, and thus experienced together with action in the same realm of being as the will to will." Section XXVIII of "Overcoming metaphysics" in Martin Heidegger, *The End of Philosophy*, (ed.) Joan Stambaugh (Chicago: University of Chicago Press, 1973) p. 110.

79 I explored this in a little more detail in the extended essay C. Dilnot, "Ethics? Design?" in *The Archeworks Papers*, 1(2), pp. 1–148. See especially pp. 54–65.

80 As Adorno pointed out, the problem is emphasized because in this case (and now in others, past and present) "The enormity of what was perpetrated works to justify [a] consciousness [that] consoles itself with the thought that such a thing surely could not have happened unless the victims had in some way or another furnished some kind of instigation, and this 'some kind of' may then be multiplied at will." Adorno, *Critical Models?*, p. 91.

81 Precisely the (deliberate) failure to acknowledge "the cause," in the sense of the cause for which one fights, in the Vietnam Veterans Memorial in Washington was one of the reasons why Mya Lin's memorial was so viciously attacked by the right on its inception.

82 Their implicit message, "See, we remember, in order that Auschwitz does not repeat," is belied by the fact that they forget the second half of Adorno's injunction: "and that nothing like it should ever exist again." Theodor Adorno, *Metaphysics: Concepts and Problems* (Stanford: Stanford University Press, 2001), p. 115.

83 The correspondence is by no means one-to-one but there is obviously overlap between the theses advanced in chapters IV and V of Scarry's *The Body in Pain,* and the Schöneberg memorial.

84 This recalls Adorno's observation that "disregard for the subject makes things easy for the administration." The line occurs in the version of "Elements of Anti-Semitism" translated in Rolf Tiedemann (ed.), *Can One Live After Auschwitz? A Philosophical Reader* (Stanford: Stanford University Press, 2003), p. 421.

85 Scarry, *The Body in Pain*, p. 291.

86 That which today "can be called moral, i.e., the demand for right living" finds its true basis "in bodily feeling, in identification with unbearable pain." Adorno, *Metaphysics: Concepts and Problems*, p. 117.

87 This is Rolf Tiedemann's useful summary of Adorno's argument on this point. See the introduction to his edited collection of Adorno's work *Can One Live After Auschwitz?*, p. xxv.

88 In a swipe as much at those who might wish to deify the Holocaust, as well as those who cynically can see nothing of value in the ordinary, Agamben adds, "this is why those who try to make the world and life sacred again are just as impious as those who despair about its profanation." See Agamben, *Coming Community*, p. 90.

89 Richard Ellmann, *Ulysses on the Liffey* (London: Faber and Faber, 1972), p. 185.

90 Conversely, it means that they had also succeeded in situating, with some acuity, the true location and agency of political evil.

91 Rose, *Mourning*, Chapter 2, p. 43.

92 One argument is that in relation to the Holocaust, banality "is the adopted disguise of a very powerful will to abolish conscience." From Saul Bellow, *Mr Sammler's Planet* (New York: Viking, 1970). If the sense of this observation is immediately apparent, conversely the turning of banality from as-such to being, as the ordinary, the location of good and evil, is the act of rescuing conscience by rescuing that on which it materially depends.

93 The difference lies, as Lacan suggested, in relation to culture as a whole, in how you take an attitude to it. Whether, in fact, you betray it, or allow yourself to betray it, or whether you resist it.

94 Žižek, *In Defence of Lost Causes*, p. 315.

95 Adorno, "Why still philosophy?," in *Critical Models* (New York: Columbia University Press, 1998) p. 17.

96 Adorno, "Why still philosophy?," p. 14.

97 Adorno, "Why still philosophy?", p. 14.

98 Badiou, *Ethics*, p. 35.

99 Bernstein, *The Fate of Art*, p. 189.

100 Heidegger, "Overcoming metaphysics", p. 110.

101 Heidegger, "Overcoming metaphysics," p. 103.

102 Heidegger, "Overcoming metaphysics," p. 14.

103 Critchley, *Infinite Thought*, p. 1.

104 Adorno, "Why still philosophy?", p. 16.

105 Badiou, *Ethics*, p. 30.

106 Badiou, *Ethics*, p. 30.

107 Badiou, *Ethics*, p. 38.

108 Badiou, *Ethics*, p. 38.

109 Badiou, *Ethics*, p. 33.

110 Simon, *Sciences*, p. 164.

111 Adorno, "Why still philosophy?", p. 16.

112 Adorno, "Why still philosophy?," p. 13.

113 Adorno, "Why still philosophy?," p. 13.

114 Adorno, "Why still philosophy?," p. 15.

115 Michael Baxandall, *Patterns of Intention: On the Historical Explanation of Pictures* (New Haven: Yale University Press, 1985), pp. 46–7.

116 Badiou, *Philosophy in the Present*, p. 2.

117 Badiou, *Philosophy in the Present*, p. 15.

118 I have benefitted greatly from observations on these essays by Susan Stewart, Komal Sharma and Veronica Uribe.

ESSAY THREE

AND SO TO ANOTHER SETTING . . .

Susan C. Stewart

1 ON CARE AND EDUCATION

There is quite a rage for design thinking these days, not only in business, but also in educational circles. That education should take up design thinking in the wake of business's enthusiasm for it simultaneously signals both cause for concern, and also what is most promising in the current state of our world.

Cause for concern is given not so much by the motives and hopes that have fueled enthusiasm for design thinking, or even by its specific content—although the well placed critique by Kimbell should be noted.[1] Rather, what is concerning, here, is the easy acceptance of a conversion of healthy and much needed questioning concerning the direction of many of our mainstream practices, into a method for producing (with relatively little expenditure) more innovative thinkers. The transformation of question into technique in the context of education is something that should indeed give us pause.

What is promising, of course, is the questioning itself; and the recognition of need from which that questioning springs.

Also promising is the turn to design. Both within and beyond design thinking as currently formulated, design brings into play a range of activities, acquired dispositions and types of engagement that are essential, I would argue, to the project of critical redirection. Among these valuable dispositions is the designer's acquired orientation to the pursuit of attentive and open-ended inquiry into the possibilities latent within lived material contexts. A second promising characteristic of design is its restless dissatisfaction with answers. Expert designers are addicted to iterative projection and critique. Equally important is the deep pleasure experienced by the designer, in the blossoming or unfolding of felicitous material conjunctions and effects; the embodied recognition of what is both transformative and fitting within the material context in question.

However, by itself, and certainly in respect of the forms it acquired within 20th-century contexts of practice, design is *not* sufficient to the task of redirection. Design will certainly be a key player in our unfolding future. Whether or not it plays to good effect will depend upon the possibilities that blossom within its own practices, carrying it in new directions. This chapter seeks to facilitate such blossoming by pointing to resonant practices and to interpretive lenses, variously drawn from philosophy and the humanities, through which design might be stimulated into new and promising paths.

Key to these lenses, and noticeably absent from discussions of design thinking, is *history*. Quite simply, the connection between the historicality of everyday being-in-the-world and understanding has not been widely recognized—either in discussions concerning design or in those concerning education more generally. However this insight, which belongs to Heidegger's early teaching and achieves its fullest articulation in *Being and Time* (1927), is only the most evident part of that which has been overlooked.

One of Heidegger's most significant contributions to 20th-century philosophy lies in his development of Nietzsche's nonlinear conception of history, a trajectory that was to be continued in the work of Foucault.[2] In Heidegger's later work, not only do we dwell historically; so do both things and the associations of things-and-practices that configure worlds. We are gathered into these associations, and share in their historicality.[3]

The shift in focus from the historicality of human-centered experience, to our participation in the historicality of worlds and things, is crucial to the understandings that inform the theory of ontological designing, as articulated by Tony Fry. This theory highlights the consequences of our participation in the historicality of worlds, and emphasizes the play of influences between design, understanding and world that shapes an historical trajectory.[4]

In short, the excision of history from design thinking isolates the understanding that informs the design act from any understanding of the temporal trajectories in which it participates. Given the ambition for design thinking—that it will nurture conceptual agility and intelligent leadership in responding to complex situations, especially those involving redirection and change—its isolation from consideration of the temporal trajectories that shape and are shaped by our actions, seems a significant omission.

To be clear: it is not that history is just one among a number of supplementary "interpretive lenses or resonant practices" that might be mobilized to revitalize and redirect design. Rather, history is *key*.

The task of this chapter is to speculate on ways of bringing what is missing from design thinking not only more prominently into design itself, but also into the translations and exportations of design into other disciplines, especially as these boundary crossings and interdisciplinary conversations inform education. As will become evident, the focus upon education within this chapter is neither a turning away from the topic of history, nor from the topic of design. Rather, it sharpens our focus upon that with which design, history and education should be equally concerned; and that, I will suggest, is character (*ethos*).

Preliminary clarifications

Character is a term that knits together the diverse threads of this chapter. In mobilizing character, I mean to invoke a cluster of terms that, within Western language traditions, have conceptualized the links between configuration, orientation and action within a performative association.[5] Important among these are the ancient Greek term *ethos* that informed the original sense of our term "ethical"; also the Latin *dispositio*, and its English derivative, "disposition."

Each of these terms—character, *ethos*, disposition—operates across diverse scales and contexts of association. In Plato's *Republic*, for example, the *ethos* of an ideal *polis* was invoked specifically for its ability to conjure, by analogy, the *ethos* of a well-disposed soul.[6] In Vitruvius's *Ten Books of Architecture*, published in ancient Rome, the disposition of a building— the arrangement of its parts and the establishment of proportionate relations between them—was to be guided by analogy with the disposition of a well-formed body.[7] Macrocosm resonated with microcosm. In each case the character of a body, association or state was understood as informed by its disposition; by the relationships established or negotiated among the constellation of parts or participants (both material and immaterial) that were gathered together in active association. Such analogies between different kinds and scales of bodies and associations are commonplace throughout the Greco–Roman tradition. My use of the term "character," then, is to be understood as applicable to diverse kinds of performative association, ranging in scale from the micro to the macro, and (as in a *polis*) encompassing all possible combinations of participants; human and nonhuman, animate and inanimate, material and conceptual, lasting and ephemeral.

An advantage of the term character is that it is understood not only as exercising a hold over the body to which it belongs and as unifying that complex entity through time and through change. Additionally, at least within contemporary contexts (and despite its association with unity and continuity), character is understood as formative; that is, open and ongoing—a work in progress. In this respect "character" invokes a temporal and historical dimension that the terms *ethos* and disposition may neglect. Finally, as reflected throughout literature and poetry, as well as in everyday experience, character, even when portrayed as belonging to an individual, is internally contested, uncertain, often astray but nevertheless capable of self-correction. When grasped as belonging to a hybrid and complex association, the internal contestations, misdirections and corrections of character at play in the interactions between the association's participants, are even more readily evident. This term, then, provides a handy means of *characterizing* the performative, open-ended and historically unfolding associations that, I will argue, should be the focus of design histories.

One final clarification may be helpful: The compound term "performative association" is an important and recurring one within the argument of this chapter. The understandings that inform this compound percolate through the history of Western thought, arcing from the texts of Plato and Aristotle to the 20th-century writings of Heidegger, Gadamer and Foucault (among others) and, more recently, the Actor–Network theorists and their associates, predecessors, allies and interlocutors.[8]

Important for this essay are the understandings developed within Heidegger's thought, especially where he speaks of "worlds worlding" and "things thinging."[9] Heidegger's use of the German term, "thing" (*ding*), is likely to have been influential in the adoption of the German neologism "*Dingpolitik*" by Latour and Weibel in their exhibition and accompanying tome: *Making Things Public: Atmospheres of Democracy* (2005). *Ding* refers to a gathering, the purpose of which is to open up and concernfully deal with something that matters, through deliberation and discussion; thus Heidegger conceived of "the thing" as that which presents itself as bearing upon or of concern within our worlds. The thing is never exhausted by its relations. Its "thinging" belongs to world as world unfolds historically, and not simply to any situated perception of it.[10] What this approach to things and gatherings achieves is a shift in the focus of discussion from individual entities to active and operative associations that stretch across and gather in time.

Latour, Callon, Law and Michael (among others) variously develop the notion of a performative association, although without necessarily adopting this terminology. Their work focusses attention not only upon the character or identity of an association, as gathered and articulated through its action, agency or performance, but upon the internal negotiations and accommodations of the various members of the association in the working out of its performance. Exemplary for my meaning are the co(a)gents playfully elaborated by Mike Michael; the couch potato and the hudogledog.[11] Importantly, as for Heidegger, neither the agency, nor the existence, of participants in any association is exhausted by the agency or existence of the association itself. Things are relational but are not exhausted by their relations.

Attaching character to such evidently contingent configurations can help to undo preconceptions about the fixed nature of things, and encourage a more active, playful and (wherever called for) subversive attitude to the associations that hold our practices in place. Such unglueing, undoing and rejigging, whether of monstrous infrastructure or of apparently innocent facilitators of business-as-usual, is essential if we are to sufficiently mobilize ourselves and our worlds to meet the challenges of the not-so-distant future.

And so, with the cast assembling, we can begin.

Performative associations 1: Hold

Ancient myths concerning origins typically point to a moment in which either absolute difference (chaos), or absolute identity (indifference) is transformed by an event or an act that introduces relationships into the preexistent; absolute difference becomes relative, absolute identity becomes differentiated, distinctions are made, allegiances are formed, meaning enters and suffuses the emergent world.

What is recognized in these ancient tales of origins is the constitutive role of relations. For relations to exist there is need for both commonality and distinction; for things to stand both together and apart. Thus in Plato's mythic account, the demi-urge who formed the world kneaded together "the same and the different" then divided and subdivided, rekneaded and redivided until the whole texture of existence was worked through with proportionate relations.[12] Creation myths from other traditions speak in other ways of the emergence of relations, whether through the giving of birth, or through making, through marking, differentiating and naming. Through the introduction of relations and distinctions each world is made articulate.

Relations between things erase neutrality and detachment. Where there are relations there are attachments, associations, lines of interest and influence. If relations are constitutive of worlds, then there is no world in which influence is not exercised. Things, within worlds, exercise a hold over other things. Beings acquire their orientations and directions from the configuration of beings around them. Thus the European Enlightenment, in its quest for detachment, for objectivity, was struggling against the tendency of the world to create binding attachments, obligations and influences.

Of course, what the Enlightenment sought to put in place was not absolute freedom but, rather, an absolute distinction; that is, it sought to clearly distinguish between relations that could be rationally accounted for, and relations arising from unreasonable influence, or for which there could be no rational account given. For Enlightenment man (and certainly men, rather than women, were the focus), only the reasoned and the reasonable would be recognized as legitimately binding.

The virtue of reason, for these thinkers, was its ability to generate stable accounts of the world. Reason was identified with a God-given capacity to identify truths that remain independent of time, place or circumstance; universal truths that correspond to some fundamental, unchanging pattern of relations that remains external to the flux of experience, free from hidden ties or undeclared allegiances. In their endeavor to isolate and validate sets of relations that might have suprahistorical validity, Enlightenment thinkers assumed the authority and priority of their project over the projects and commitments commanded within the worlds of others. The Enlightenment project aimed at attainment of an ultimate measure of the validity of all experience and understanding, regardless of world. Ironically, this commitment to the isolation of rational relations from the tugs and ties of worldly involvements established a profound hold of its own over the understanding of Enlightenment thinkers and their heirs; a hold that was all the more influential for the freedom it promised from influence itself.[13] If the task of philosophy in the wake of Nietzsche has been to challenge the assumptions of the Enlightenment project (in its crystallization of the overarching trajectories of Western thought), it has done so in part by revisiting ancient insight into the hold that exists between beings and world. A significant move in this direction was made by Martin Heidegger.

Performative associations 2: Care

Heidegger saw clearly that worldly engagements unfold within a relational complex that has historical dimension; what is delivered into the present from the past includes not only configurations of the material, conceptual and practical worlds that we inhabit, but also orientations and assumptions that project us towards particular futures.

This recognition of the hold that is exercised by and within worlds is likely to have been prompted by Heidegger's early engagement with the works of Aristotle, especially the *Ethics, Physics* and *Metaphysics*. Certainly Aristotle's conception of *phronesis*, the virtue of judging well in practice, is a constitutive influence in Heidegger's magnum opus of 1927, *Being and Time*.[14] Both Aristotle's account of *phronesis* and Heidegger's argument in *Being and Time* play an important role in the argument of this chapter, and so need preliminary introduction.

The cultivation of a capacity to judge well in practice, or *phronesis*, may well be, at bottom, the goal at which advocates of design thinking aim. That this aim is articulated, by them, as a desire to foster innovation, reflects recognition of the need for a shift in our practices; however mobility without wisdom is surely the blight of our time, and certainly not what is desired. *Phronesis*, then, provides a necessary underpinning for the innovation or redirection of practice.

Certainly, in classical times, the cultivation of good judgment was understood to be the highest aim of education.[15] And the capacity to hold to what one grasped as being the right thing to do within each situation, was understood to be the essential mark of character. The man or woman of character was one who possessed *phronesis*, who was able to judge well concerning what needed to be done, was able to act on that judgment and hold to it.[16] And then, as now, the arts of making, of *techne* and *poesis*, were seen as providing a guide; a clue to the direction to be taken in education to this end.[17]

In Aristotle's account, the exercise of good judgment in practice arises from a disposition of the soul; and this disposition to judge well needs to have been established, over time, through the inculcation of good habits. As Aristotle observed, the repeated performance of a task establishes a habit. Becoming habituated to the way a task *should* be performed develops a feel for the right way of doing it. Once a good habit is established, to perform the task carelessly or incorrectly would simply feel wrong; would in fact cause discomfort or distaste.[18]

This embodied feel for what is right or wrong with respect to a way of working, with respect to materials, tools and practices, is what informs expertise. The expert craftsman or poet can extend the experimental edge of their craft, push the boundaries of what can be done in their field, by exercising this attuned, embodied feel for what will work; for what will produce good results. In the midst of such experimentation the expert also has a feel for where to draw the line. Instinctively they are able to avoid excess or the pursuit of a wrong path.[19]

By analogy, Aristotle argued, good habits exercised in public life are an essential part of an education into citizenship.[20] A feel for what action will be right within each situation is cultivated through the performance of right actions within other situations. The exercise of good habits establishes a hold over the embodied soul, and disposes it to right action. The virtue of *phronesis* is attained once one's soul has been so inculcated with a disposition to do right that one is not only able to recognize what *is* right, but would feel distaste for acting otherwise. In other words, an ethical disposition is registered and played out in embodied understandings and reactions. The hold exercised by the ethical disposition of the soul is inseparable from embodied experience.

Stimulated in his early years by Aristotle's account of the virtue of *phronesis*, but taking issue with what he felt to be the ancient's failure to root the ontological unity of human existence in *temporality*, Heidegger focused his first major work upon an account of the historicity of human practices, motivations and understandings.[21] Central to this work was an articulation of "care" (*Sorge*). By *care*, Heidegger meant an appetitive attunement to the situation that one is in; a "being-out-toward" or "reaching towards" the possibilities of the situation.[22] It is care that directs and gives moment to this reaching out toward. What is reached towards, or hearkened to, is that to which care is attuned.

The temporal structure of care is tripartite: care is defined by Heidegger as "to-be-ahead-of-itself-Being-already-in-(the world) as Being-alongside (entities encountered within-the-world)."[23] This can be broken into:

- Being-ahead-of itself, or, being already projected into possibilities; i.e., being oriented to, and already under-way in respect of possibilities for the future;

- Being-already-in, which Heidegger elsewhere speaks of as "throwness"; i.e., cast without choice into a world that is already configured by complex ways of operating, assumptions, structures and trajectories that are established and under way; i.e., being the heir to a past;

- Being-alongside, not as separate from, but entangled and involved with, other entities insofar as they present themselves to us; i.e., being with others and with things in this moment, the present.

Thus the temporality of care means that we are always already projected into the possibilities that the world we have inherited, and are in the midst of, presents to us. Every moment thus draws together future and past through what presents itself in *this* moment as worth engaging with or orienting oneself to. Temporality is "stretched along" a span of time;[24] past and future are drawn into and through the present. No temporal moment or trajectory can be grasped or experienced except insofar as these three meet within it.

The temporality of care needs to be grasped in the context of Heidegger's denomination of human being as *Da-sein* "Being *there*." The "*there*" is the situated moment into which we are thrown, within which certain possibilities present themselves and within which certain kinds of engagement are already underway. The handiness of the things, the tools and materials that are there in the doing of something, is inseparable from the "at-handness" of the possibilities that present themselves in the course of doing, and a handiness of the understandings (delivered from previous doings) that are *there* when needed. Situated doing is not just spatial, it is temporal. It includes not only things, but understandings, expectations and preconceptions. An orientation in time is just as crucial to our doing, as orientation in space.

Being-*there, Da*-sein, is to be *in* the moment that stretches across time, and that brings close and makes-handy the understandings that experience and anticipation offer. Heidegger refers to this temporal structure that stretches to encompass past experience and anticipation of the future in the present moment, as *ecstatic*.[25] The term "ecstatic" means to be outside of oneself. Care, as being-out-toward, and as hearkening, being attuned, alert to, and reaching out for the possibilities within a situation, is projected beyond itself; is ecstatic. *Da*-sein is not a unified subject, distinct from and observant of the objects of this world; not an identity located inside an individual, independent "self" but, rather, is Being-*there*; that is, *there*, in the moment, in the situation.

Of course *Da*-sein is not always alert and attuned to what is given in the moment. Much of the time we just go along with whatever presents itself. This going-along-with is what Heidegger refers to as *falling*.[26] The temporal structure of care is operative both in the distracting busyness of falling, and in hearkening-attunement of attentiveness. In both cases the situation is interpreted through what both past and anticipated future have already delivered into it. However, the everyday going-along-with is a falling away from the possibility of recognizing the character of what the moment offers, and to what it tends. This latter recognition, which Heidegger speaks of as being disclosed in the glance-of-an-eye, an *Augenblick*, represents a translation of *phronesis*; the moment of vision in which the situation is truly grasped, and it is clear what kind of response is called for.[27] Crucially, for Heidegger, this disclosure/clearing that occurs within the temporal ecstasies of care is *historical*; the arc of experience and anticipation informs what is recognized within the trajectory of the present. The historical and futural are fused in what presents itself as the right thing to do.[28] This ecstatic vision, then, this moment of clearing, is Heidegger's reconfiguration of the experience of *phronesis* within an historical conception of Being.

Thus the ecstatic temporality of *Da-sein*, given in care, is the basis for being historical and for being true, both to one's own-most possibilities and to the moment. The moral compass provided by *phronesis* is re-presented, in *Being and Time*, as bound to the historicity of our Being *there*, in the world.

After the publication of *Being and Time*, Heidegger shifted his focus from the temporality that informs *Da*-sein, to the locatedness of those involvements within a particular historical epoch. His earlier concern to articulate the understanding that operates within Being *there*, gives way to an exploration of the overarching assumptions and orientations that unify the epoch within which *Da*-sein's situated engagements unfold. Consonant with this shift in focus from the immediate to the epochal, is a change in the way that things—equipment, poetic works, designed infrastructure and environments—enter into Heidegger's essays. No longer are they presented only insofar as they participate in the immediate engagements of *Da*-sein, but rather they are seen to hold a place in and configure worlds across multiple scales of involvement, from the intimate to the structural.[29]

In this later work, the existential language of care—circumspection, conscience, resoluteness and authenticity—disappears. However, the temporality of care that incorporates future, past and present in the "Being *there*" of *Da*-sein, enabling the *Augenblick*, the possibility of vision—of an uncovering/disclosing of what matters, of what is worth holding to within the situation in question—*this* remains central to his thinking.[30] As Being-*there* is always situated within a particular historical epoch, the temporality that informs the moment is constituted by the dynamic of the epoch itself. Care, which is always temporal, takes on a particular form within each epoch. The care with which we comport ourselves within the world, our attunement to things (which is directed by a sense of what matters), our instincts concerning what is worth striving for and what we should hold to—all are shaped by the historical epoch in which that care arises. Heidegger's ontology of history; his positing of a succession of historical epochs with radically different interpretive structures, is thus also an ontology of care.

The character of the epoch into which we are thrown, within which we orient ourselves to particular possibilities and activate particular futures, is thus of the utmost moment. If the futures into which we are headed and to which we orient ourselves seem particularly bleak, then we urgently need to understand the mode of care that is propelling the unfolding of these futures. Understanding our epoch, understanding it historically, is the first step to be taken in attuning ourselves to the more promising possibilities that may be latent, and currently neglected, within the situations that we find ourselves.

Here, then, is the most compelling argument for prioritizing historical understanding within education. Without a sense of the historical those who project futures, who innovate or seek to lead, will be doing so with no perception of the way in which their understanding is historically constituted. They will be unaware that the things that seem to matter most to them, are given *as* mattering by the care structure of the epoch within which they are situated. They will be unaware that the possibilities for action to which they are instinctively oriented, are likely to be those that belong within, and give weight to, the ongoing, unfolding, historical trajectory of that epoch. If we have doubts about that trajectory, as we might justly do, we should not want our innovators or our leaders to be unaware of its hold upon them.

Performative associations 3: Ontological design

If historical understanding is of crucial importance to the education of those who must judge well in what they do, it is not just any kind of history that will furnish this understanding. Rather, it is *design* history that is crucial. As the arguments of this book have made clear, human history cannot be disentangled from the shaping force of design; it cannot be understood except in relation to what it has made.

Tony Fry has previously shown that the activity of designing is inseparable from what it is to be human and that, in *fact*, the project of becoming human (as yet incomplete) is being accomplished in and through our designing; we are always in the process of becoming what we will have been, by design.[31] If Heidegger pointed to the centrality of *temporality* to the way we care, to the way things matter to us, then Fry's important insight, crystallized from Heidegger's later work, is that that care is materialized and given force within the world in the things we *design*. Designed things, once released into the world, add weight and momentum to the trajectories of care that have informed them. It is not just history, or care, that is ontological, but design.

Anne-Marie Willis has succinctly articulated "the double movement of ontological designing—we design our world while our world acts back on and designs us."[32] This means that the legacy of our previous designing is always a part of what is acting upon us; shaping our horizons and our understandings, and informing our ongoing judgments as we navigate current concerns, activities and productions.

Designed things are of all kinds. The macro structures that hold our practices in their current trajectories are always being worked upon, reinforced, supplemented, and facilitated or, occasionally, undermined and redirected by our designing for meso- and micro- operations and pleasures. The hold of these macro structures is ever more deeply inscribed through our everyday embodied engagements with the equipmental, sensory and communicative complex that they enable and give meaning to.

A banal but pervasive example is given in the technologies of flow that have been a focus of our designing for the past century or so. The infrastructure of flow—whether it be directed to the redistribution of persons, goods and services, materials and waste, of capital and status, or of images, ideas and information; whether it operates through tangible, material networks as in highways or plumbing, or whether it be immaterial and ubiquitous—whatever form it takes, this infrastructure is ever more deeply embedded in our world by our participation in, and designing for, the multitude of performances that it variously supports and requires. Human lives that are stretched across and played out within the pervasive and interwoven technologies of flow have a different character to lives of the ancient world that were gathered and held in place by *polis* or by the presence of the gods.

But why have we made such an investment in flow? Certainly it was not because we truly grasped the kinds of beings that would emerge and flourish, or the ways of being that would disappear, in the wake of that investment. Certainly it was not by intention or choice that we brought this world into being, but it *was* through a myriad of designings, small and large, set in motion in response to the possibilities that appeared within the worlds in which we were engaged.

Heidegger's ontology of care would point to the role played, in these transforming worlds, by the Cartesian separation of space from place, or Galileo's separation of movement from essence.[33] While the understanding of motion that had informed Aristotle's thought assumed movement to be informed by essence—either a motion towards, a realization of, or a falling away from the essential mode of being to which the thing, by nature, belonged—Galileo thought of motion purely in relation to position. Position, as opposed to place, is content-free. The natural world—emptied of concepts of belonging, emptied of essences through which things participate in, belong to and have their place within larger relational complexes—was made newly available to the ordering projects of man. Nature, in its newly defined neutrality and availability, was set over against humankind, now recognized as the sole (or divinely ordained) source of projection, intention, and interest. Thus mathematization of position and motion went hand in hand with the setting apart of human consciousness from the natural world, the latter now reconceived as objective, measurable and calculable. Heidegger notes that for Newtonian physics: "All bodies are alike. No motion is special. Every place is like every other, each moment like any other."[34] Human consciousness was distinguished by its capacity to observe, grasp and articulate this physical order; to project redistributions and to realize intended ends. The activity of projection and reconfiguration became man's task.

The Enlightenment epoch thus came to experience temporality in terms of technological progress. Time, reconceived as unidirectional flow, became a vessel for the realization of projects. The care structure of the technological epoch of the Enlightenment oriented *Da*-sein to the past as to that-which-has-been-surpassed, and to the future as to that-which-will-certainly-be-different. The temporal "there" of Enlightenment *Da*-sein, was reduced to the fleeting; sometimes exhilarating but always precarious. Like the aesthetic of the sublime that accompanies it, temporal experience in the wake of the Enlightenment (at least in its moments of self-consciousness) walks a tightrope between terror and an exhilarating sense of power.

What kind of care is exercised by beings so situated? A history of design would bear witness to a reordering of the world in favour of the predictable, the disciplined and self-controlled. Roles are redistributed. Things are positioned in readiness for the labors to which they have been assigned. The energies and potential of the natural world are aligned with human projects; directed to the realization of human comfort and security. Designed environments, equipment, interactions and communications neutralize, or package and commercialize, bodily experience. Fear, ever-present, is either defiantly invoked, kept at bay by the stockpiling of power, or blanked out by the elimination of difference. Busyness supplies distraction, and entertainment, escape.

Technologies of flow have provided essential infrastructure for this reordering of the world. They have made possible a "readiness" of the world for participation in our projects. This readiness, this instant and ubiquitous availability of things for deployment in service to our purposes, has given things the character of being ready-to-hand; and this has changed the world for us, changed the relationship that we have to the material and sensuous presence of beings other than ourselves. As recognized by Heidegger in *Being and Time*, things that are ready-to-hand disappear in use. Even more significantly, they disappear when not in use. The equipment that we are about to use is peripherally present in its handiness and readiness. The equipment that we have finished with is no longer present, even though it sits there, where we have left it. As the *"there"* in which *Da*-sein is involved becomes more and more narrowly project-oriented, our awareness of the things of the world is ordered in terms of the needs of each project. Things must appear when needed, perform efficiently, retire discretely. Our concernful engagement with them is limited to their participation in what we are doing.[35]

Technologies of flow that have ordered the things of the world as ready-to-hand, play into and add weight to a deficient mode of care; to a care for things to appear only insofar as they supply our need; to carelessness concerning the trajectory of things beyond their participation in this moment, this project of ours. In a world where everything has been interpreted in advance as material for deployment, we are increasingly unobservant of the materiality of things, of their existence *as* things apart from us and our immediate needs. The sensuous nonhuman world, with its myriad interactions, exchanges, exuberant flourishings and rich transformations, for the most part appears only insofar as it serves our project-oriented horizons.

Hand-in-hand with this reduction of things to resources, is a similar reduction of relations between humans.[36] Not only things, but fellow humans, are interpreted in advance as standing reserve; optimized, ready for deployment. We have devised technologies that order us into instant and ongoing availability, and demand from us continuous attention.[37] We are monitored within vast bureaucracies through a coding of measurable attributes. Our achievements are judged against productivity indexes, digitized and distributed within further orderings. There is little distinction here between our narrow and exhaustive exploitation of the nonhuman world, and the ways in which our "human resources" are managed.[38] The care structure through which the world is currently interpreted delivers all that is, human and nonhuman, to the project of making-available, monitoring and exploiting. And in so delivering it, there is also a covering over of all else that it is or could be.

As well as participating in the project of making things available, design is actively involved in the project of making things, whether human or nonhuman, disappear when not needed or wanted. Ironically, this could even be said to be one of the roles of "human-centered design," which empathizes with we humans equally in our desire to be independent, and in our isolation from caring communities—which is the corollary of independence. Nonhumans, shaped by human-centered design, release us from the need for collaboration with, and dependence upon, other humans. While such release certainly smooths relations—nonhumans being more predictable and less demanding, for the most part, than fellow humans—it allows us to forget, or to become unobservant of, the humanity of the other; it deprives us of warmth and companionship as well as of difficulty and challenge in our relations, encouraging us to narrow our horizons to that which is both easy and easily assimilable.

Similarly the smoothing of environmental experience, accomplished by design, reduces our capacity to deal with the difficult and the unpredictable. The covering over of environmental untowardness, its apparent compliance with all our projects, has fooled many into believing that the environment is or can be, only what we will it to be.

If this project-oriented ordering of the world has followed from its objectification, an equally powerful effect has followed from the rendering of human consciousness as the subject that encounters this objectively knowable world. The special position of the subject, its capacity to experience, to know, to intend and to project, presents the flip side of Cartesian subject–object dualism. From optimization of the world, we turn to the optimization of ourselves; the optimization of our bodies, our skills, and our capacity for accumulating knowledge and experiences. These days it seems that the optimization of ourselves and of our children is the sole endeavor that contemporary humankind attends to seriously, as a responsibility. This is the task in which we invest most, and which we would most vehemently defend as our rightful pursuit.

If design plays a central role in rendering the world ready-to-hand and available for our projects, it plays an equally important, if different, role in the optimization of our selves. Both avant-garde and mainstream design supply an image-based context within which self-optimization can be pursued. Models and guidelines are provided by the media, accessories are mass produced and commercially distributed, environments for acquisition or performance are made available. Here, even more evidently than in our ordering of the world, design designs us. Not only does it design our appearance and our accomplishments, but it determines what we attend to, spend time on, what we notice and discuss. Although self-optimization may be presented, and may appear, as the realm of choice, intention, and self-determination, in fact most performances keep closely to the designed pathways on offer.

Unlike the designing that configures the world as ready-to-hand, however, design for self-optimization is not discrete, does not withdraw from our awareness but, rather, makes its effects present as intense, aesthetic and sensuous embodied experience, or as consciously reviewed, measurable achievement.

Care—as an attunement to, and reaching out toward, the things that appear to matter within our worlds—is here oriented to achievement measured against pleasures delivered or credits awarded, against the standards that circulate within the media or those that configure our institutions. The past, which is responsible for the world we are thrown into, is grasped as a record of previous strivings for the kind of goal to which we are oriented.[39] The future that we anticipate in our strivings is one in which we will somehow measure up. Just as we are attuned to and notice the possibilities offered by the human and nonhuman resources of the world for utilization in our projects, so too are we attuned to and reaching out towards possibilities for realization of our own potential to be what the world would have us be. As for the care with which we encounter the world as resource, the care with which we tend to our self-fashioning springs from temporal experience that is always precarious, never secure.

These days, in most advanced capitalist countries, education is grasped as belonging to each individual's project of self-optimization. It is conceived primarily as a responsibility to oneself, not to the community; a private good, not a public one; an economic good, not a cultural one. As such, education has become a service industry catering to the anxious striving of individuals who fear that they will not measure up to the demands of a world in which there is little community, little sympathy for the unproductive or the unconforming, little hope for those who cannot keep up. Both the fear and the hope that fuel the client base of educational institutions, have been manufactured by, and perpetuate, our deficient care structure.

It has been suggested that design, especially as informed by design history, might play a role in education of the future. While design thinking as currently formulated is likely to be seized upon solely as another counter in the game of optimization, we would like, here, to point in a different direction.

Learning

Both Dilnot and Fry represent us as in the midst of epochal change, driven by the radical defuturing of worlds initiated by the optimization projects of the Enlightenment, and accelerated by the onset of Nietzschean nihilism. The damage done by the progressive technological ordering, stripping and plundering of the world over past centuries has been evidenced most forcefully in environmental stress and in disruption of the ecological systems that have supported terrestrial life in its current form. It is equally evident in the nihilistic will to will that currently propels global political and economic life. What seems increasingly certain is that we face rapid and difficult change. What has yet to be determined is the way we will navigate that change, and what will follow. Fry advocates an activism toward the opening up of a new epoch of sustainment.[40] In order to open up the possibility of sustainment, what needs to be learned is a different kind of care.

We need to learn to be attuned to the world not for the ways in which it might offer itself up to either anxious or triumphant projects of optimization and control. Rather, we should seek to be attuned in other ways. The *Augenblick* that currently delivers a flash of insight into how to reconfigure atoms to set vast reserves of energy at our disposal, or that informs a sure instinct for the cosmetic purchase that will make the most of our appearance on this or that occasion, needs to be recognized for what it is; as problematic, as arising out of narrowly defined, project-oriented care. A different kind of *Augenblick* would arise out of a different kind of care.

The particular character of care that informs our orientation to the world is given by the epoch within which we dwell. Heidegger argued, however, that although epochs unfold historically, it is possible to access epochs other than the one that is dominant at any time. Not only are there periods of overlap in which more than one epochal mode is available but, also, an epoch that has passed does not dissolve, but merely withdraws.[41] The multiplicity of different worlds in which we engage each provides a different context for the activation of care.

The possibility of accessing different epochal modes of care makes possible a critical consciousness of, and engagement with, the form of care that currently orients us. Learning takes place when the contingency of the assumptions and presuppositions that orient us is revealed, and the possibility of other orientations is recognized.

Heidegger and, following him, Gadamer, saw learning as taking place through the hermeneutic circle; that is, through the back and forth play of interpretation.[42] The hermeneutic circle is set in motion when we engage with a situation or a text that calls for understanding. In many ways the action of the hermeneutic circle is an everyday affair. We are always interpreting the situations we find ourselves in and the texts that we engage with; and in much of our everyday interpretive activity the understanding that takes place arises unproblematically out of the assumptions, fore-understandings and prejudices that we bring to the situation. In such cases the hermeneutic circle closes on itself without initiating questioning. It is only when we truly attend to the nuances of a situation or a text, when we hearken to what it might have to say to us other than what is expected, that real questioning is set in motion.[43]

If the situation or text that we are interpreting belongs to an epoch other than our own, the questioning that arises can spring from what seems strange in the particular configurations of relations set in motion in the worlds of those historical or cultural others; from the unfamiliar ways in which they orient themselves to the world, care for things, spend their time and direct their energies. Such questioning can alert us to the presuppositions that we have brought to the interpretive process, and in so doing make us more aware of the action of our care structure upon our orientations and understanding.

Snodgrass and Coyne have argued that designing is hermeneutical; that the attentive exploration of a situation that takes place in designing, the open-ended questioning and alertness to what might emerge, is exemplary of the interpretive process.[44] Designing is always (or should always be) learning, and this is one of the things that makes it interesting. However, design these days is rarely informed by the kind of *historical* questioning that Gadamer advocates. Design certainly questions, and is attuned to, the material and embodied contexts that it designs for. Certainly, the designer attentively seeks to learn what the design situation offers. However, for the most part such questioning remains within the framework of Cartesian dualism. A reasoning or intuitive consciousness is understood as reaching out toward—"getting a feel for"—an aspect of the world. Within this framework what is grasped as imperfectly understood is the world, not the self. What is thrown into question is, for the most part, only that preliminary set of suppositions through which the designer has grasped the situation in question. The presuppositions informing designing itself remain largely unobserved within the hermeneutic activity of the design process.

Given the ontological significance of design and the weight that it gives to the care structures that configure our worlds, design uninformed by historical questioning and unattuned to its own historicality is likely to further bind us to the problematic paths that we currently tread, rather than offer a way of rethinking or redirecting those paths. Nevertheless, that design is characterized by attentive and open-ended inquiry into the possibilities latent within lived material and communicative contexts, certainly suggests an opening for learning. That expert designers are addicted to iterative projection and critique, that they are dissatisfied with gestures that don't quite fit, or that fail to move—all of these qualities of design are promising.

What is essential, however, is the reinstatement of historical questioning in relation to design. Current design histories are not oriented to this task. A different approach is needed. It is here that the emerging focus upon performative association may offer a foothold.

Performative association, character and design history

Patterns of belonging within the world exercise a hold upon the things that participate in those patterns. That this is the case was accepted as given within the Aristotelian understandings that dominated pre-Enlightenment Western thought. It is also a given within non-Western cultures that each, in different ways, have conceived of their world as made meaningful through the relations that constitute it.

Enlightenment belief in the rational independence of things from unaccountable influence, thus represented an event of understanding that opened a new epoch, radically shifting the way the world is interpreted. Heidegger saw the epoch that had been opened by Enlightenment commitment to objective detachment as characterized by a care structure that is deficient; that cultivates carelessness of things, and exploitation of them as mere resource.

In returning to the Aristotelian account of *phronesis*—an account of good judgment exercised within a relational context—Heidegger initiated a recovery of the ancient recognition of the hold that is exercised by patterns of relations that have been established within worlds. From Aristotle, Heidegger also understood the performative nature of character. A pattern of activity that is repeatedly performed establishes a hold upon those who participate in that performance. Repeated performance brings a particular *ethos*, a particular character, into being, and gives that character a hold upon those who have participated in bringing it into being. Unlike Aristotle, however, Heidegger saw particular performances as an expression of epoch. They arise out of, and repeatedly realise, the character of their time.

The idea of performativity is thus an ancient one, recovered and reconfigured within Heidegger's thought, and increasingly taken up in late-20th and early-21st-century understandings.

In opposition to the Enlightenment notion that objects in the world are independent, rationally intelligible entities, it is now grasped that things—animate and inanimate, material and immaterial, remembered, anticipated or present—appear within, act within and are encountered as meaningful within the various performative associations into which they enter or within which they are taken up. Performative associations are not neutral—the participants gathered within the performance exercise a hold upon one another, and these participants include patterns of behavior, orientations to the world, expectations, modes of caring, and attitudes to what matters. In entering into a performative association, one enters into its patterns and, through participation, perpetuates them.

Hybrid collections of participants are gathered within and contribute to performances that have already been taken up, repeated and given weight within the world. What is repeatedly performed can range in scale from the game that arises between a child, a ball and a hard surface, to the performance of the economy, with its myriad human and nonhuman participants, its global reach and seemingly unstoppable trajectories and effects.[45] What is brought into being and sustained through repeated performance includes modes of action, attitudes and dispositions, concrete and communicative productions, and a collection of trajectories, affects, concepts, and things. Insofar as either humans or designed things participate in performative associations, one thing among the others that will be brought into and sustained in being is a particular mode of care, arising out of and reflecting the care structure of the epoch upon which the performance draws.

Performative associations have diverse temporalities. Mike Michael's "hudogledog"—an association (or co(a)gency) comprised of a human, a dog lead and a dog, has the temporality of a pulse, coming together once or twice a day, morning or evening, and lasting from half an hour to an hour. While gathered into association, the hudogledog brings into being a particular mode of behavior and sensibility, a particular experience of space, time and body, a particular set of relationships with the wider world—with trees and posts, with other hudogledogs (or partial hudogledogs), with plastic bags and neighborhood responsibilities. These relationships and affects are lively for the time of the association, and variously withdraw or linger when the association breaks apart.[46]

Recognizing the hudogledog as a performative association that brings into being a particular mode of being in the world, alerts us to the ease with which we step in and out of different associations, participate in their character, and either retain or discard their lingering effects within our other doings and associations. Everything we do is done in association with others, whether human or nonhuman. Every performance participates, knowingly or unknowingly, in multiple others. And in every case, the performance itself and the various things it brings into being have character.

Some associations may appear frugal in character, some may appear generous, some sloppy, some disciplined, some greedy or selfish, some efficient and useful. However, the things that are brought into being through their performance may reveal unexpected dimensions to their character. The frugality of the monastery is inflected by the richness and nuance of its choral performances; the luxury of a spa retreat is betrayed by the poverty of the conversations it harbors. The efficiency of bureaucracy is revealed as monstrous in its administration of genocide. In each case the performances that an association gives rise to betray the character of the care structure in which they participate.

A design history that is capable of informing us of the shifts in character that follow upon changes in the composition of a performative association; that is capable of alerting us to the character of the associations we are thrown into, and come to participate in; would be one that contributed to a tracing of performances across different epochs or across cultural divides. Michel Foucault's histories of the exercise and distribution of power can be read as a contribution here, charting epochal shifts within the Western tradition.[47]

On a smaller scale, Alex Preda's account of the introduction of the stock ticker (2005) records a dramatic shift in the character of participation in the stock market, following from the introduction of a communications technology that dramatically altered patterns of attention to market fluctuation.[48]

Similarly, Shove and Southerton's history of the introduction and normalization of the household freezer, and Chappells and Shove's history of changing household waste disposal arrangements, chart the changing character of domestic life as household members, spaces and equipment become participants in macro technological networks that supply food and remove waste.[49] Ellen Lupton charts the shift that brings bathrooms and kitchens (as essential participants in these networks of supply and removal) from the periphery to the center of domestic design.[50] These histories document the multiple ways that new technologies, backed by design, trigger multiple shifts in the character of everyday life.

These latter contributions to design history—although hardly recognized as such—barely nibble at the edge of what needs to be done. They are suggestive of the territory, they provide cameo insights into significant performative shifts, however, despite their suggestiveness, in isolation they fail to communicate the scale of the reconfiguration of worlds in which the performances they speak of, participate. Much more needs to be done.

The ontological role of design positions designed things at the center of performative associations. Changes in design, sometimes quite subtle, may significantly shift the character of a performance; may gently nudge the association into a different epoch, a different form of care. If we are to understand how to do this, as designers, as innovators, or as leaders; if we are to understand what may be at stake in the innovations we make; then we need to cultivate an attunement to the character of associations, an alertness to the participants that are gathered in a performance, and an appropriate delicacy or determination in engagement with them.

Not only designers, but all of us, need to start to read the world in terms of the character of what is brought into being, and what participates in bringing it into being. The performative habit that we should cultivate in those we educate should be a habit of reading the world as association, performance, character and care. Design history is an essential player, needing to be mobilized to bring into being this educational *ethos*, this attunement to what matters. Informed by design history, and attuned to character, design thinking may indeed begin to deserve the attention it has been getting.

NOTES

1 Lucy Kimbell, "Rethinking design thinking: part 1," *Design and Culture*, 3 (2011), pp. 285–306.

2 Martin Heidegger, 'On the essence of truth', translated by John Sallis, in *Basic Writings: from Being and Time* (1927) to *The Task of Thinking* (1964), David Farrell Krell, ed. (San Francisco, CA: Harper & Row, 1977), pp. 117–41.

Stuart Elden outlines the trajectory of thinking on history that runs through Nietzsche, Heidegger and Foucault in S. Elden, *Mapping the Present: Heidegger, Foucault and the Project of a Spatial History* (London and New York: Continuum, 2001).

3 See, for example, Heidegger's treatment of the bridge in M. Heidegger, "Building dwelling thinking," *Poetry, Language Thought*, trans. Albert Hofstadter (New York: Harper & Row, 1952, 1971), pp. 152–4.

4 The theory of ontological designing is succinctly explained by Anne-Marie Willis in "Ontological designing—laying the ground," in Anne-Marie Willis, ed., *Design Philosophy Papers Collection Three* (Ravensbourne, Queensland: Team D/E/S Publications, 2007), pp. 80–98.

5 I understand performativity in the sense developed within Science and Technology Studies (STS) and Actor–Network Theory (ANT), especially as illustrated in essays by Bruno Latour, Michel Callon, and John Law. For these thinkers performativity is a quality of hybrid associations of humans and non-humans, hence the reference to "performative associations."

6 Plato, *The Republic*. The analogy between State and soul, which informs the entire text, is introduced in Book II (Socrates – Adeimantus), explicitly articulated in Book IV (Socrates – Glaucon) and restated at the beginning of Book V. Plato (1994), *The Republic*, translated by B. Jowcett (South Bend IN: Infomations).

7 Vitruvius, "On symmetry: in temples and in the human body," in *Ten Books on Architecture*, trans. Morris Hicky Morgan (Cambridge, MA: Harvard University Press and London: Oxford University Press, 1914), Book 3, Chapter 1.

8 Examples I draw upon include those developed in the collection of essays in Bruno Latour and Peter Weibel, eds, *Making Things Public: Atmospheres of Democracy* (Cambridge, MA: MIT Press and Karlsruhe, Germany: ZKM/ Centre for Art and Media, 2005). See also Mike Michael's series of essays in his *Reconnecting Culture, Technology and Nature: From Society to Heterogeneity* (London: Routledge, 2000); Jane Bennett's "Thing-power," in Bruce Braun and Sarah Whatmore, eds, *Political Matter: Technoscience, Democracy and Public Life* (Minneapolis, MN: University of Minnesota Press, 2010), pp. 35–62; and Karen Barad's "Posthumanist performativity: towards an understanding of how matter comes to matter," *Signs*, 28/3 (Spring 2003), pp. 801–831.

9 Martin Heidegger, "The thing," in *Poetry, Language, Thought* pp. 174–5.

10 Bruno Latour, "From realpolitik to dingpolitik: or how to make things public," in Bruno Latour and Peter Weibel, eds, *Making Things Public: Atmospheres of Democracy* (Cambridge, MA: MIT Press and Karlsruhe, Germany: ZKM/Centre for Art and Media, 2005), p. 14. See also Graham Harman's essay "Heidegger on objects and things," in *Making Things Public, Atmospheres of Democracy* (Cambridge, MA: MIT Press and Karlsruhe, Germany: ZKM/Centre for Art and Media, 2005), pp. 268–72.

11 See Mike Michael's essays "Disciplined and disciplining co(a)gents: the remote control and the couch potato," in *Reconnecting Culture*, pp. 96–116, and "Narrating co(a)gents: the case of the hudogledog," in *Reconnecting Culture*, pp. 117–39. See also Michel Callon, "What does it mean to say that economics is performative?," in Donald Mackenzie, Fabian Muniesa and Lucia Siu, eds, *Do Economists Make Markets?: On the Performativity of Economics* (Princeton, NJ: Princeton University Press, 2007), pp. 311–57; and Alex Preda, "The stock ticker," in Bruno Latour and Peter Weibel, eds, *Making Things Public: Atmospheres of Democracy* (Cambridge, MA: MIT Press and Karlsruhe, Germany: ZKM/Centre for Art and Media, 2005), pp. 622–7.

12 Plato (2008) 'Timaeus', in *Timaeus and Critias*, translated by R. Waterfield (Oxford: Oxford University Press), pp. 23–24, sections 35a–36c.

13 Recognition of the hold exercised upon our "pre-judgments" by the worlds we participate in, is an important thesis of Hans-Georg Gadamer's *Truth and Method*, trans. Joel Weinsheimer (London: Sheed & Ward, 1993).

14 That Heidegger's extensive engagement with Aristotle throughout his formative years as a philosopher shaped his teaching in both Freiburg (1919–23) and at Marburg (1923–8) and paved the way for *Being and Time* (1927), is strongly argued by Franco Volpi, "In whose name? Heidegger and practical philosophy," *European Journal of Political Theory*, 6/1, trans. Niall Keane, pp. 31–51; Daniel L. Smith, "Intensifying phronesis: Heidegger, Aristotle and rhetorical culture," *Project Muse: Philosophy and Rhetoric*, 36/1, pp. 77–102; and Matthew C. Weidenfeld, "Heidegger's appropriation of Aristotle: phronesis, conscience and seeing through the one," *European Journal of Political Theory*, 10/2, pp. 254–76, among others.

15 Aristotle (1953) *The Ethics of Aristotle: The Nicomachean Ethics*, translated by J. A. K. Thomson (Harmondsworth: Penguin Books), Bk X, Ch.9, 1179b1–1180b26, pp. 335–40.

16 Aristotle, *The Nicomachean Ethics*, Book VI, Chapter 5, 1140a24–1140b33. See also Hans-Georg Gadamer, *The Idea of the Good in Platonic-Aristotelian Philosophy*, trans. P. Christopher Smith (New Haven, CT and London: Yale University Press, 1986), p. 96.

17 I have written of this relationship in Susan C. Stewart, "Phronesis, praxis and techne: the politics of Sir Henry Wotton's distinction between architect and critic," in *Proceedings of the 19th Annual Conference of the Society of Architectural Historians of Australia and New Zealand* (Brisbane: 2002),

pp. 77–84, https://www.academia.edu/1008060/Phronesis_Praxis_and_
Techne_the_politics_of_Sir_Henry_Wottons_distinction_between_
architect_and_critic and http://epress.lib.uts.edu.au/research-publications/
handle/10453/1382

18 Aristotle, *The Nicomachean Ethics*, Book II, Chapter 1–3, 1103a14–1105a9.

19 Aristotle, *The Nicomachean Ethics*, 1106b1–10a. Hubert Dreyfus makes the
same point in his discussion of expertise in H. Dreyfus, *On the Internet:
Thinking in Action* (New York: 2001), p. 34.

20 Aristotle, *The Nicomachean Ethics*, 1180a15.

21 Franco Volpi, "In whose name?", p. 38.

22 Daniel L. Smith, "Intensifying phronesis," p. 80.

23 Martin Heidegger, *Being and Time*, 7th edn (Oxford: Blackwell; New York:
Harper & Row, 1962), H 192.

24 Heidegger, *Being and Time*, H 410.

25 Heidegger, *Being and Time*, H 329–331.

26 Heidegger, *Being and Time*, H 179, 347–349.

27 Heidegger, *Being and Time*, H 328 and 338. The connection between
phronesis, the moment of vision, and care is argued by Smith in "Intensifying
phronesis," p. 90.

28 Pierre Keller and David Weberman argue that for Heidegger, intelligibility is
given through the temporal structure of care: P. Keller and D. Weberman,
"Heidegger and the source(s) of intelligibility," *Continental Philosophy
Review*, 31 (1998), pp. 369–86. See especially pp. 379–83.

29 This is evident in Heidegger's treatment of things, equipment and poetic
works in his essays "The origin of the work of art," "Building, dwelling
thinking," and "The thing," all in *Poetry Language Thought*.

30 See Matthew C. Weidenfeld, "Heidegger's appropriation of Aristotle," and
Stuart Elden, *Mapping the Present*, pp. 44–9.

31 Tony Fry, *Becoming Human by Design* (London and New York: Berg, 2012).

32 Anne-Marie Willis, "Ontological designing," p. 80.

33 Martin Heidegger, 'Modern Science, Metaphysics, and Mathematics',
reprinted section from *What is a Thing?* Translated by E.T. Gendlin (Chicago,
IL: Henry Regnery & Co. 1967), pp. 66–108, in *Basic Writings: Writings from
Being and Time (1927) to The Task of Thinking* (1964), ed. David Farrell Krell
(San Francisco, CA: Harper & Row, 1977), pp. 247–82.

34 Heidegger, "Modern science," p. 291.

35 Heidegger, *Being and Time*, H 102.

36 Martin Heidegger, "The question concerning technology," in M. Heidegger,
The Question Concerning Technology and Other Essays (New York: Harper &
Row, 1977), pp. 3–35.

37 Alex Preda gives an account of the gradual establishment of a hold upon the attention of its users, by one particular device: "The stock ticker," in Bruno Latour and Peter Weibel, eds., *Making Things Public: Atmospheres of Democracy* (Cambridge, MA: MIT Press and Karlsruhe, Germany: ZKM/Centre for Art and Media, 2005). pp. 622–7.

38 See Richard Sennett's critique of contemporary management attitudes to "human resources" in R. Sennett, *The Culture of the New Capitalism* (New Haven, CT: Yale University Press, 2006).

39 Typical of this tendency are many influential design histories, such as Nikolaus Pevsner's *Pioneers of Modern Design* (originally published as *Pioneers of the Modern Movement*, 1936; 2nd edn. New York: Museum of Modern Art, 1949; revised and partly rewritten, Harmondsworth: Penguin Books, 1960).

40 Tony Fry, "The voice of sustainment: an introduction," *Design Philosophy Papers*, 1 (2003), http://www.desphilosophy.com.ezproxy.lib.uts.edu.au/dpp/dpp_journal/back_issues/feature_first/dpp_feature.html

41 See the concluding arguments in Iain Thomson's "Ontotheology? Understanding Heidegger's *Destruktion* of metaphysics," *International Journal of Philosophical Studies*, 8/3, (2000), pp. 297–327.

42 Martin Heidegger articulates the hermeneutic circle of understanding in *Being and Time*, H 150–154. Gadamer develops the hermeneutic circle as the basis of historical understanding in *Truth and Method*, trans. Joel Weinsheimer (London: Continuum, Sheed & Ward, 1989 revised edn), p. 267.

43 Gadamer, *Truth and Method*, p. 267.

44 Adrian Snodgrass and Richard Coyne, "Is designing hermeneutical?," *Architectural Theory Review*, 2/1 (1997), pp. 65–97.

45 This is an important focus of Michel Callon's work. See, in particular, Michel Callon, "What does it mean to say that economics is performative?," in Donald Mackenzie, Fabian Muniesa and Lucia Siu, eds, *Do Economists Make Markets?: On the Performativity of Economics* (Princeton, NJ: Princeton University Press, 2007), pp. 311–56.

46 Michael, "Narrating co(a)gents", pp. 117–39.

47 Exemplary is Michel Foucault's *Discipline and Punish* (London and New York: Allen Lane and Pantheon Vintage, 1977).

48 Preda, "The stock ticker," pp. 622–7.

49 Elizabeth Shove and Dale Southerton, "Defrosting the freezer: from novelty to convenience: a narrative of normalization," *Journal of Material Culture*, 5/3 (2000), pp. 301–319. Heather Chappells and Elizabeth Shove, "The dustbin: a study of domestic waste, household practices and utility services," *International Planning Studies*, 4/2 (1999), pp. 267–80.

50 Ellen Lupton, *The Bathroom, the Kitchen, and the Aesthetics of Waste: A Process of Elimination* (Cambridge, MA and New York: The Center; Princeton Architectural Press, 1992).

INDEX

early humans 69–70
economy 54, 209, 295
    see also capitalism
ecstasy 283–4
education 277, 281, 285, 286, 291, 297
    critique of 15–23
    unlearning process 20, 65
Ellman, Richard 235
emancipation 59–60
end of history 33–4, 35
Endstate (Hegel) 33
Enlightenment 12–13, 65, 280, 287–8,
    291, 294–5
environment 290
epochal change 291
epochs 284–5, 291–2, 294–7
ethical/ethical disposition 277, 281–2
ethics 43, 60–1, 106–10, 160, 197–8,
    200–1
    politics 190–3, 200–3
    the situation as site of 197–200
    subjectivity of 198
ethnocentrism 10–11
ethos 277–8, 294
eugenics 79
Eurocentrism 32, 77
euthanasia institutes 79
"the event" 73
evil 236
existence, structure of 133–40
experience 14–15
expertise 282

"facts" 73
falling 284
Fascism 228
"ficticity" 73–4
fiction, history as 72, 73–4
flow 286–9
Flusser, Vilém 135, 136
food prices 55
forgetting 11–12, 35, 39
formalism 158
formative experience 14
Forty, Adrian 150
fossil fuels 173

Foucault, Michel 12, 41, 46–9, 276,
    278, 296
fracturing of history 33
free market 54–5
freedom 280
Fukuyama, Francis 33–4
the future 66–7, 105, 133–4, 136,
    140–6, 158–63, 165–6
futuring 109–10

Gadamer, Hans-Georg 36, 73, 278,
    292–3
Galileo 287
gas chambers 83
genealogy 47–8
genocide 76–7, 80, 102, 233
genuine design 207–8
German Ideology (Benjamin) 45
Germany 39, 79, 214–16
ghetto/concentration camp,
    Theresienstadt 89–93
global capitalism 55
Goodman, Nelson 211, 224–5
Grossraum 53
growth, ideology of 50

habit 282, 297
habitus concept 20, 28, 46
Haeckel, Ernst 44
Hall, David 70–1
Hanssen, Beatrice 44
Haraway, Donna 185
Harr, Michel 11
Hegel, Georg Wilhelm Friedrich 10,
    33, 34, 169, 241
Heidegger, Martin 10, 141, 288,
    292, 294
    care 282–5
    destructiveness 188, 189
    historicity theory 27–8, 29,
        36–7, 41–3, 284
    law 178
    ontological education 13,
        22–3
    paideia concept 17
    ready-to-hand 288–9

Joyce, James 198, 235
Jullien, François 179
Jus Publicum Europaeum 53

Kant, Immanuel 43, 239
knowledge 19–20, 24, 28, 39, 46, 48,
        69, 160, 239
Kojève, Alexandre 34
Kraft, Julius 38
Kristeva, Julia 167–8
Kundera, Milan 155, 160

LaCapra, Dominick 72, 73, 78
language 185–6
Latour, Bruno 278
law 56, 172, 174, 177–81, 229–31
learning 292
Lederer, Zdenek 82, 88, 90, 92
Levi, Primo 82
Levinas, Emmanuel 11
li (pattern) 70–1
Libeskind, Daniel 156, 218, 224
lightness 155–6
logocentrism 45
Lyotard, Jean-François 5

McNeill, William H. 99–100
Magnus, Bernd 49
making 153, 187–8
Marx, Karl 45, 49–58, 59
Mauthausen concentration/work
        camp 83–8
measurement/measuring 158–63,
        174
mediation 184, 186, 187, 192–3,
        210
medical experimentation, Dachau
        83–4
memorials 217–18, 224–7
        see also Schöneberg memorial
memory 12, 14, 35, 217–18, 224–7
Mesoamerica 77
Mesopotamia 70
metaphysics 18–19, 21, 141
Miami 159
Michael, Mike 279

Milgram, Stanley 107
modernity 10–11, 31, 101–4, 165
Monroe Doctrine 53
monumental history 40
morality 235
Mourning Before the Law (Rose) 199
'Muselmann' term 96

narratives, historical 71–5, 99
nation states 102
"natural history" 43–6
natural law 172, 177–8
nature 13, 37, 43–4, 45, 101, 173,
        178, 191–2
Nazis 86, 214–16
Near East 70
negative futures 18
negotiation 181–4, 193
neoliberalism 174–5
Netherlands 158–9
Newtonian physics 287
Nietzsche, Friedrich 25, 38–41, 47,
        172, 193, 276
"Nietzsche, genealogy, history"
        (Foucault) 47
nihilism 41, 66, 148, 166, 194–5,
        240, 291
the nonhuman 289, 295
novels 160
now 15, 30–1
nuclear power 183–4
nuclear weapons 55
Nuremburg trials 86–7

object and subject 192, 284, 290
objectification, modes of 48
objectivity 29–30, 280, 287, 294
Olympics 215
*On the Advantages and Disadvantages
        of History for Life* (Nietzsche)
        38, 39, 40, 47
ontological design 276, 286, 293, 297
ontology 13–15
optimization 290, 291, 292
organic history ("natural history")
        43–6

CPSIA information can be obtained
at www.ICGtesting.com
Printed in the USA
LVHW010450120620
657871LV00019B/741

9 780857 854773